GRUMBLE™

VOLUME II
RAISING HELL IN THE GARDEN STATE

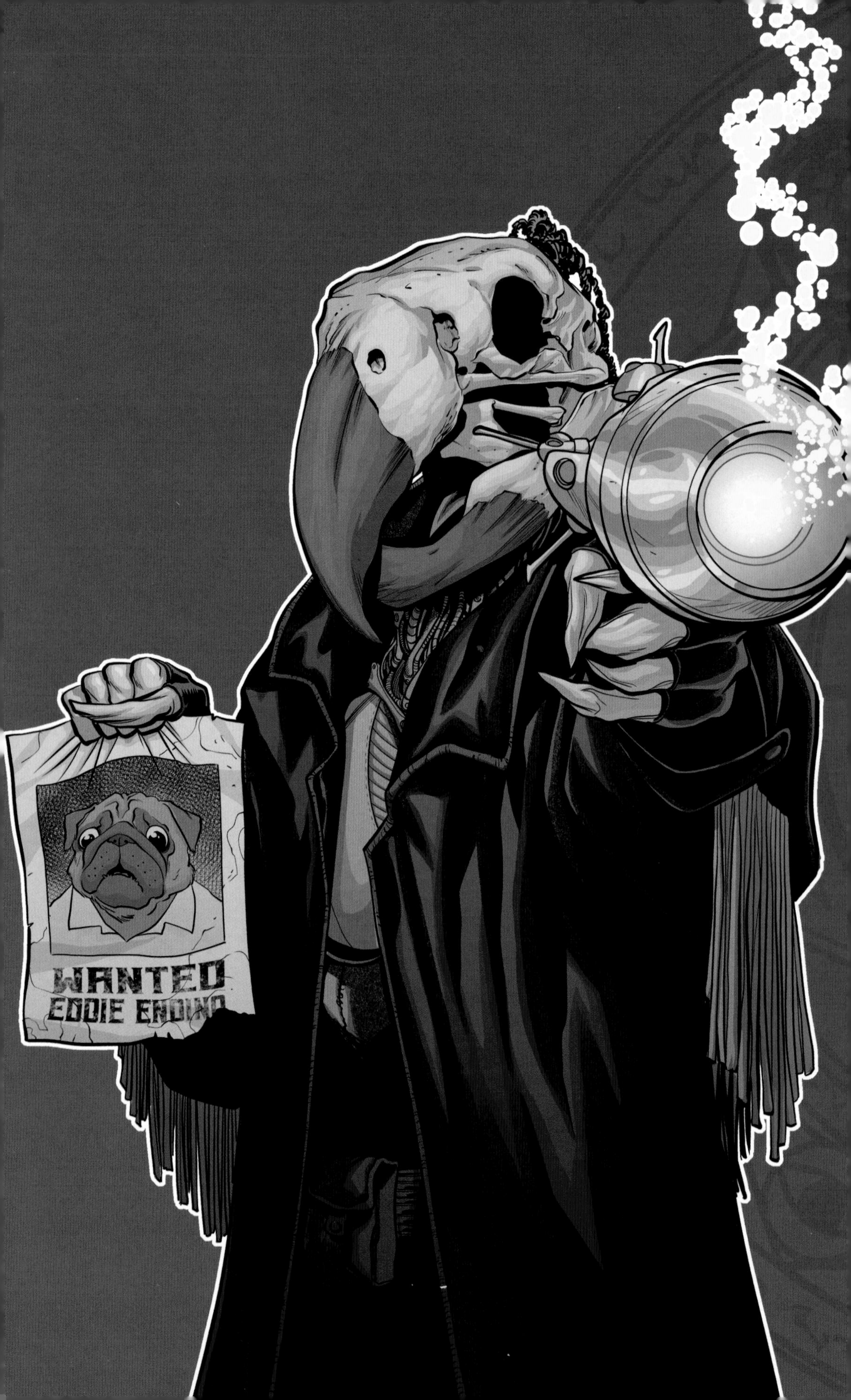
WANTED
EDDIE ENDINO

ALBATROSS FUNNYBOOKS PRESENTS

GRUMBLE ™

VOLUME II
RAISING HELL IN THE
GARDEN STATE

CREATED BY

RAFER ROBERTS - WRITER   MIKE NORTON - ARTIST

MARISSA LOUISE - COLOR ARTIST

CRANK! - LETTERER

ALEJANDRO ARBONA - EDITOR

COVERS BY
MIKE NORTON, MARISSA LOUISE & ADDISON DUKE

This volume collects GRUMBLE issues 6-10 and GRUMBLE vs. THE GOON published by Albatross Funnybooks.

GRUMBLE: RAISING HELL IN THE GARDEN STATE Published by ALbatross Funnybooks, PO Box 60627, Nashville TN 37206. Grumble™&© 2020 Mike Norton and Rafer Roberts. All contents and related characters™&© Mike Norton and Rafer Roberts. All rights reserved. No portion of this product may be reproduced or transmitted, by any form or by any means, without express written permission of Mike Norton and Rafer Roberts. Albatross Funnybooks and the Albatross Funnybooks logo are registered trademarks of Eric Powell. Names, characters, places, and incidents featured in this publication are fictional. Any similarity to persons living or dead, places and incidents is unintended or for satirical purposes.   Printed in Canada.

BOOK ONE

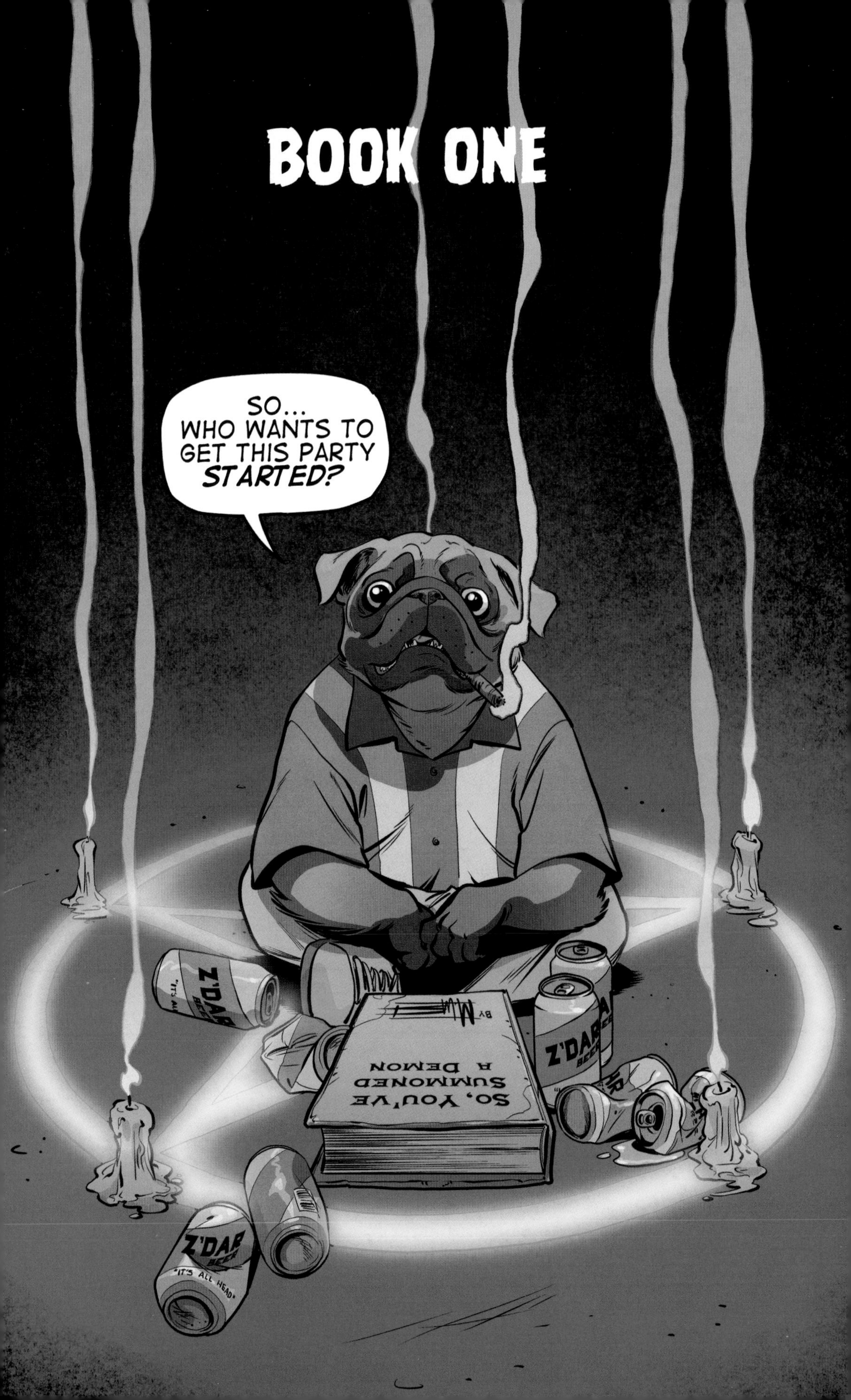
SO... WHO WANTS TO GET THIS PARTY *STARTED?*
SO, YOU'VE SUMMONED A DEMON
Z'DAR BEER
"IT'S ALL HEAD"

SO... WHO WANTS TO GET THIS PARTY *STARTED?*
SO, YOU'VE SUMMONED A DEMON

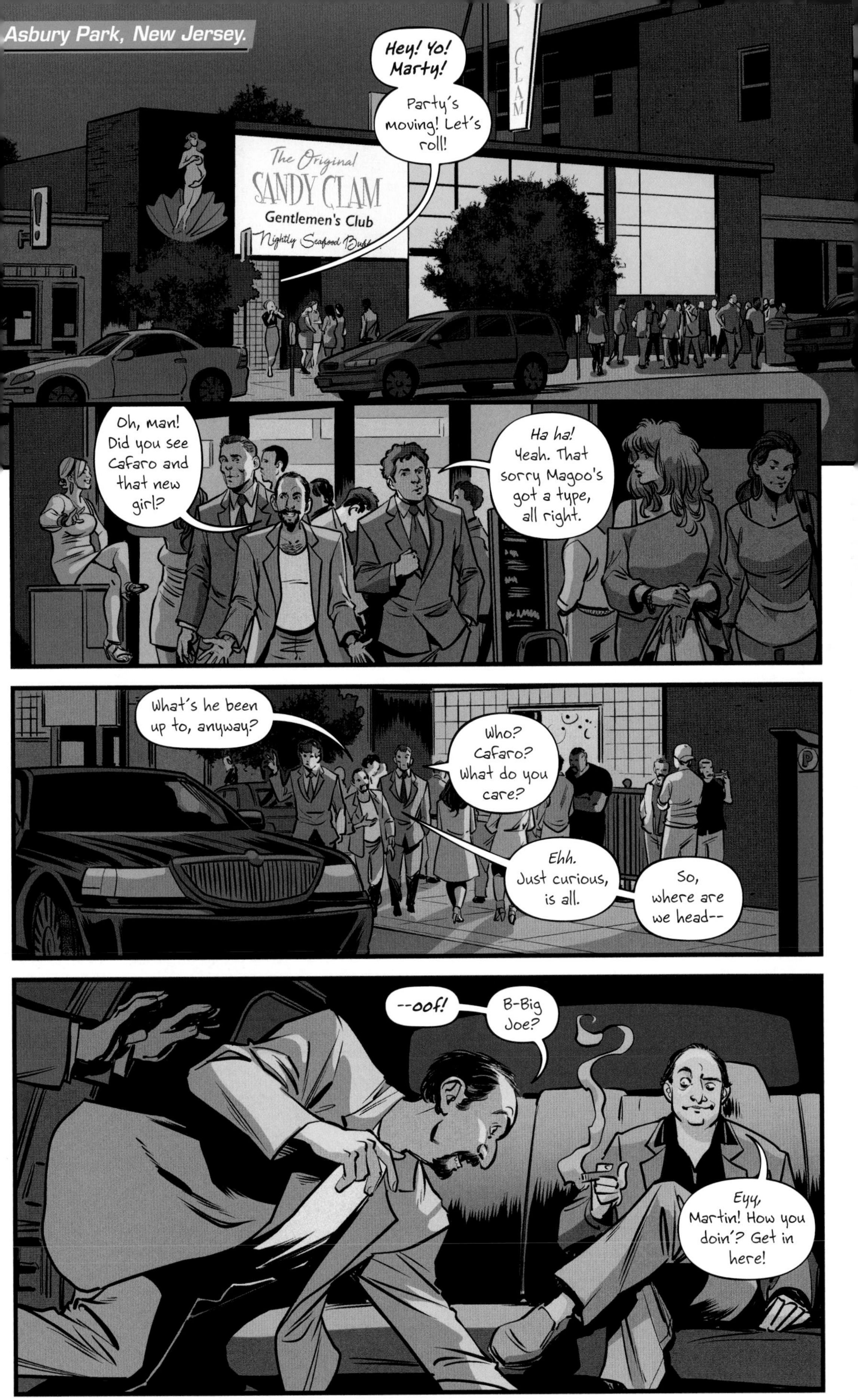

Asbury Park, New Jersey.
Hey! Yo! Marty!
Party's moving! Let's roll!
The Original SANDY CLAM Gentlemen's Club Nightly Seafood Buff
Oh, man! Did you see Cafaro and that new girl?
Ha ha! Yeah. That sorry Magoo's got a type, all right.
What's he been up to, anyway?
Who? Cafaro? What do you care?
Ehh. Just curious, is all.
So, where are we head--
--oof!
B-Big Joe?
Eyy, Martin! How you doin'? Get in here!

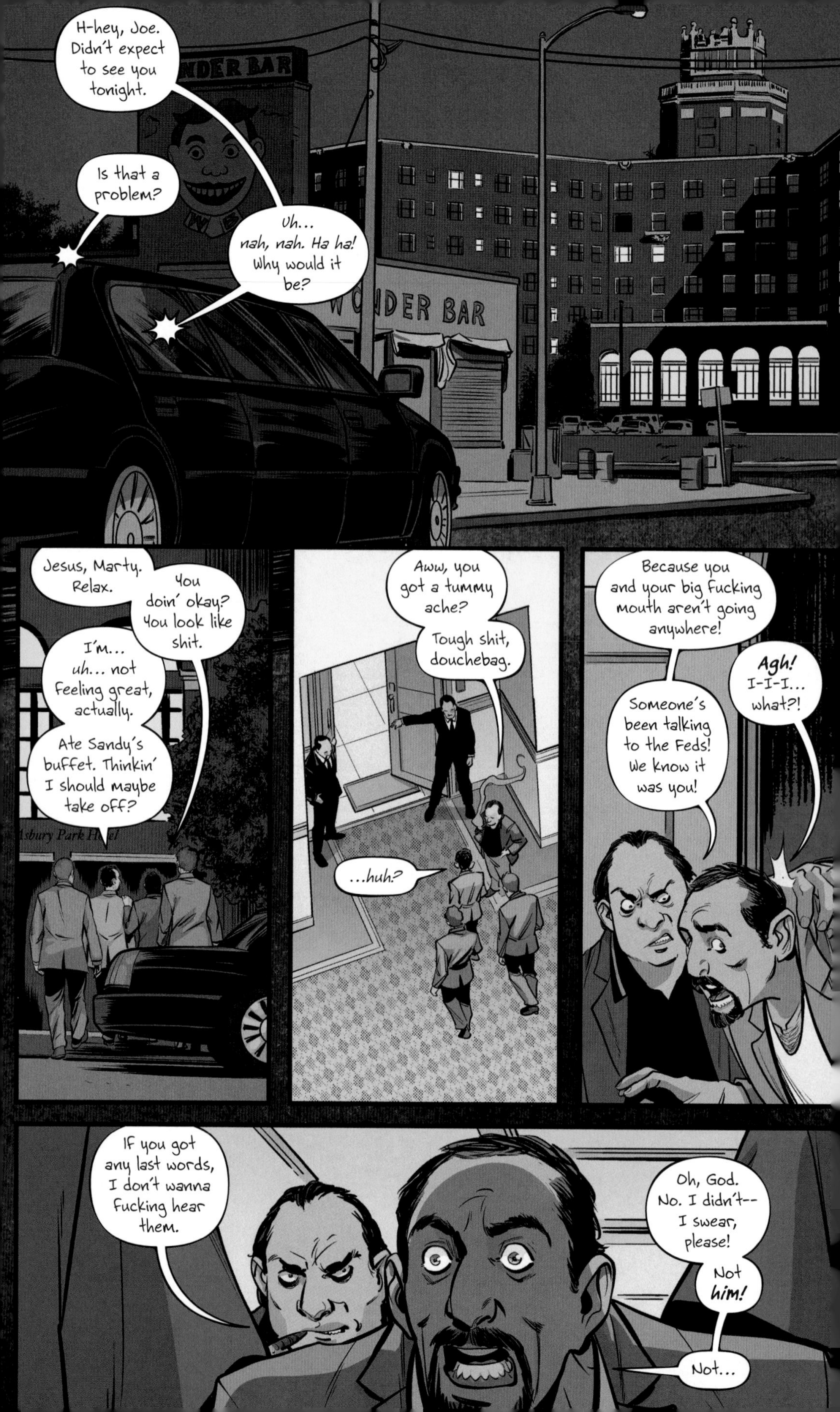

H-hey, Joe. Didn't expect to see you tonight.
Is that a problem?
Uh... nah, nah. Ha ha! Why would it be?
Jesus, Marty. Relax.
You doin' okay? You look like shit.
I'm... uh... not feeling great, actually.
Ate Sandy's buffet. Thinkin' I should maybe take off?
Aww, you got a tummy ache?
Tough shit, douchebag.
...huh?
Because you and your big fucking mouth aren't going anywhere!
Agh! I-I-I... what?!
Someone's been talking to the Feds! We know it was you!
If you got any last words, I don't wanna fucking hear them.
Oh, God. No. I didn't-- I swear, please!
Not *him*!
Not...

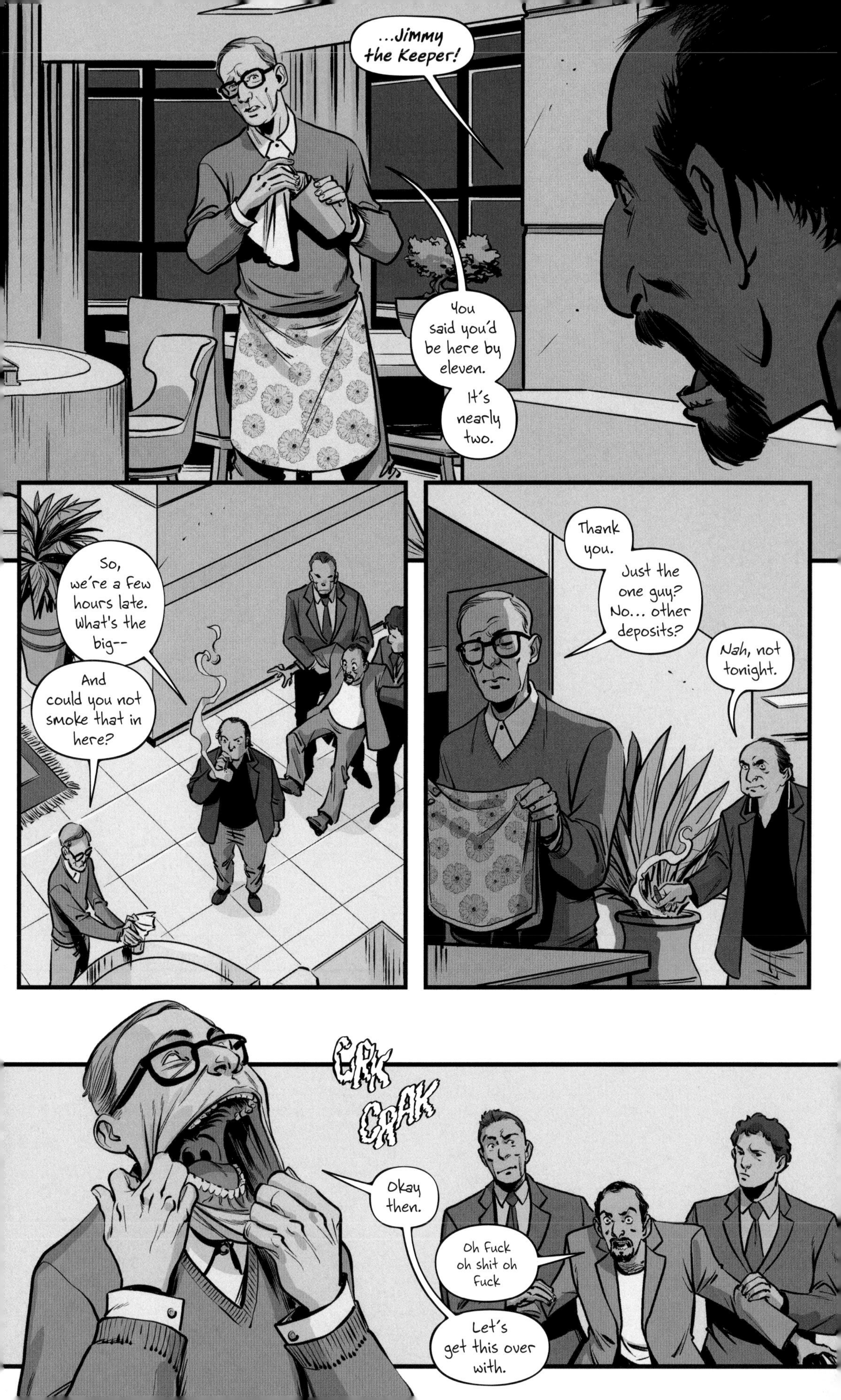
...Jimmy the Keeper!
You said you'd be here by eleven.
It's nearly two.
So, we're a few hours late. What's the big--
And could you not smoke that in here?
Thank you.
Just the one guy? No... other deposits?
Nah, not tonight.
CRK
CRAK
Okay then.
Oh fuck oh shit oh fuck
Let's get this over with.

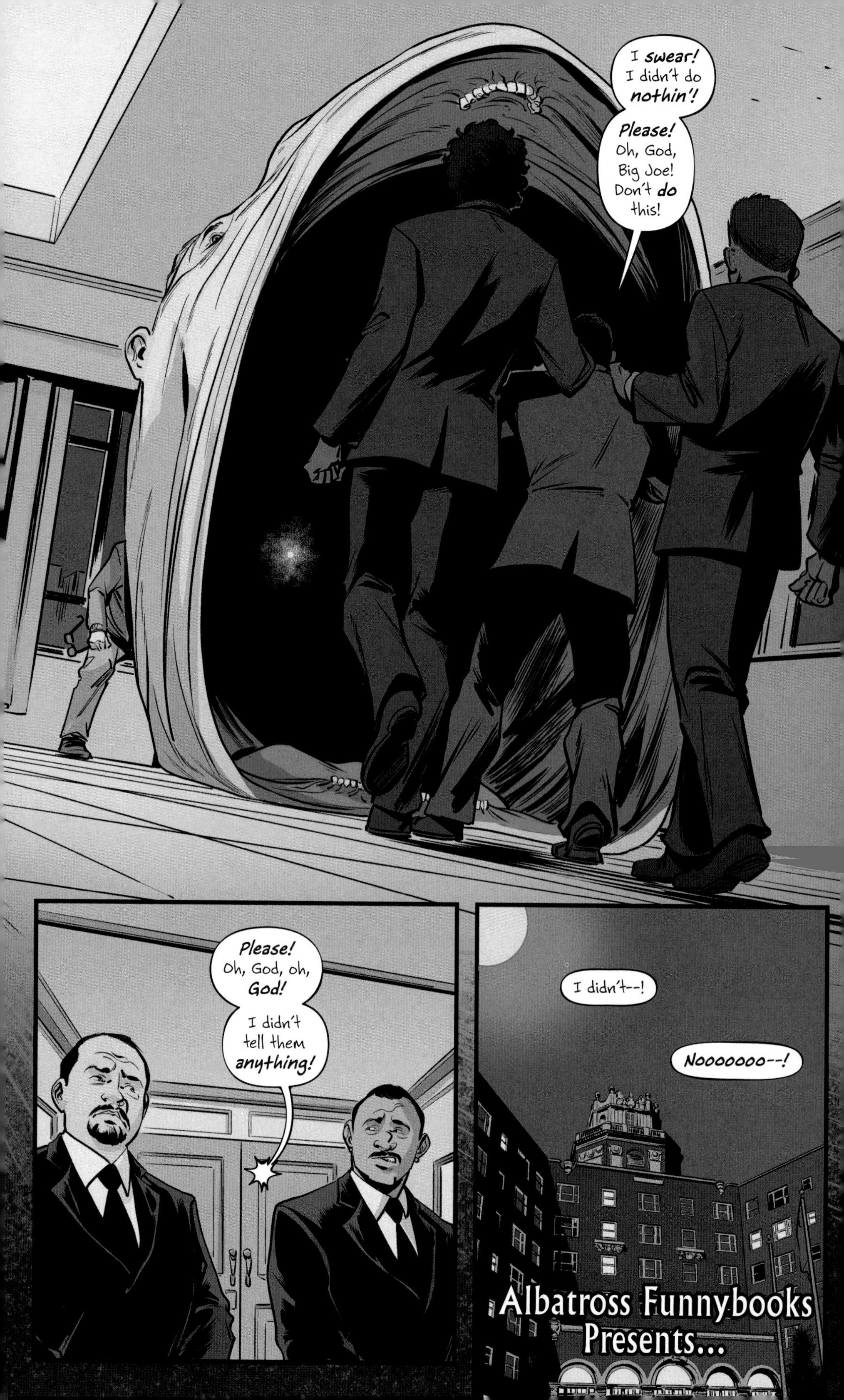
I swear! I didn't do nothin'!
Please! Oh, God, Big Joe! Don't do this!
Please! Oh, God, oh, God!
I didn't tell them anything!
I didn't--!
Noooooooo--!
Albatross Funnybooks Presents...

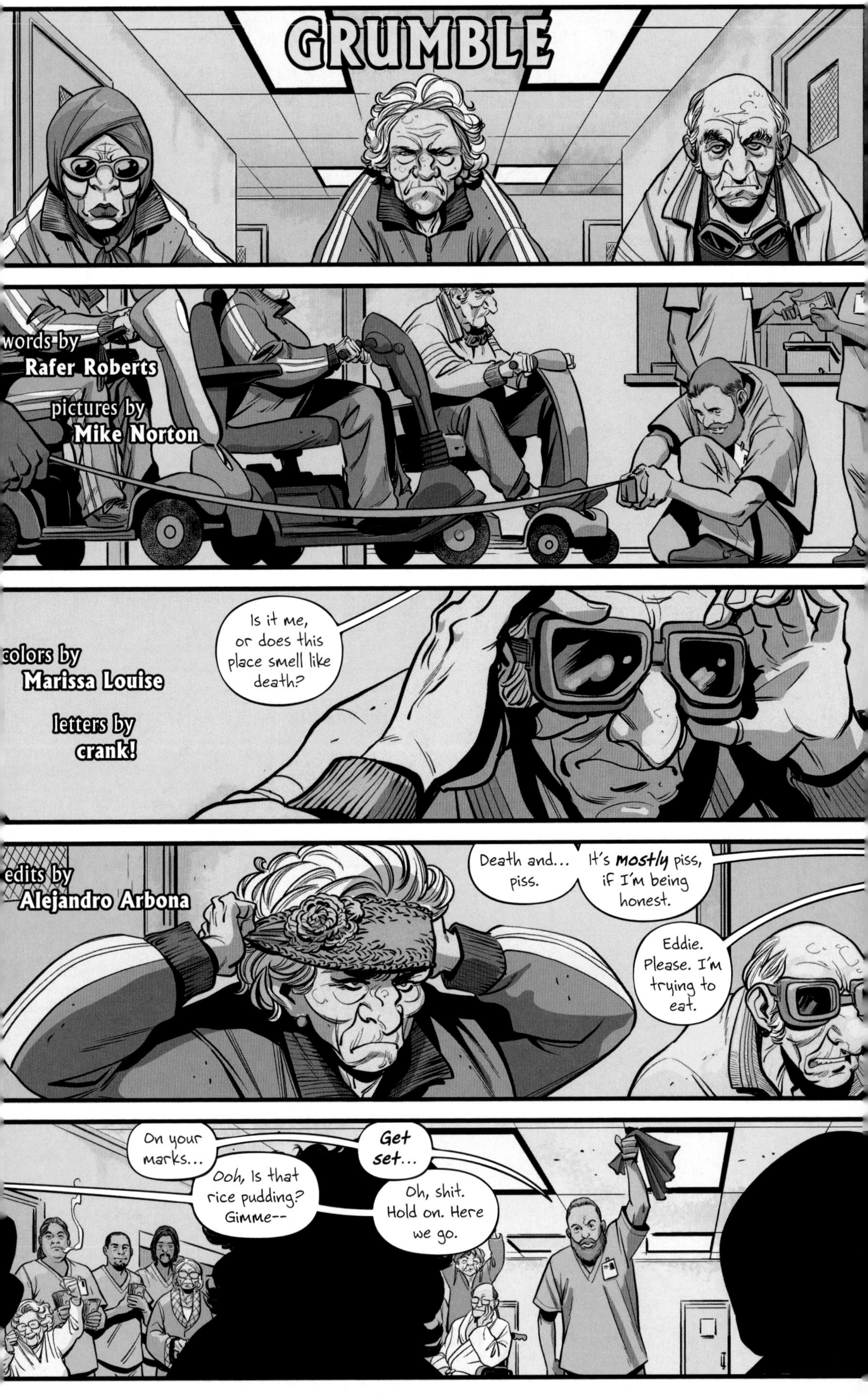

GRUMBLE
words by
Rafer Roberts
pictures by
Mike Norton
colors by
Marissa Louise
letters by
crank!
Is it me, or does this place smell like death?
edits by
Alejandro Arbona
Death and... piss.
It's *mostly* piss, if I'm being honest.
Eddie. Please. I'm trying to eat.
On your marks...
Ooh, Is that rice pudding? Gimme--
Get set...
Oh, shit. Hold on. Here we go.

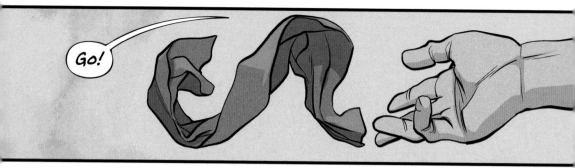

Go!

Philadelphia, Pennsylvania.

Go get 'em, Gertie!

Ooh, hurry up, Esther!

Floor it, Jerry! Move your wrinkly ass!

Go, Gertie, go!

That's the stuff, Jerry!

Hooray! Yay!

Come on, you sonnavabitch! Come on!

Winner! Jerry!

Hell yeah!

Let's go, kid.

Congratulations. You hit the long shot.

Had a hunch.

Uh, Eddie?

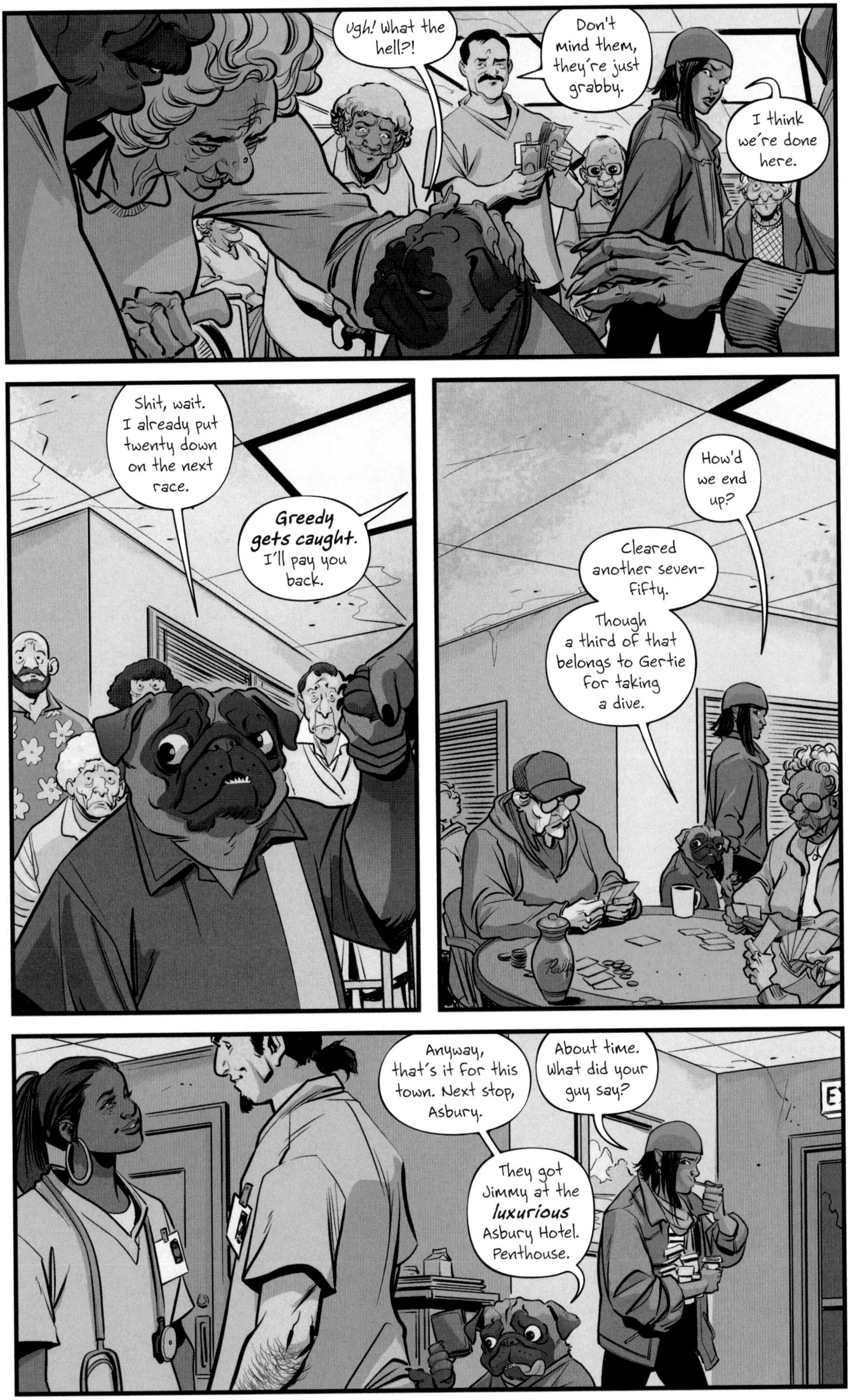

Ugh! What the hell?!
Don't mind them, they're just grabby.
I think we're done here.
Shit, wait. I already put twenty down on the next race.
Greedy gets caught. I'll pay you back.
How'd we end up?
Cleared another seven-fifty.
Though a third of that belongs to Gertie for taking a dive.
Anyway, that's it for this town. Next stop, Asbury.
About time. What did your guy say?
They got Jimmy at the ***luxurious*** Asbury Hotel. Penthouse.

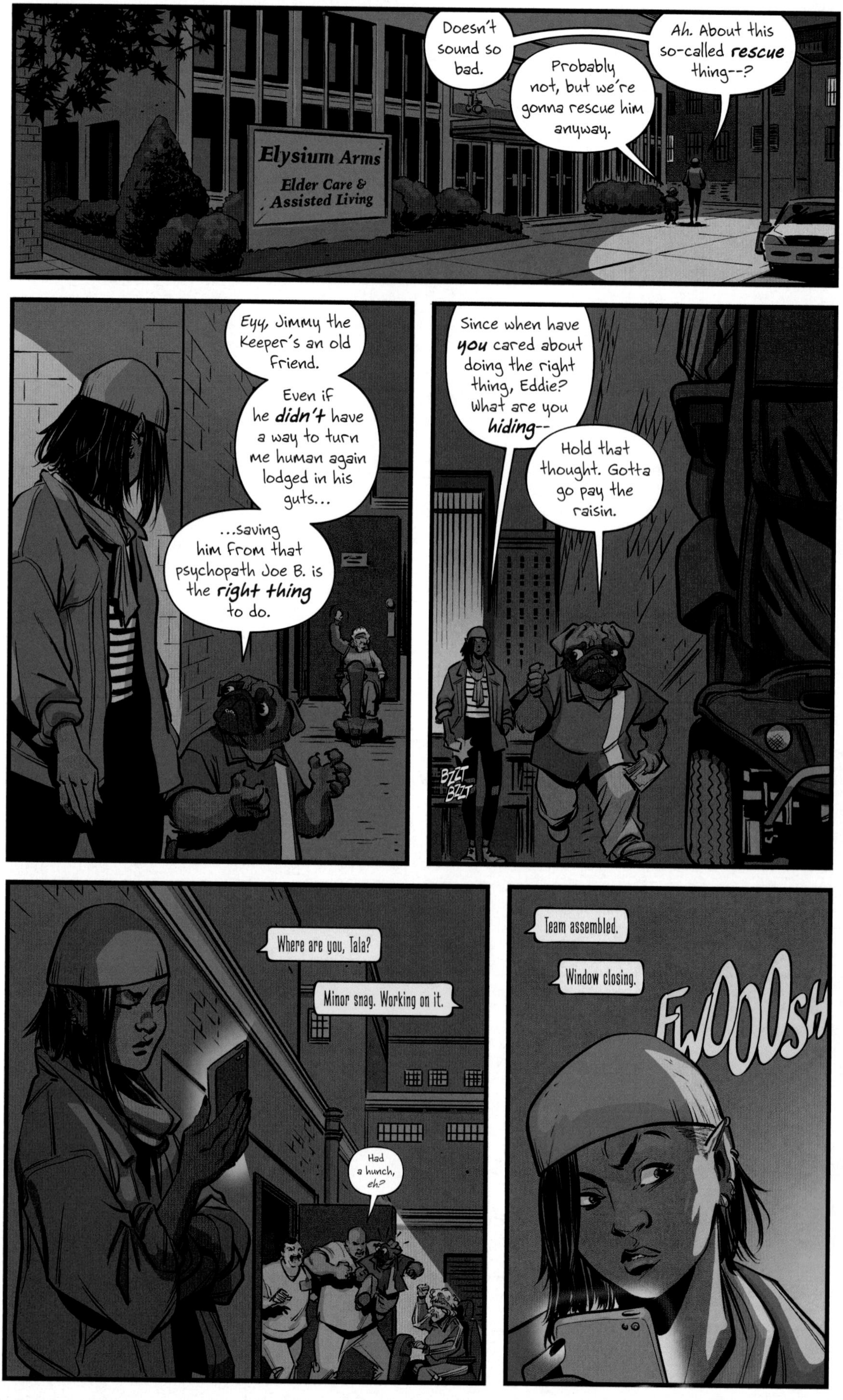
Elysium Arms
Elder Care & Assisted Living
Doesn't sound so bad.
Probably not, but we're gonna rescue him anyway.
Ah. About this so-called **rescue** thing--?
Eyy, Jimmy the Keeper's an old friend.
Even if he **didn't** have a way to turn me human again lodged in his guts...
...saving him from that psychopath Joe B. is the **right thing** to do.
Since when have **you** cared about doing the right thing, Eddie? What are you **hiding**--
Hold that thought. Gotta go pay the raisin.
BZZT BZZT
Where are you, Tala?
Minor snag. Working on it.
Had a hunch, eh?
Team assembled.
Window closing.
FWOOOSH

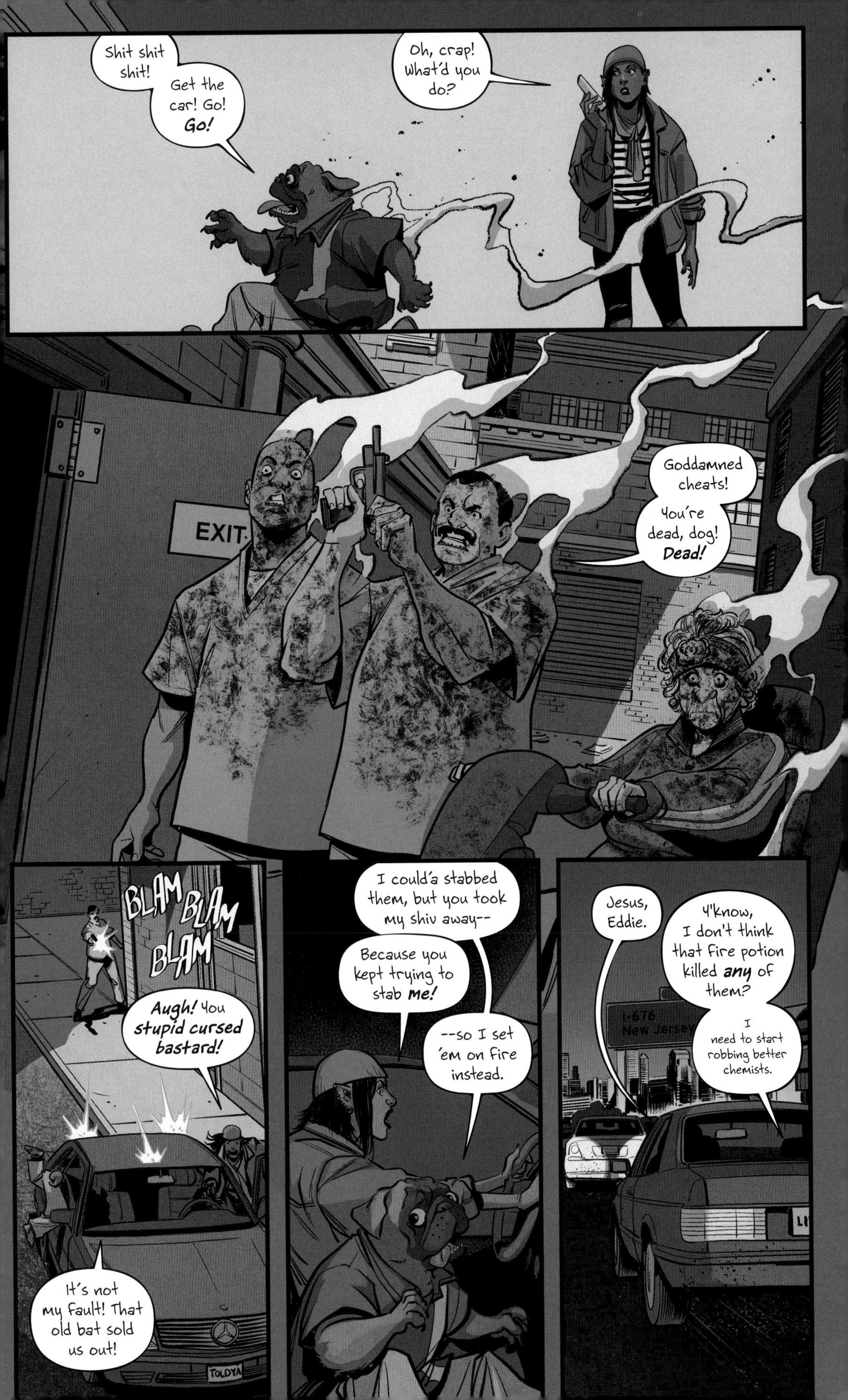
Shit shit shit!
Get the car! Go! **Go!**
Oh, crap! What'd you do?
Goddamned cheats!
You're dead, dog! **Dead!**
EXIT
BLAM BLAM BLAM
Augh! You **stupid cursed bastard!**
It's not my fault! That old bat sold us out!
TOLDYA
I could'a stabbed them, but you took my shiv away--
Because you kept trying to stab **me!**
--so I set 'em on fire instead.
Jesus, Eddie.
Y'know, I don't think that fire potion killed **any** of them?
I need to start robbing better chemists.
I-676
New Jersey

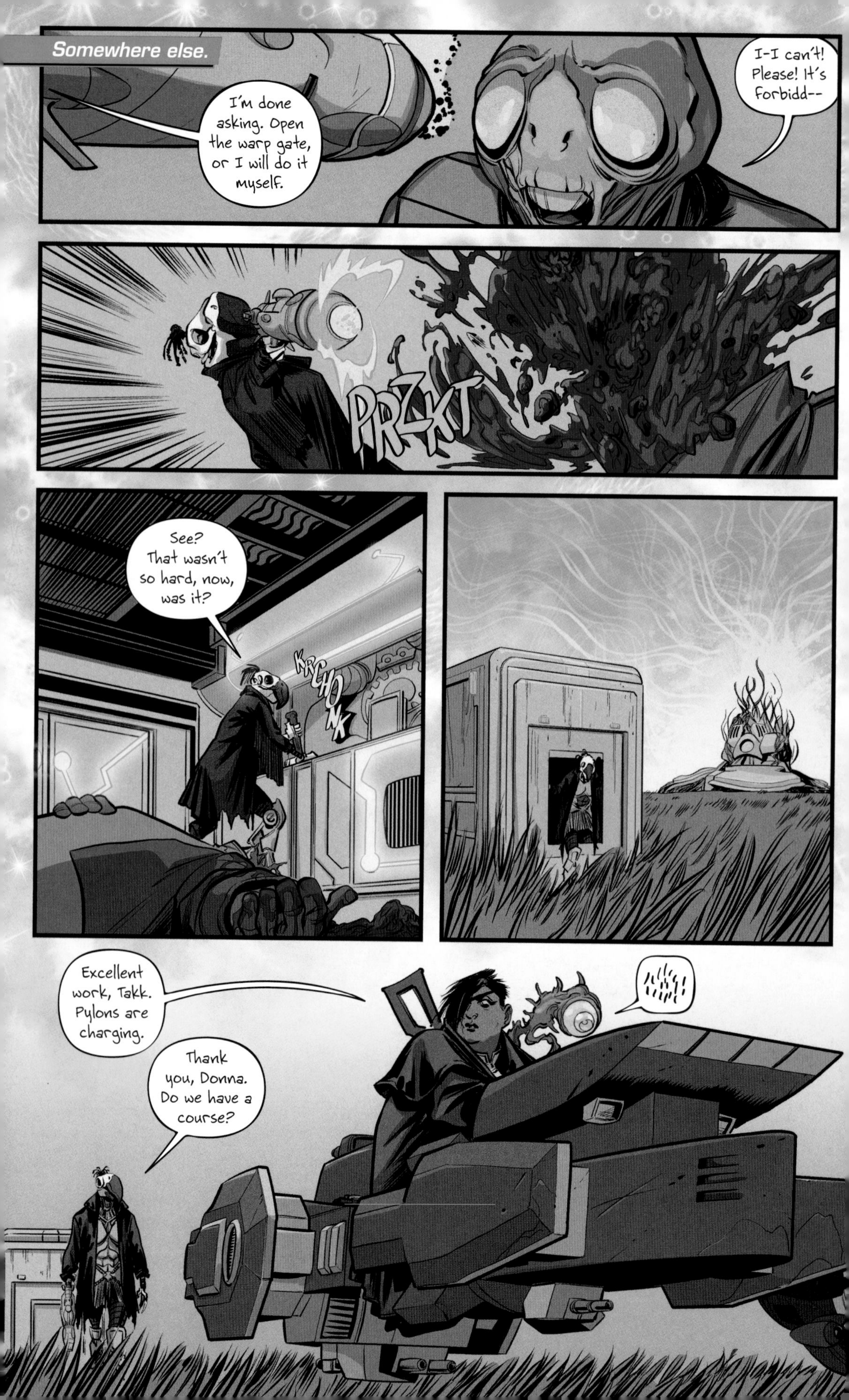
Somewhere else.
I'm done asking. Open the warp gate, or I will do it myself.
I-I can't! Please! It's forbidd--
PRZKT
See? That wasn't so hard, now, was it?
KRCHONK
Excellent work, Takk. Pylons are charging.
Thank you, Donna. Do we have a course?

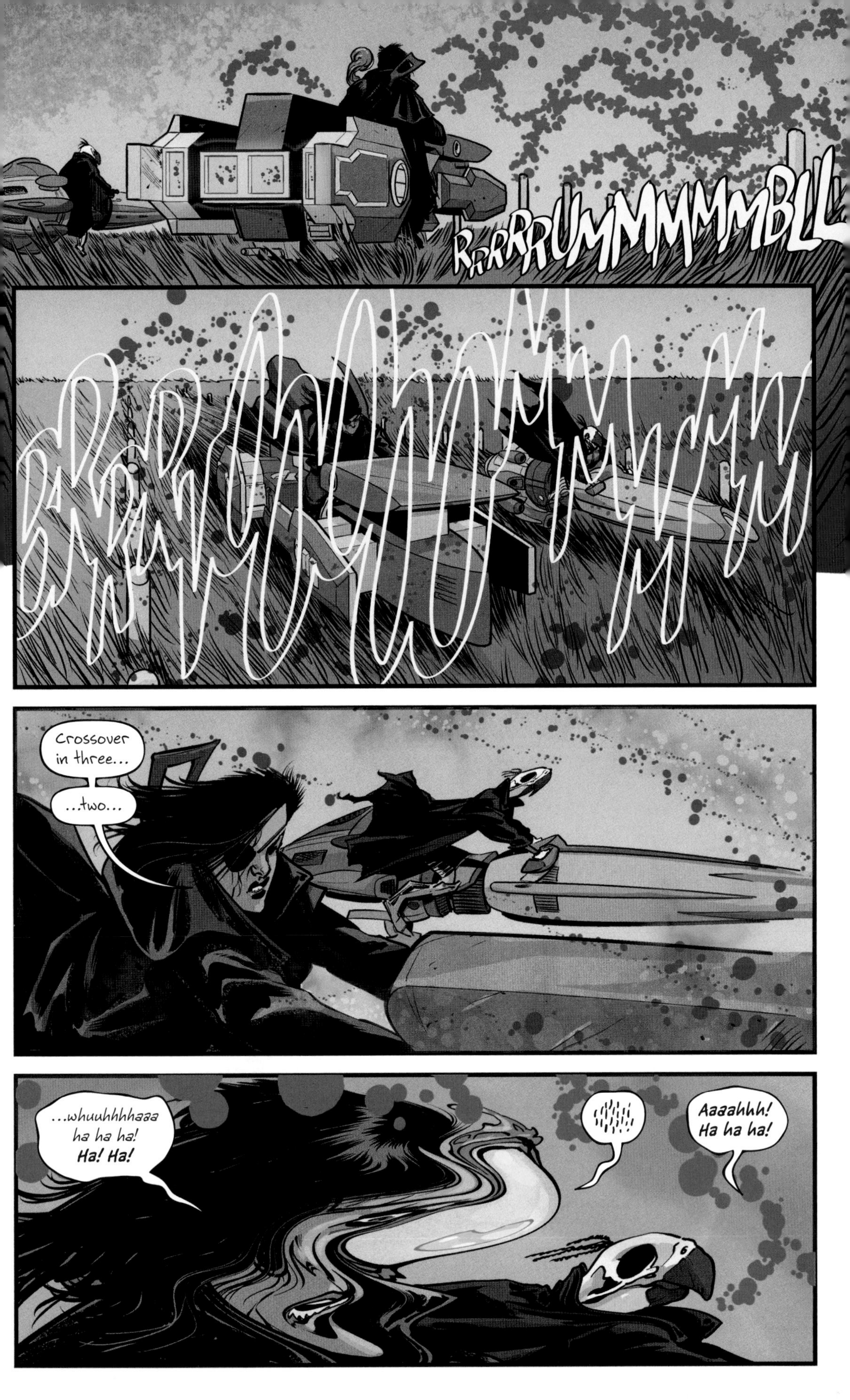
RRRRRUMMMMMMBLL
Crossover in three...
...two...
...whuuhhhhaaa ha ha ha! **Ha! Ha!**
Aaaahhh! Ha ha ha!

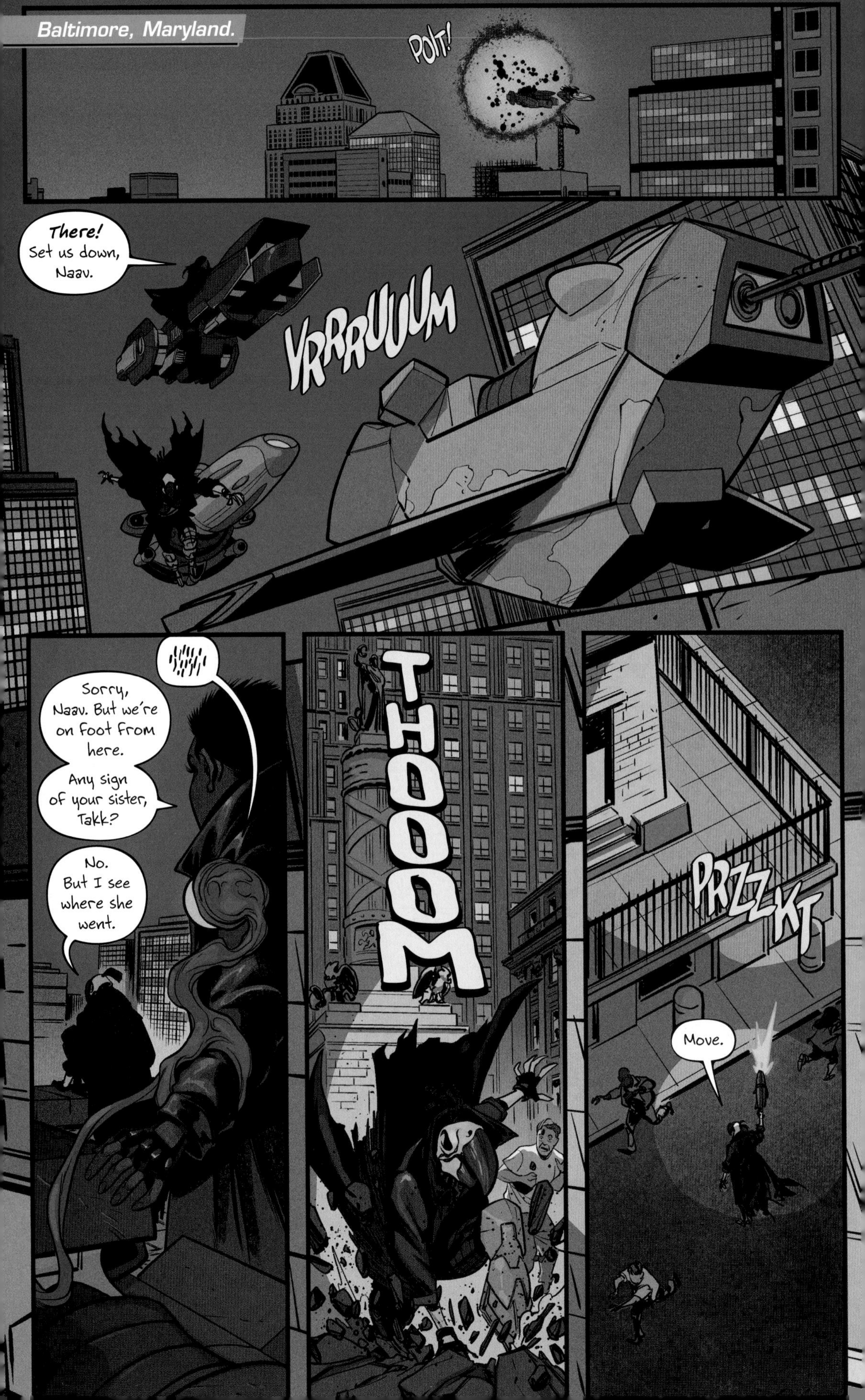
Baltimore, Maryland.
POIT!
There! Set us down, Naav.
VRRRUUUM
!!!
Sorry, Naav. But we're on foot from here.
Any sign of your sister, Takk?
No. But I see where she went.
THOOOM
PRZZKT
Move.

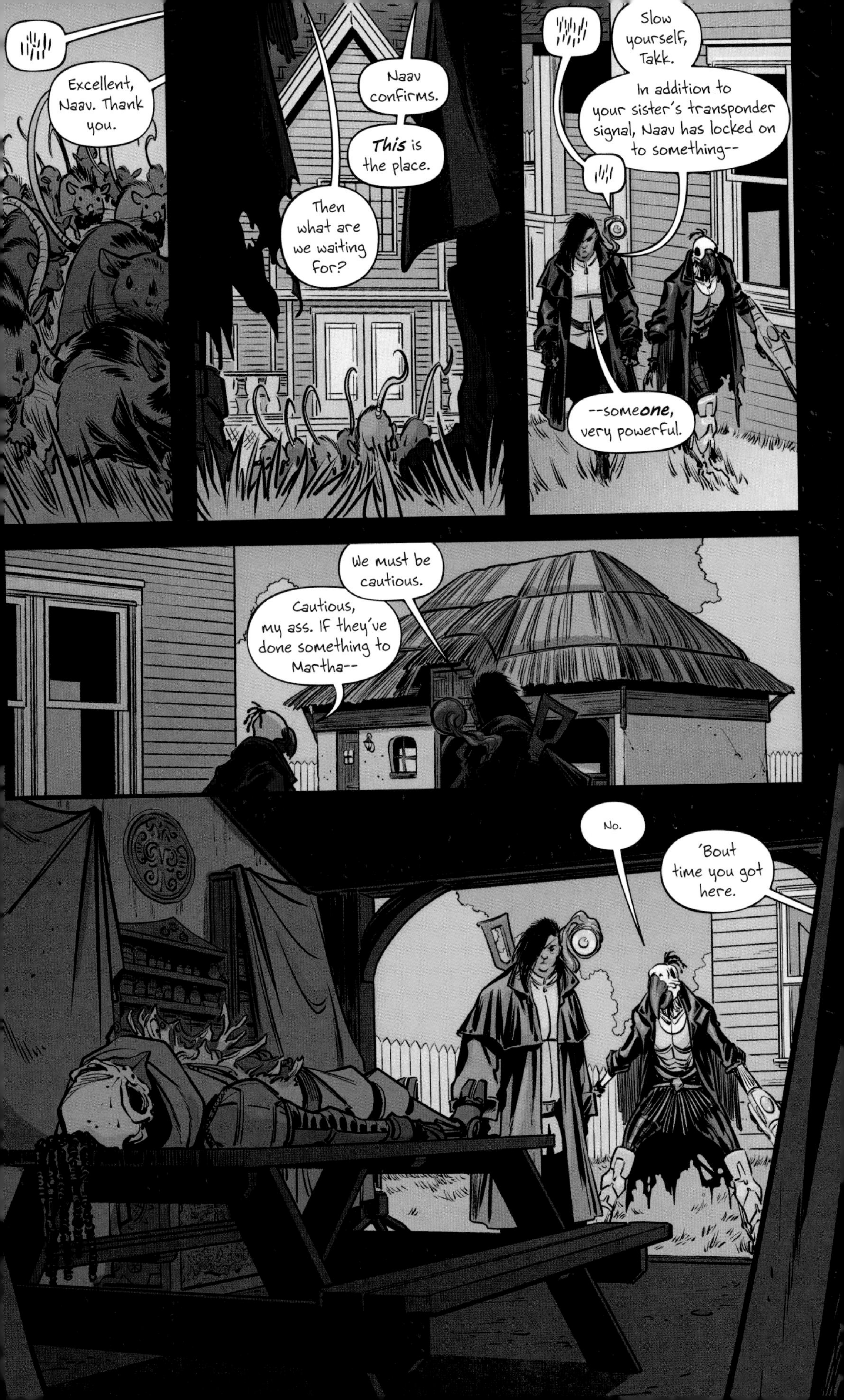
Excellent, Naav. Thank you.
Naav confirms.
This is the place.
Then what are we waiting for?
Slow yourself, Takk.
In addition to your sister's transponder signal, Naav has locked on to something--
--someone, very powerful.
We must be cautious.
Cautious, my ass. If they've done something to Martha--
No.
'Bout time you got here.

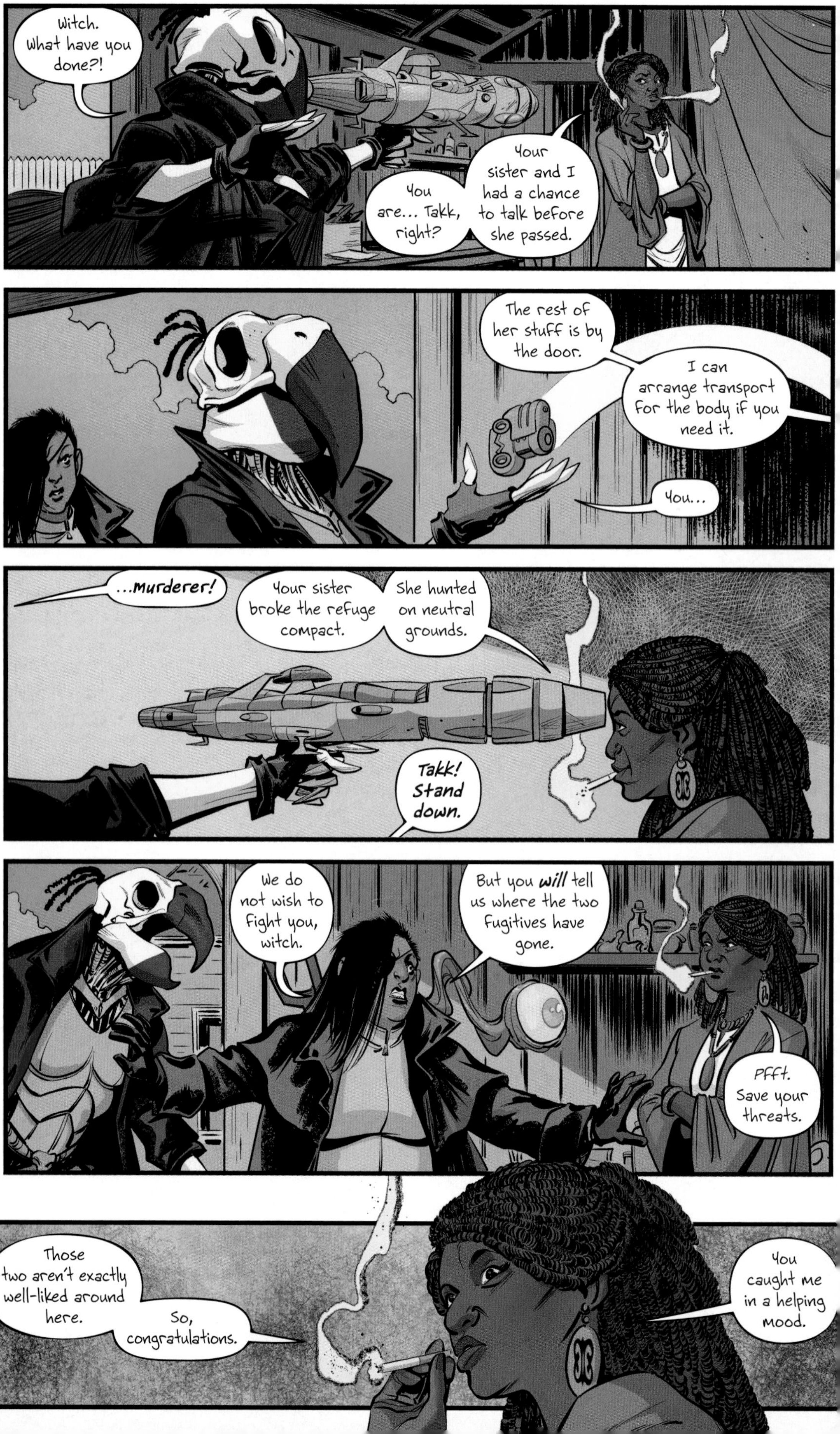
Witch. What have you done?!
You are... Takk, right?
Your sister and I had a chance to talk before she passed.
The rest of her stuff is by the door.
I can arrange transport for the body if you need it.
You...
...murderer!
Your sister broke the refuge compact.
She hunted on neutral grounds.
Takk! Stand down.
We do not wish to fight you, witch.
But you will tell us where the two fugitives have gone.
Pfft. Save your threats.
Those two aren't exactly well-liked around here.
So, congratulations.
You caught me in a helping mood.

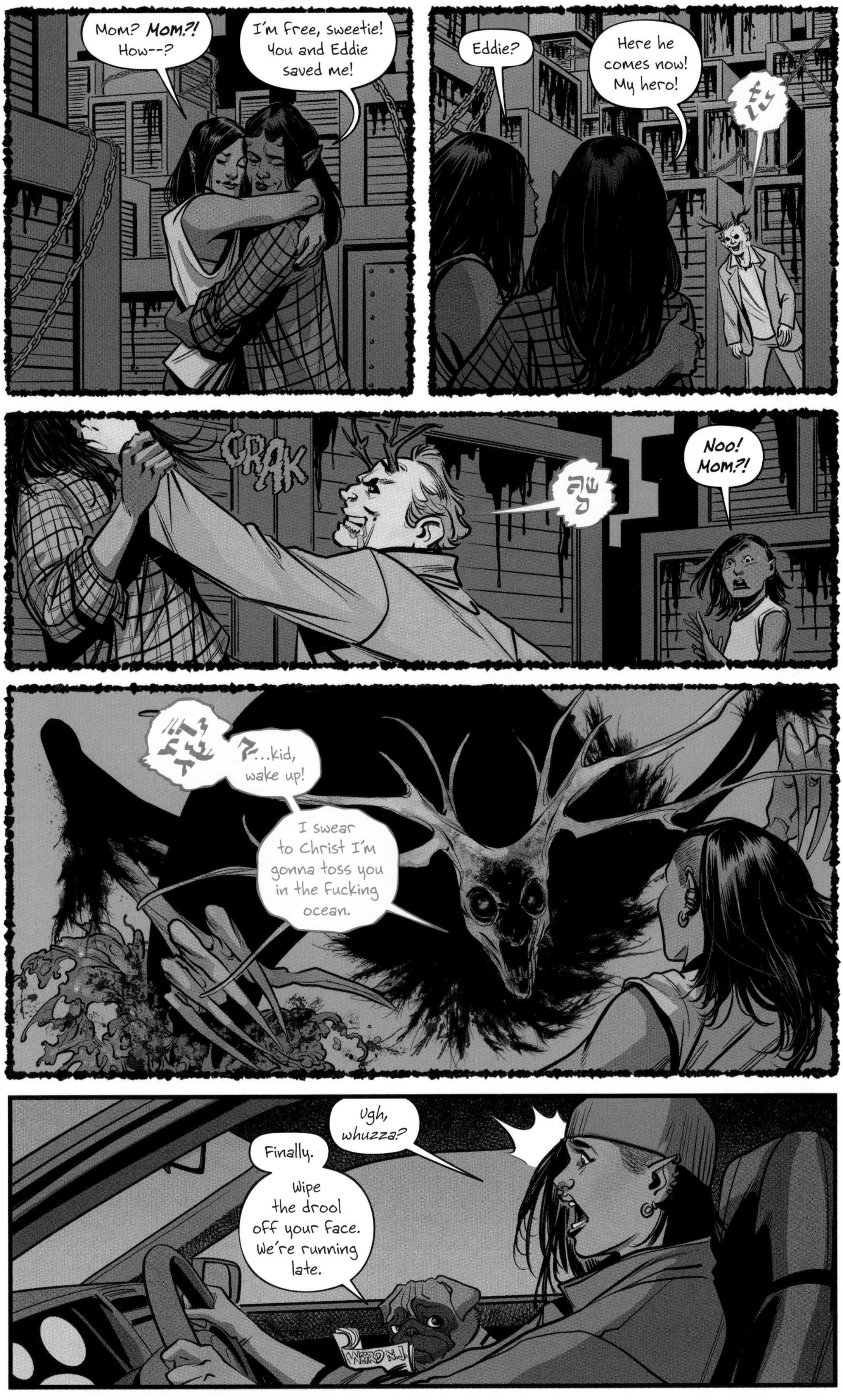
Mom? MOM?!
How--?
I'm free, sweetie! You and Eddie saved me!
Eddie?
Here he comes now! My hero!
CRAK
Noo! Mom?!
...kid, wake up!
I swear to Christ I'm gonna toss you in the fucking ocean.
Ugh, whuzza?
Finally.
Wipe the drool off your face. We're running late.
WEIRD N.J.

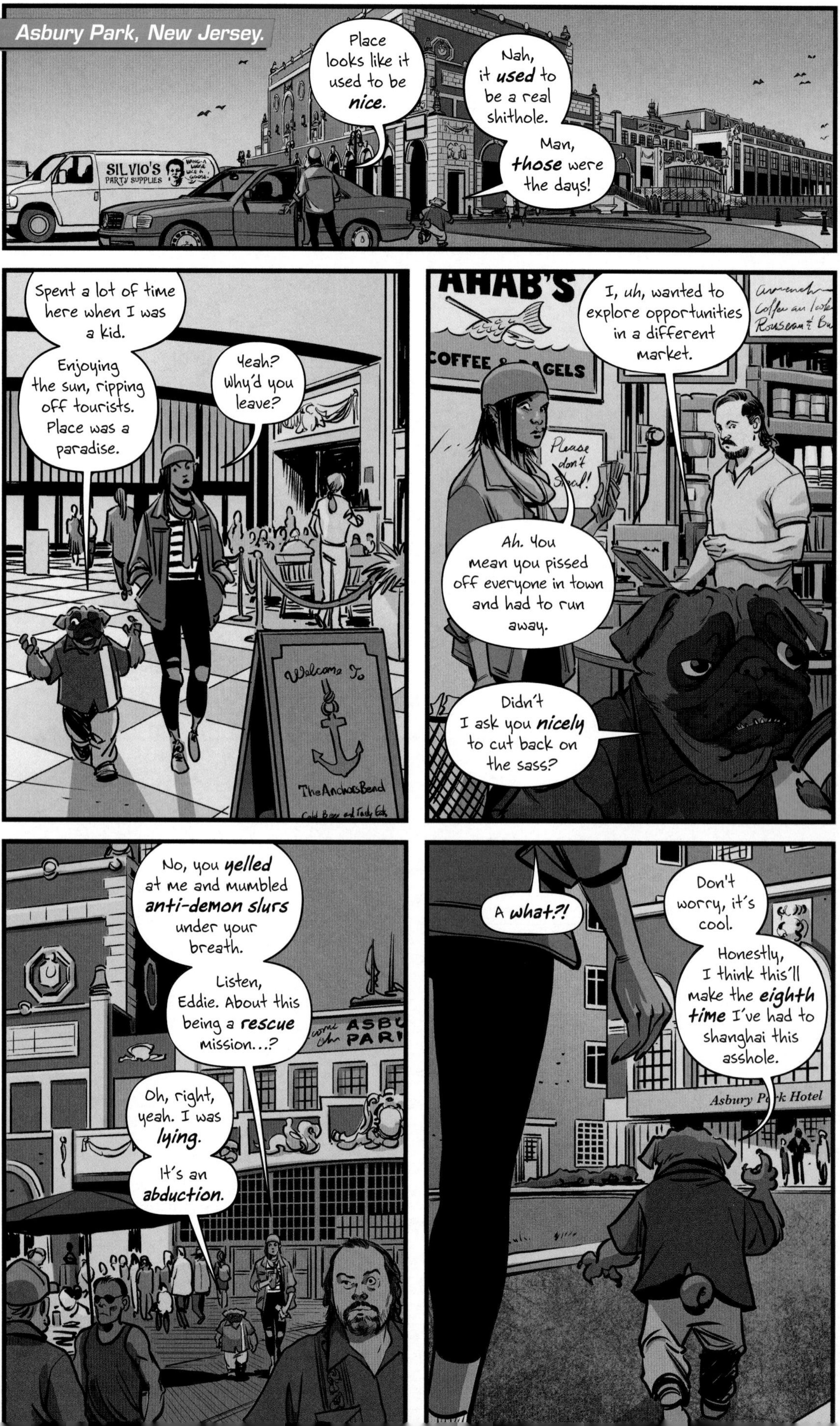
Asbury Park, New Jersey.
Place looks like it used to be **nice**.
Nah, it **used** to be a real shithole.
Man, **those** were the days!
SILVIO'S PARTY SUPPLIES
Spent a lot of time here when I was a kid.
Enjoying the sun, ripping off tourists. Place was a paradise.
Yeah? Why'd you leave?
Welcome To
The Anchors Bend
AHAB'S
I, uh, wanted to explore opportunities in a different market.
Please don't Steal!
Ah. You mean you pissed off everyone in town and had to run away.
Didn't I ask you **nicely** to cut back on the sass?
No, you **yelled** at me and mumbled **anti-demon slurs** under your breath.
Listen, Eddie. About this being a **rescue** mission...?
Oh, right, yeah. I was **lying**.
It's an **abduction**.
A **what?!**
Don't worry, it's cool.
Honestly, I think this'll make the **eighth time** I've had to shanghai this asshole.

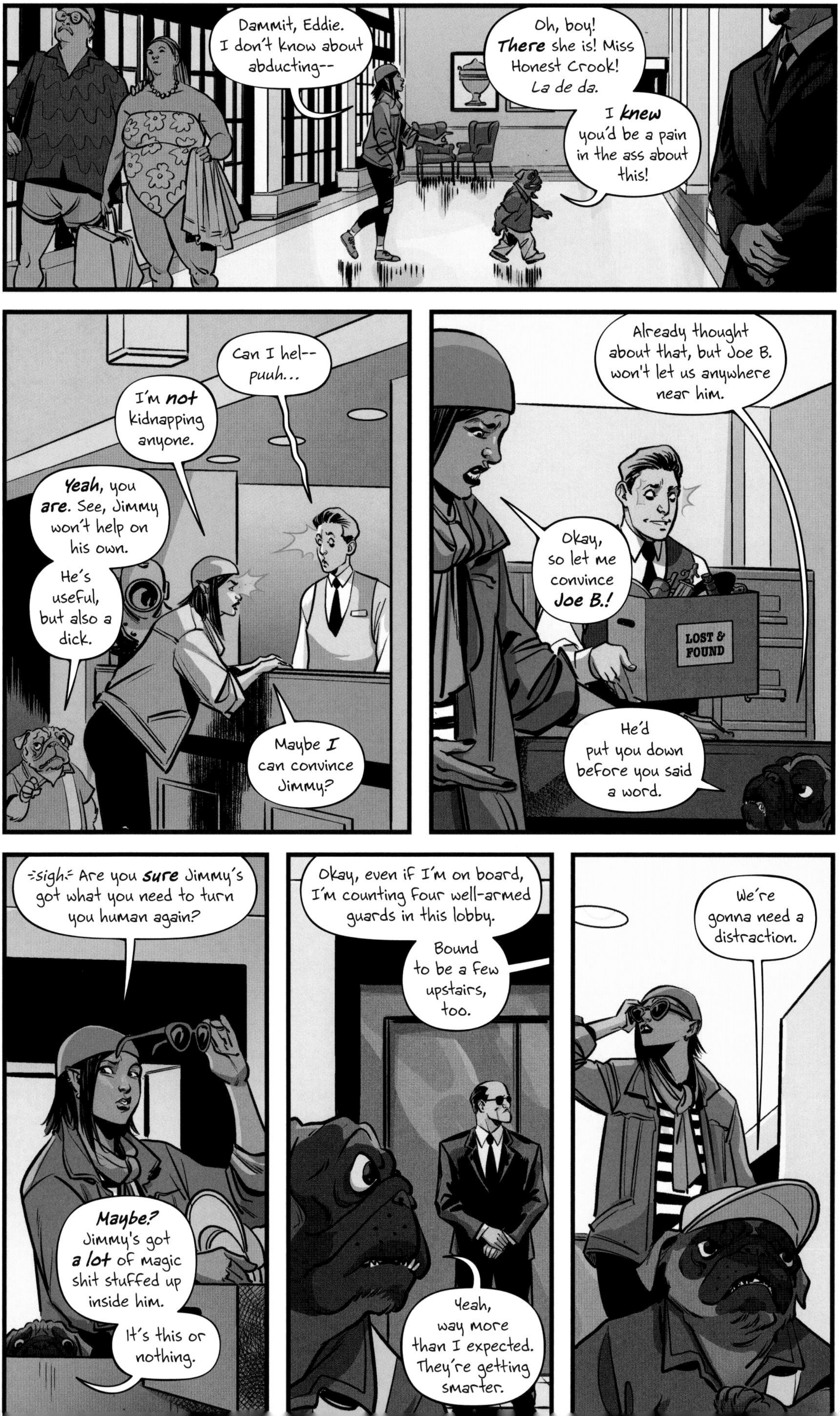
Dammit, Eddie. I don't know about abducting--
Oh, boy! There she is! Miss Honest Crook! La de da.
I knew you'd be a pain in the ass about this!
Can I hel-- puuh...
I'm not kidnapping anyone.
Yeah, you are. See, Jimmy won't help on his own.
He's useful, but also a dick.
Maybe I can convince Jimmy?
Already thought about that, but Joe B. won't let us anywhere near him.
Okay, so let me convince Joe B.!
LOST & FOUND
He'd put you down before you said a word.
=sigh= Are you sure Jimmy's got what you need to turn you human again?
Maybe? Jimmy's got a lot of magic shit stuffed up inside him.
It's this or nothing.
Okay, even if I'm on board, I'm counting four well-armed guards in this lobby.
Bound to be a few upstairs, too.
Yeah, way more than I expected. They're getting smarter.
We're gonna need a distraction.

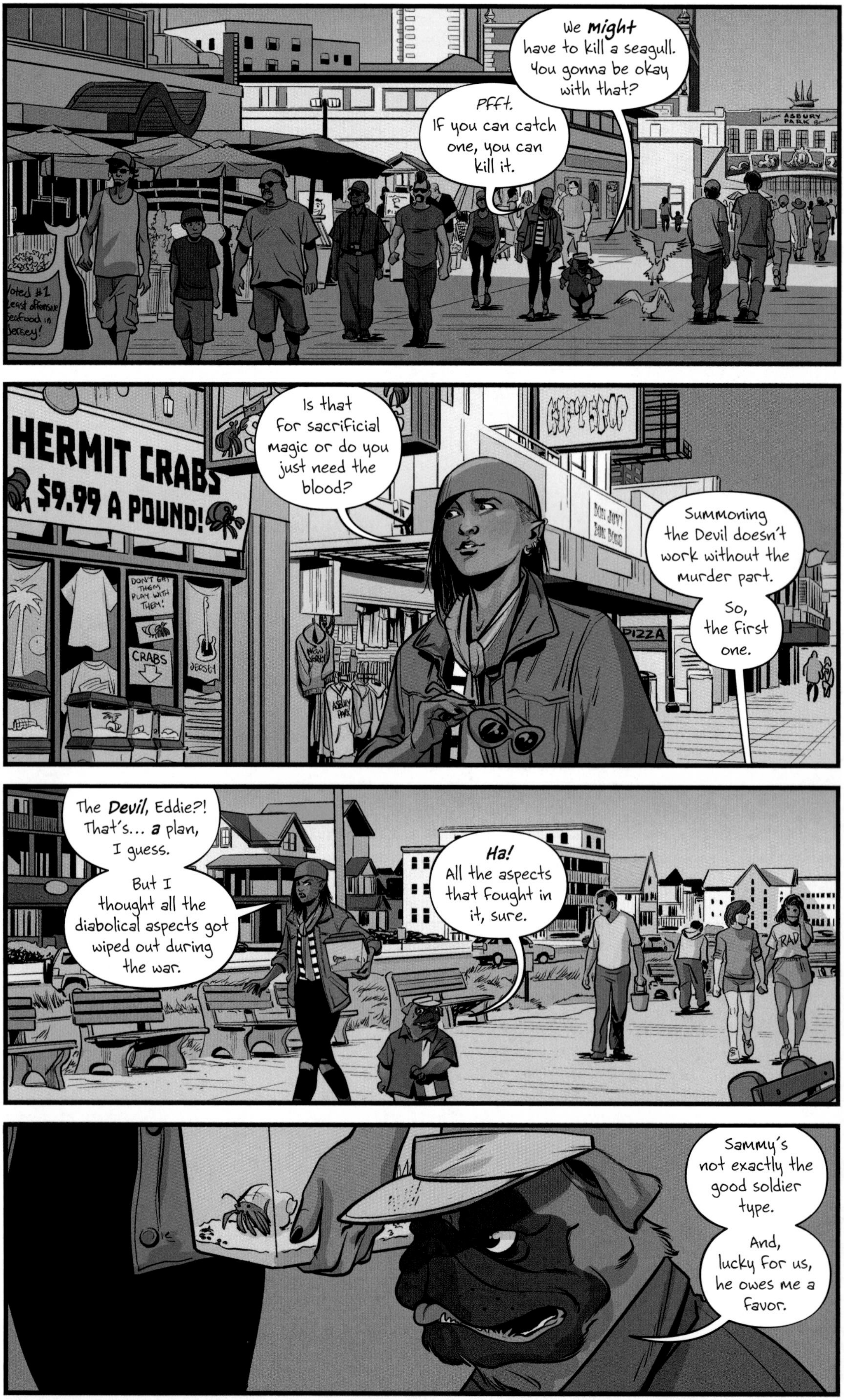

Voted #1 Least offensive Seafood in Jersey!
We **might** have to kill a seagull. You gonna be okay with that?
Pfft. If you can catch one, you can kill it.
HERMIT CRABS $9.99 A POUND!
DON'T EAT THEM PLAY WITH THEM!
CRABS
JERSEY
NEW JERSEY
ASBURY PARK
GIFT SHOP
BON JOVI! BON BONS
PIZZA
Is that for sacrificial magic or do you just need the blood?
Summoning the Devil doesn't work without the murder part.
So, the first one.
The ***Devil***, Eddie?! That's... ***a*** plan, I guess.
But I thought all the diabolical aspects got wiped out during the war.
Ha! All the aspects that fought in it, sure.
RAD
Sammy's not exactly the good soldier type.
And, lucky for us, he owes me a favor.

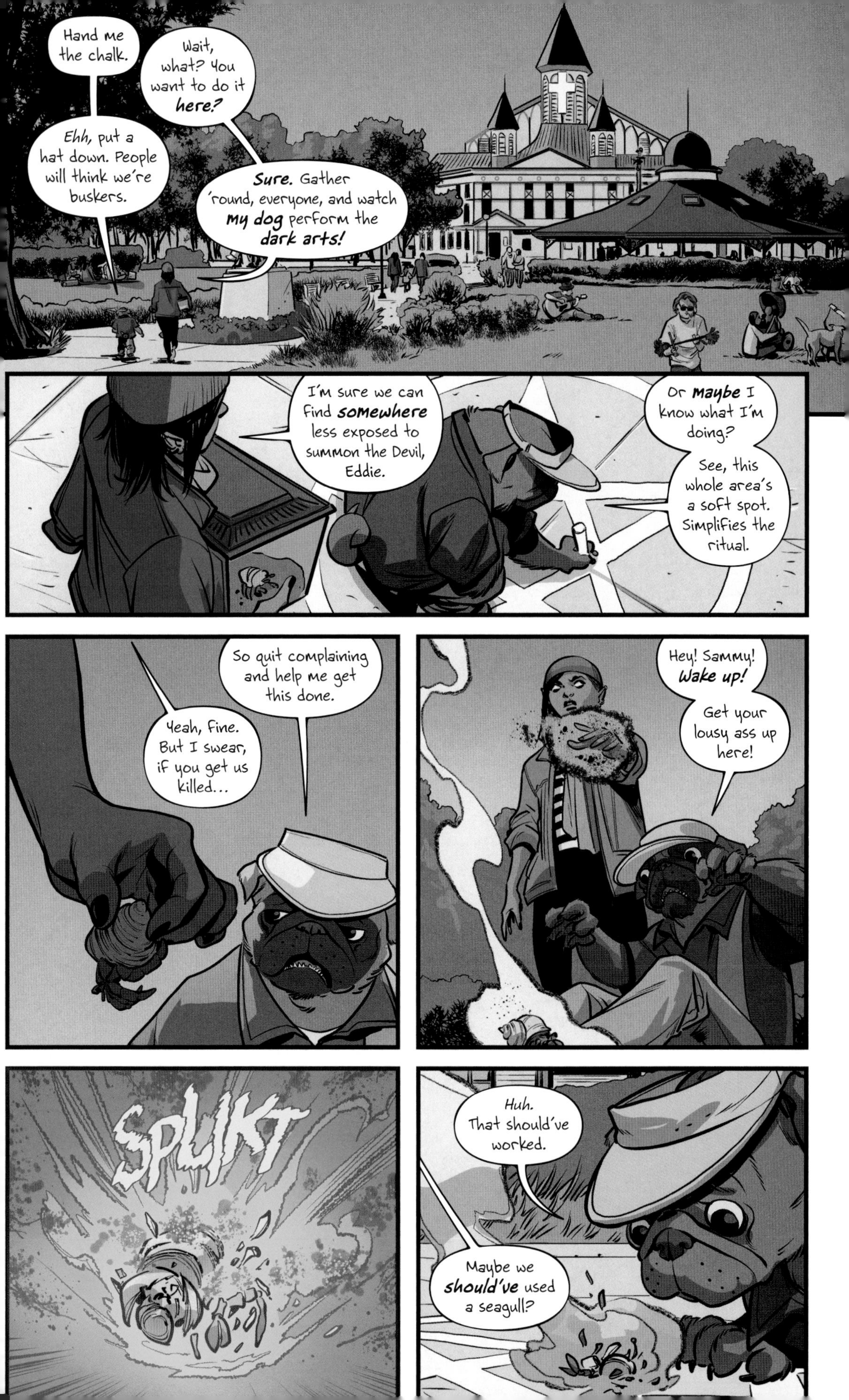
Hand me the chalk.
Wait, what? You want to do it here?
Ehh, put a hat down. People will think we're buskers.
Sure. Gather 'round, everyone, and watch my dog perform the dark arts!
I'm sure we can find somewhere less exposed to summon the Devil, Eddie.
Or maybe I know what I'm doing?
See, this whole area's a soft spot. Simplifies the ritual.
So quit complaining and help me get this done.
Yeah, fine. But I swear, if you get us killed...
Hey! Sammy! Wake up!
Get your lousy ass up here!
SPLIKT
Huh. That should've worked.
Maybe we should've used a seagull?

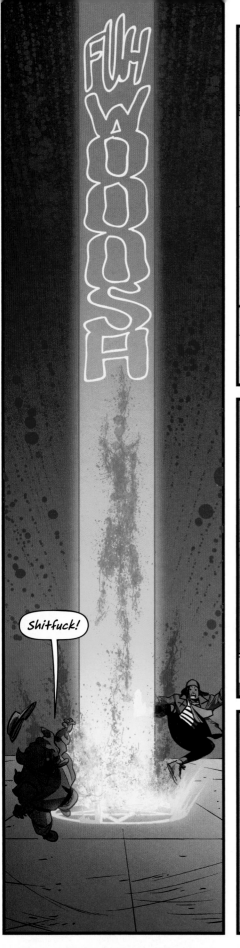

FUH WOOSH

Shitfuck!

=uuf=

Wha' th'... Who--

Eyy! Sammy! How's it hangin'?

Oh, Fuck. Eddie? You're a **dog** now?

Long story. I'm calling in a favor.

Oh, yeah? How 'bout you go fuck yourself instead?

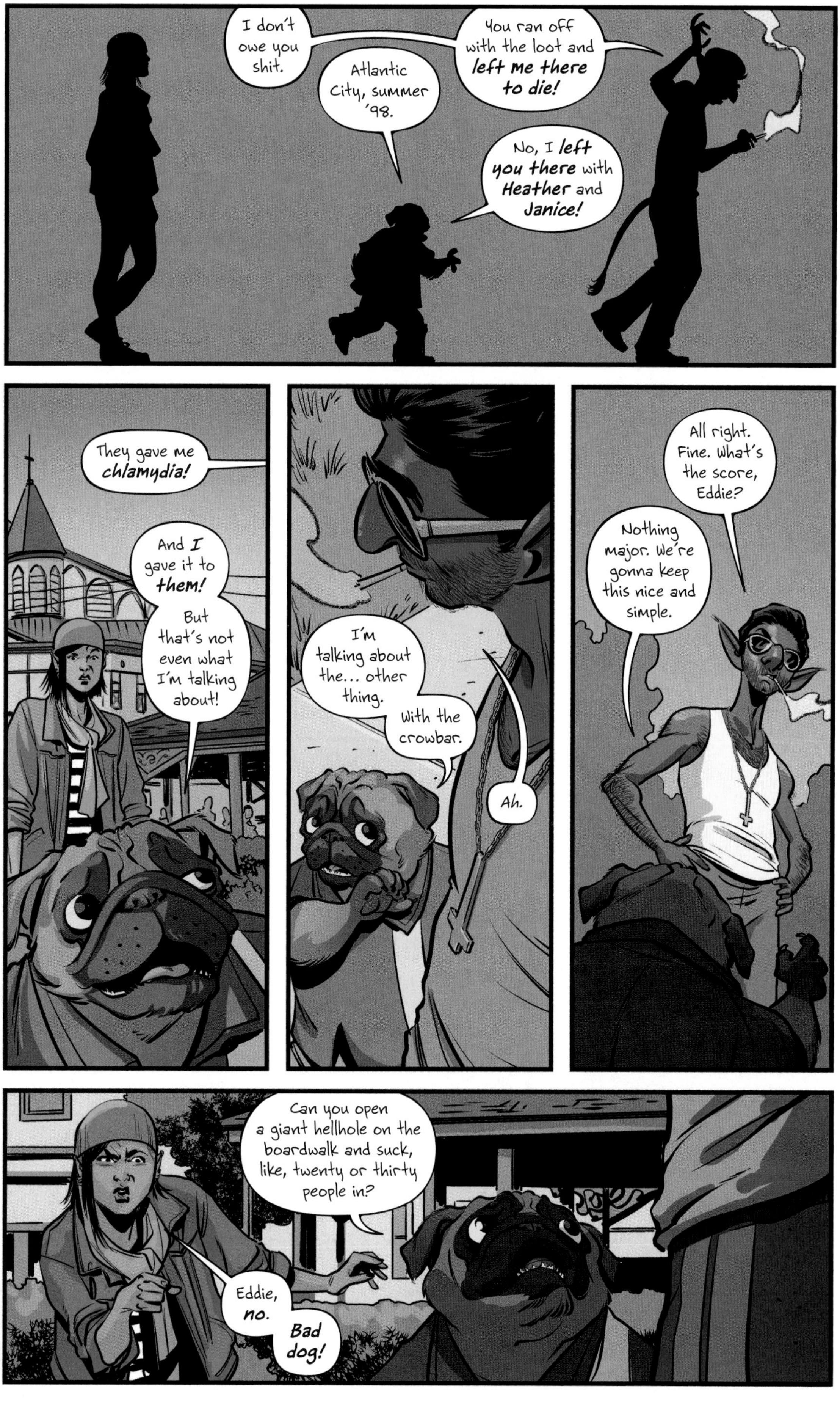
I don't owe you shit.
You ran off with the loot and left me there to die!
Atlantic City, summer '98.
No, I left you there with Heather and Janice!
They gave me chlamydia!
And I gave it to them!
But that's not even what I'm talking about!
I'm talking about the... other thing.
With the crowbar.
Ah.
All right. Fine. What's the score, Eddie?
Nothing major. We're gonna keep this nice and simple.
Can you open a giant hellhole on the boardwalk and suck, like, twenty or thirty people in?
Eddie, no.
Bad dog!

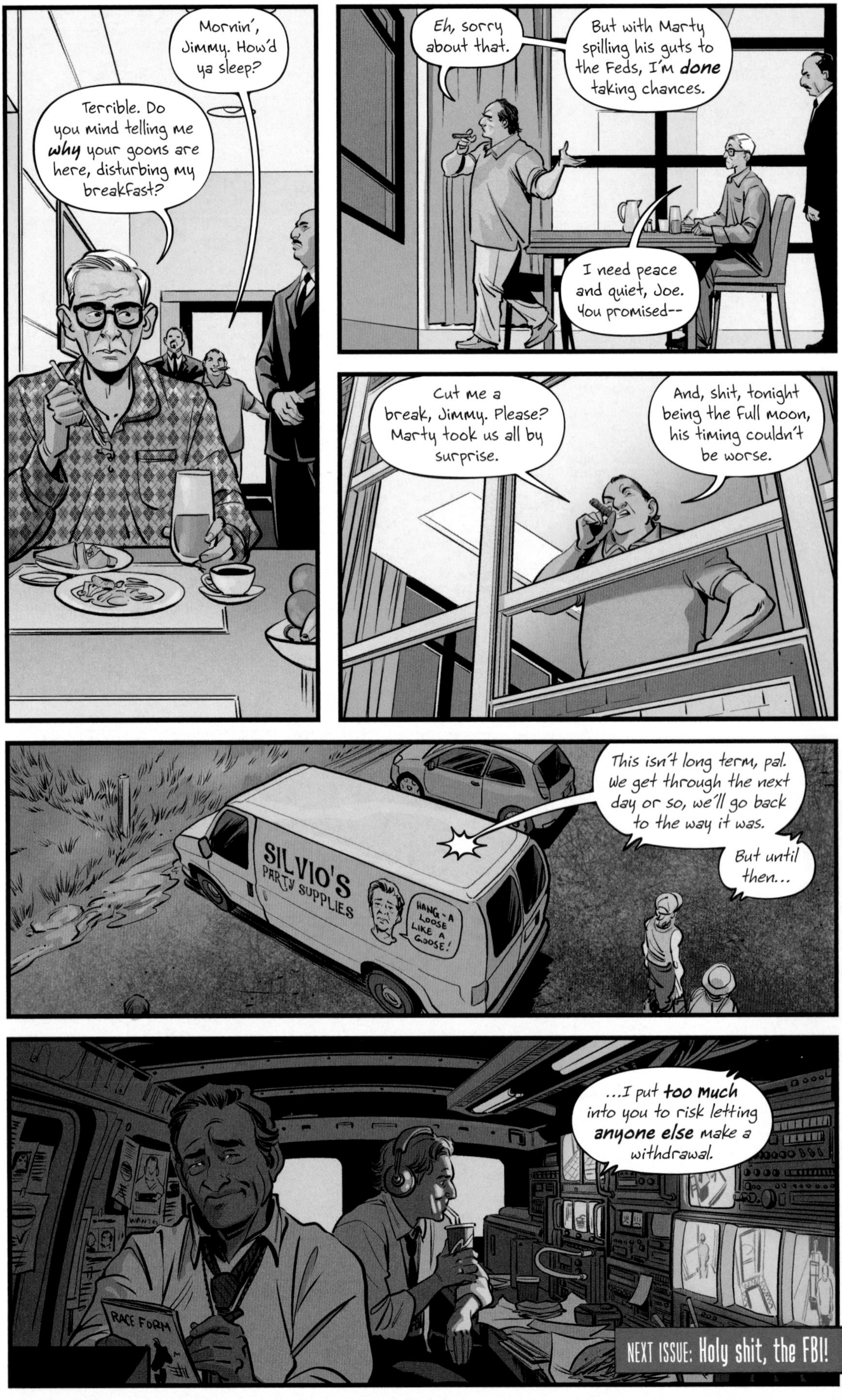
Mornin', Jimmy. How'd ya sleep?
Terrible. Do you mind telling me **why** your goons are here, disturbing my breakfast?
Eh, sorry about that.
But with Marty spilling his guts to the Feds, I'm **done** taking chances.
I need peace and quiet, Joe. You promised--
Cut me a break, Jimmy. Please? Marty took us all by surprise.
And, shit, tonight being the full moon, his timing couldn't be worse.
This isn't long term, pal. We get through the next day or so, we'll go back to the way it was.
But until then...
SILVIO'S PARTY SUPPLIES
HANG-A LOOSE LIKE A GOOSE!
...I put **too much** into you to risk letting **anyone else** make a withdrawal.
RACE FORM
NEXT ISSUE: Holy shit, the FBI!

BOOK TWO

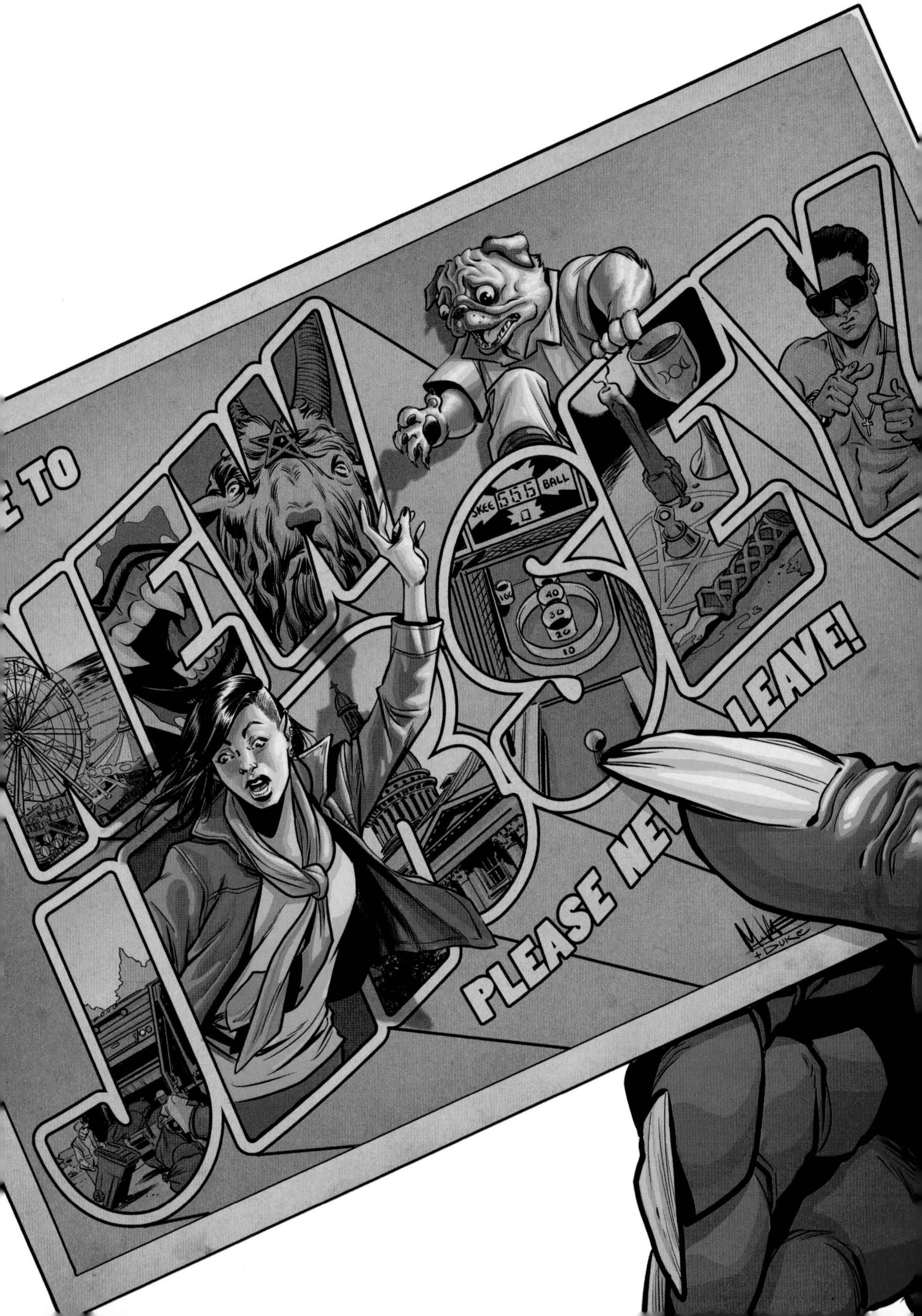
E TO
SKEE 666 BALL
PLEASE NE
LEAVE!

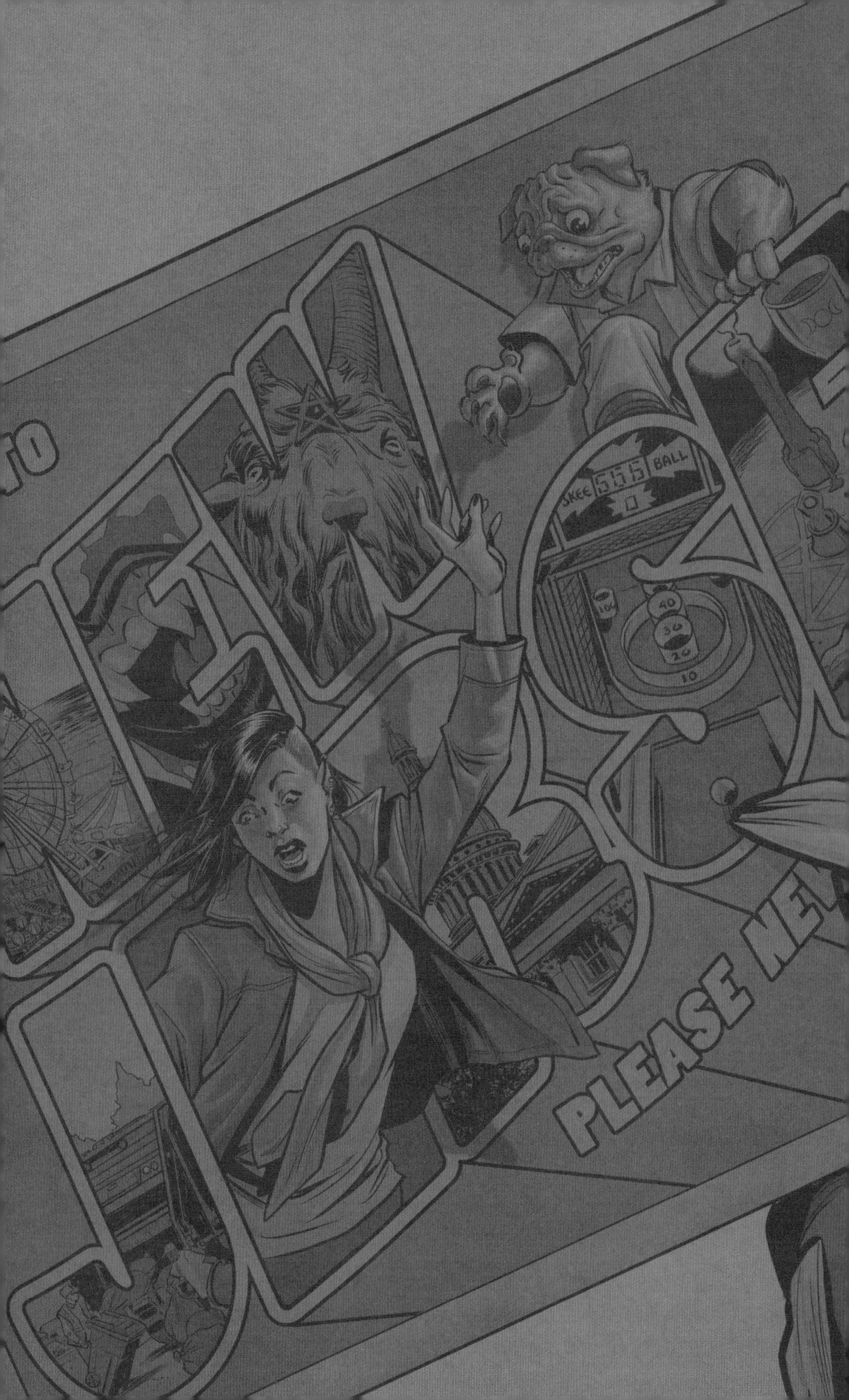
TO
SKEE 555 BALL
PLEASE NE

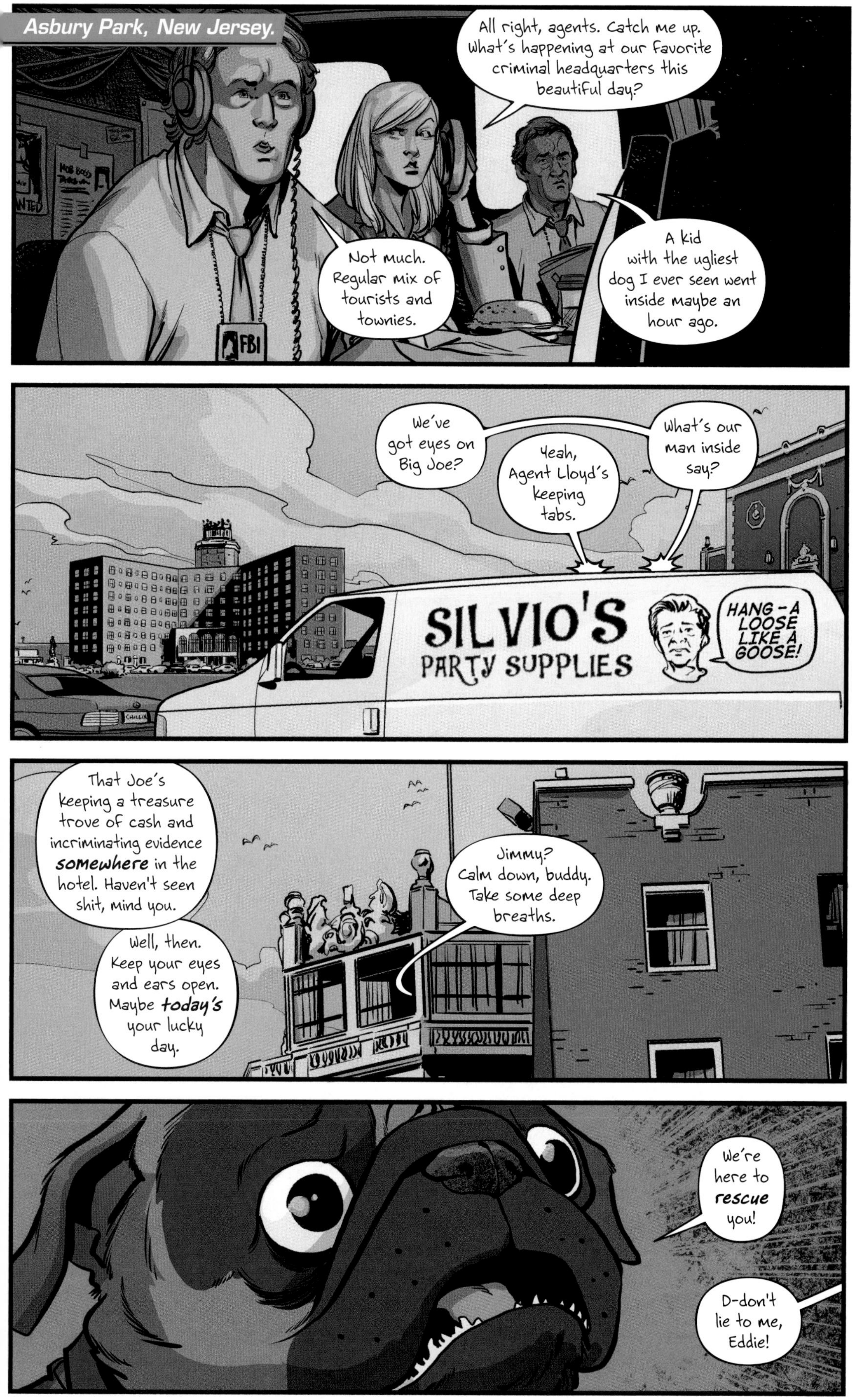
Asbury Park, New Jersey.
All right, agents. Catch me up. What's happening at our favorite criminal headquarters this beautiful day?
Not much. Regular mix of tourists and townies.
A kid with the ugliest dog I ever seen went inside maybe an hour ago.
FBI
We've got eyes on Big Joe?
Yeah, Agent Lloyd's keeping tabs.
What's our man inside say?
SILVIO'S PARTY SUPPLIES
HANG-A LOOSE LIKE A GOOSE!
That Joe's keeping a treasure trove of cash and incriminating evidence somewhere in the hotel. Haven't seen shit, mind you.
Well, then. Keep your eyes and ears open. Maybe today's your lucky day.
Jimmy? Calm down, buddy. Take some deep breaths.
We're here to rescue you!
D-don't lie to me, Eddie!

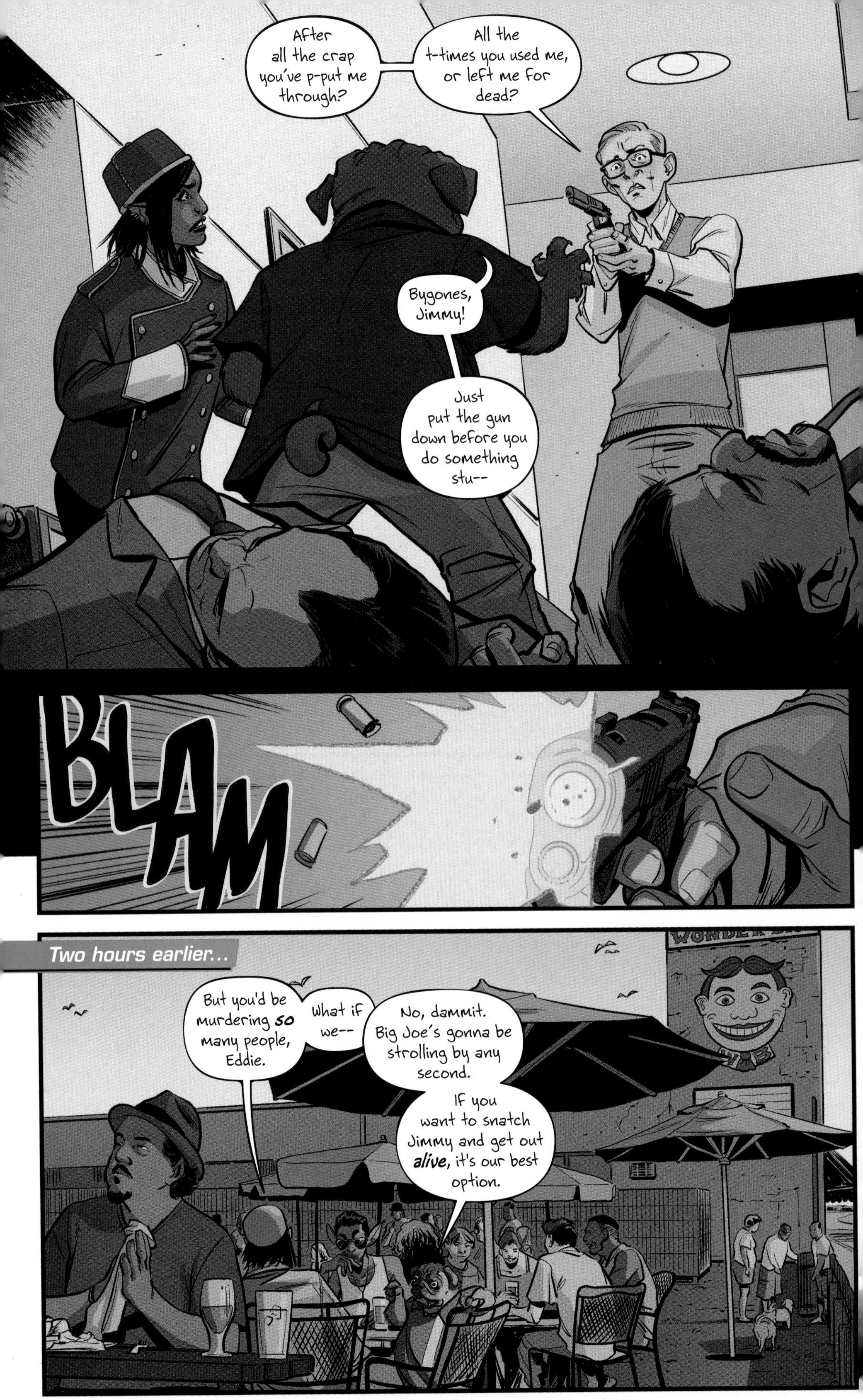

After all the crap you've p-put me through?
All the t-times you used me, or left me for dead?
Bygones, Jimmy!
Just put the gun down before you do something stu--
BLAM
Two hours earlier...
But you'd be murdering *so* many people, Eddie.
What if we--
No, dammit. Big Joe's gonna be strolling by any second.
If you want to snatch Jimmy and get out ***alive***, it's our best option.

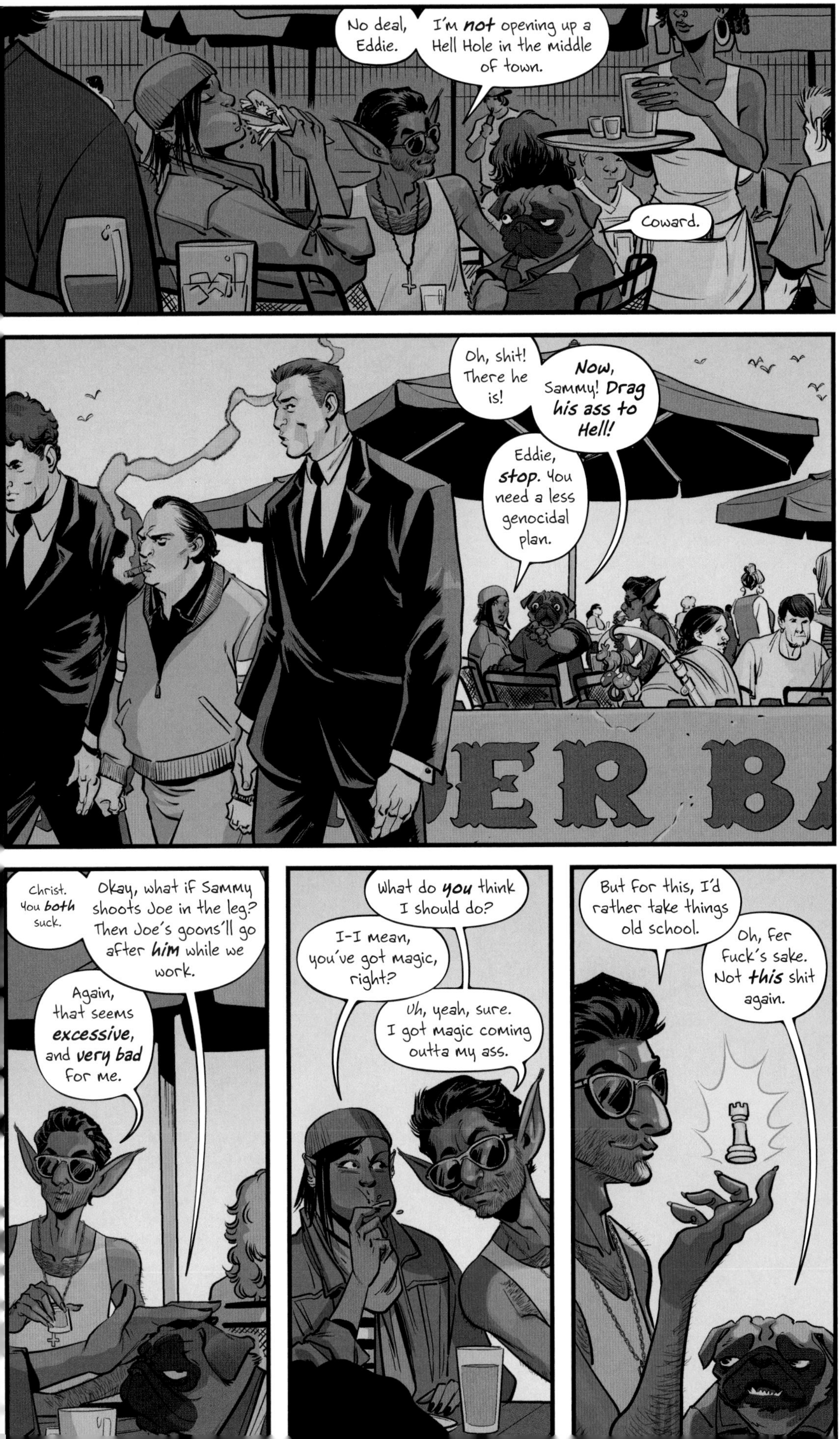
No deal, Eddie.
I'm **not** opening up a Hell Hole in the middle of town.
Coward.
Oh, shit! There he is!
Now, Sammy! **Drag his ass to Hell!**
Eddie, **stop.** You need a less genocidal plan.
Christ. You **both** suck.
Okay, what if Sammy shoots Joe in the leg? Then Joe's goons'll go after **him** while we work.
Again, that seems **excessive,** and **very bad** for me.
What do **you** think I should do?
I-I mean, you've got magic, right?
Uh, yeah, sure. I got magic coming outta my ass.
But for this, I'd rather take things old school.
Oh, fer fuck's sake. Not **this** shit again.

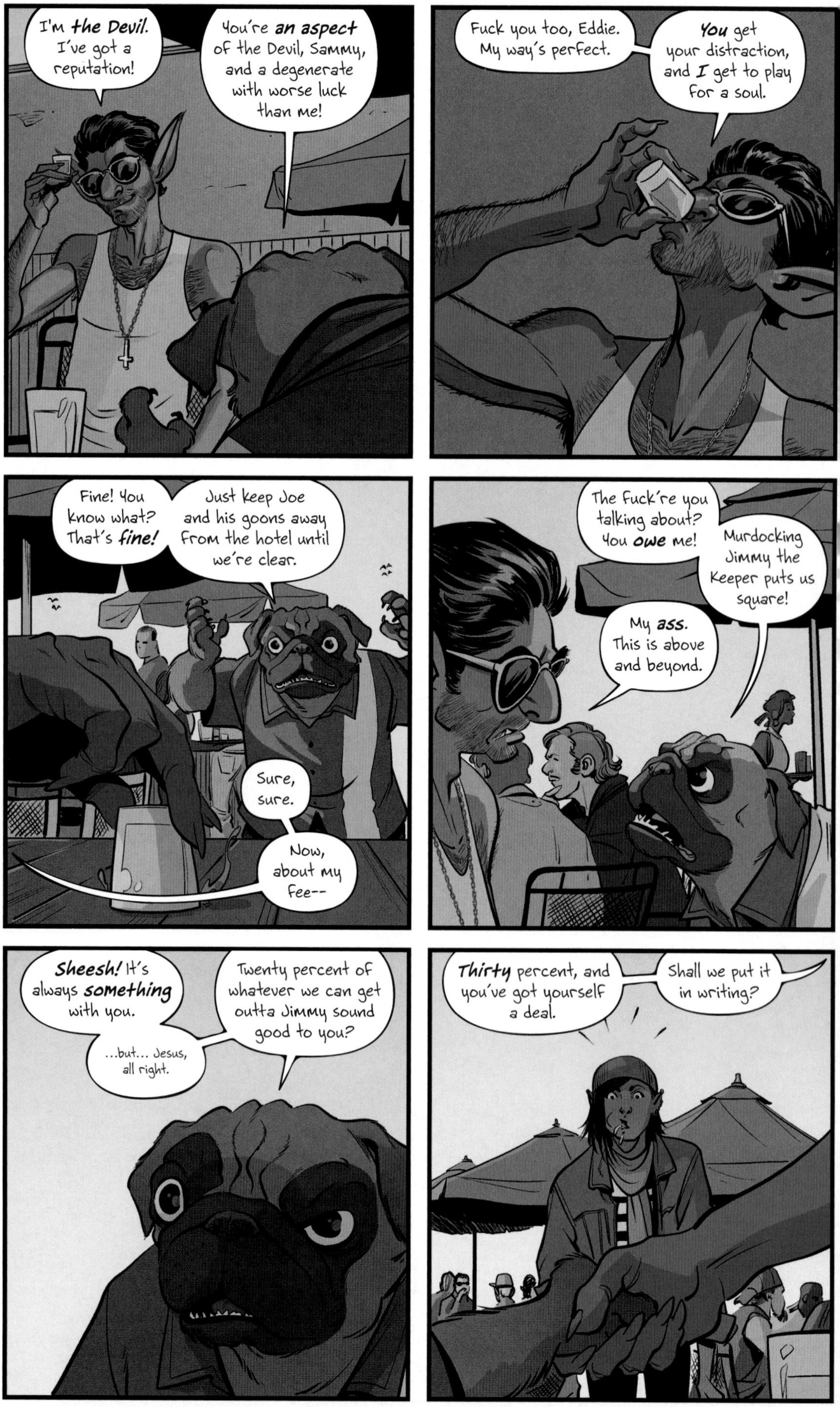
I'm **the Devil.** I've got a reputation!
You're **an aspect** of the Devil, Sammy, and a degenerate with worse luck than me!
Fuck you too, Eddie. My way's perfect.
You get your distraction, and **I** get to play for a soul.
Fine! You know what? That's **fine!**
Just keep Joe and his goons away from the hotel until we're clear.
Sure, sure.
Now, about my fee--
The fuck're you talking about? You **owe** me!
Murdocking Jimmy the Keeper puts us square!
My **ass.** This is above and beyond.
Sheesh! It's always **something** with you.
...but... Jesus, all right.
Twenty percent of whatever we can get outta Jimmy sound good to you?
Thirty percent, and you've got yourself a deal.
Shall we put it in writing?

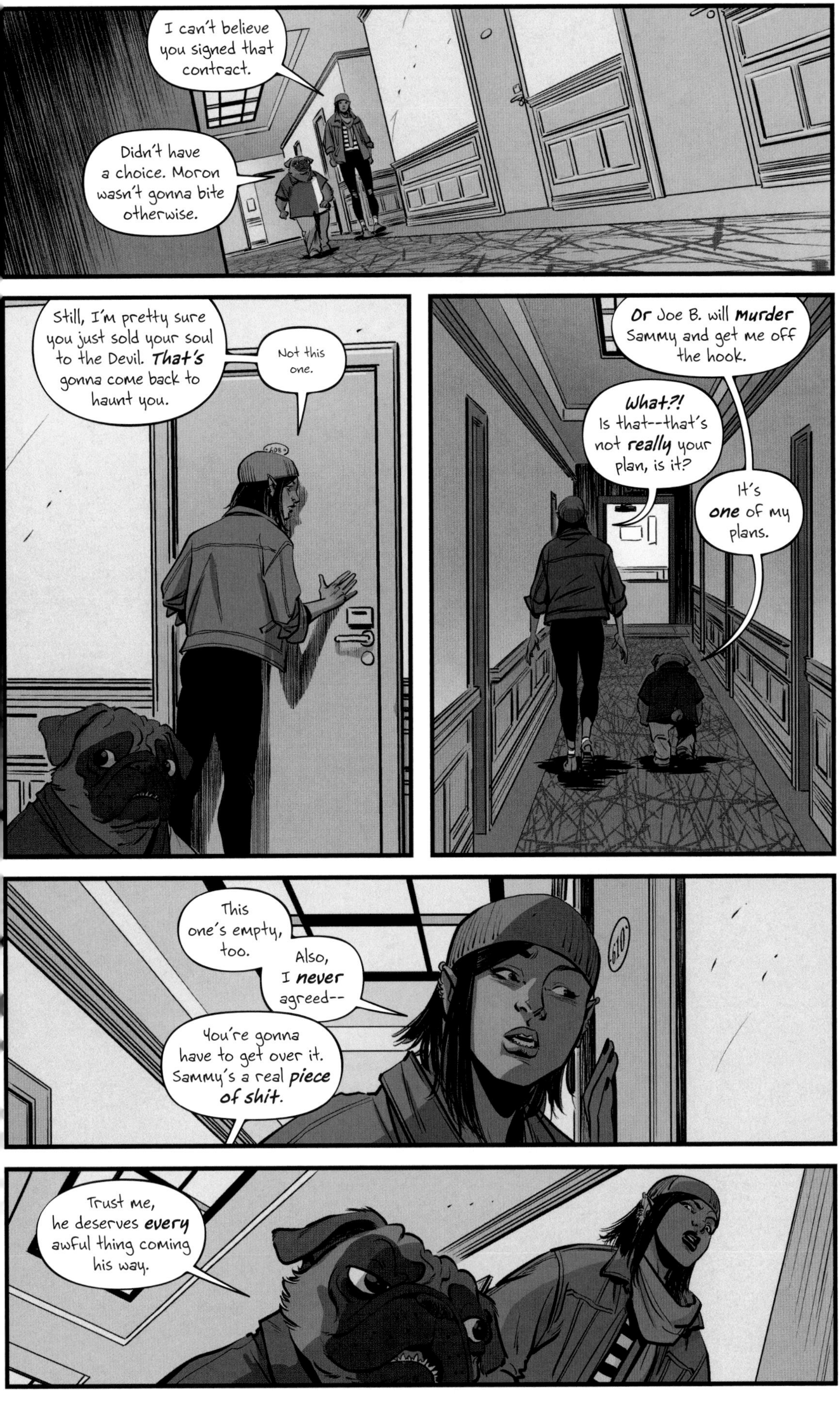
I can't believe you signed that contract.
Didn't have a choice. Moron wasn't gonna bite otherwise.
Still, I'm pretty sure you just sold your soul to the Devil. That's gonna come back to haunt you.
Not this one.
608
Or Joe B. will murder Sammy and get me off the hook.
What?! Is that--that's not really your plan, is it?
It's one of my plans.
This one's empty, too.
Also, I never agreed--
610
You're gonna have to get over it. Sammy's a real piece of shit.
Trust me, he deserves every awful thing coming his way.

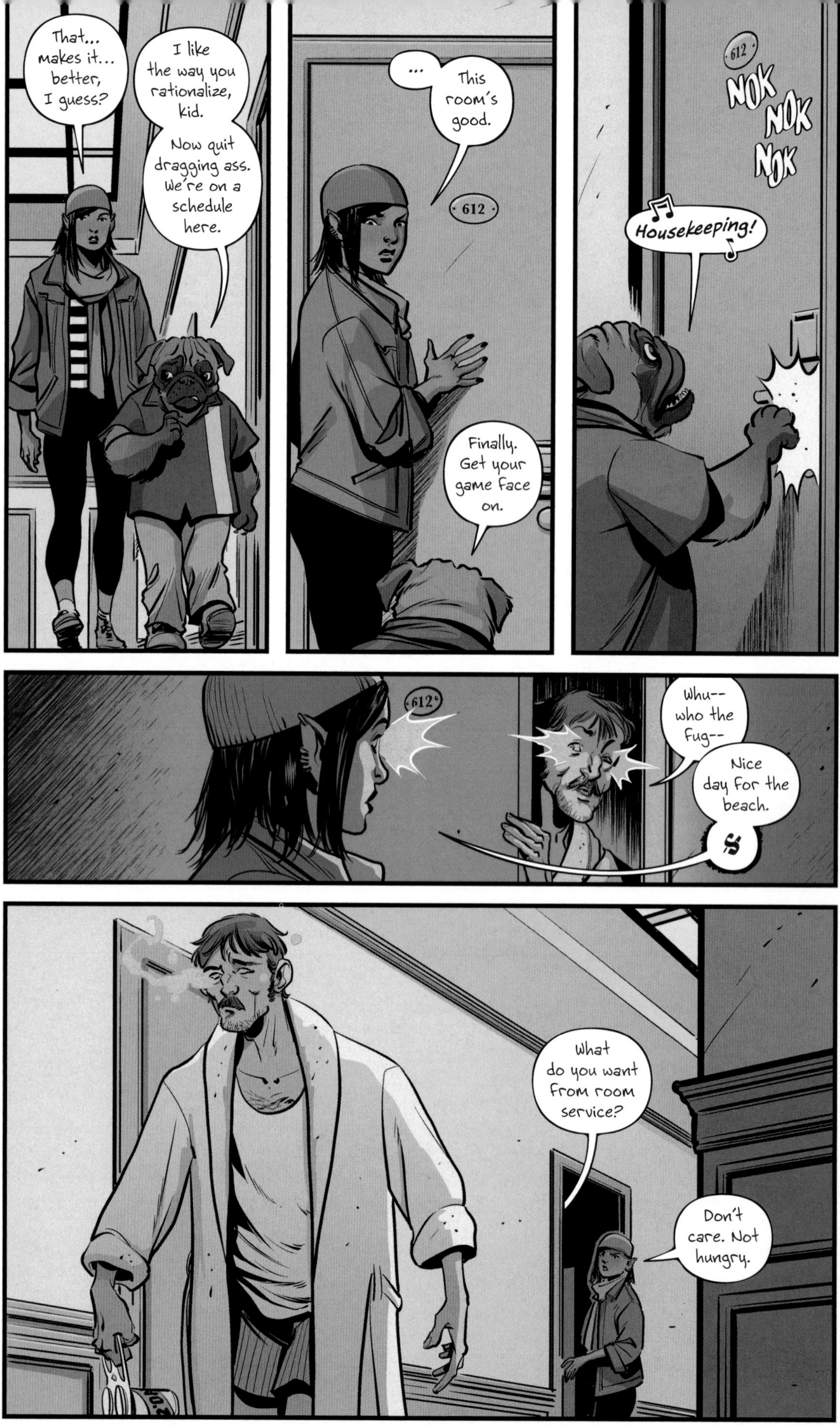

That... makes it... better, I guess?
I like the way you rationalize, kid.
Now quit dragging ass. We're on a schedule here.
...
This room's good.
612
Finally. Get your game face on.
612
NOK NOK NOK
Housekeeping!
612
Whu-- who the fug--
Nice day for the beach.
What do you want from room service?
Don't care. Not hungry.

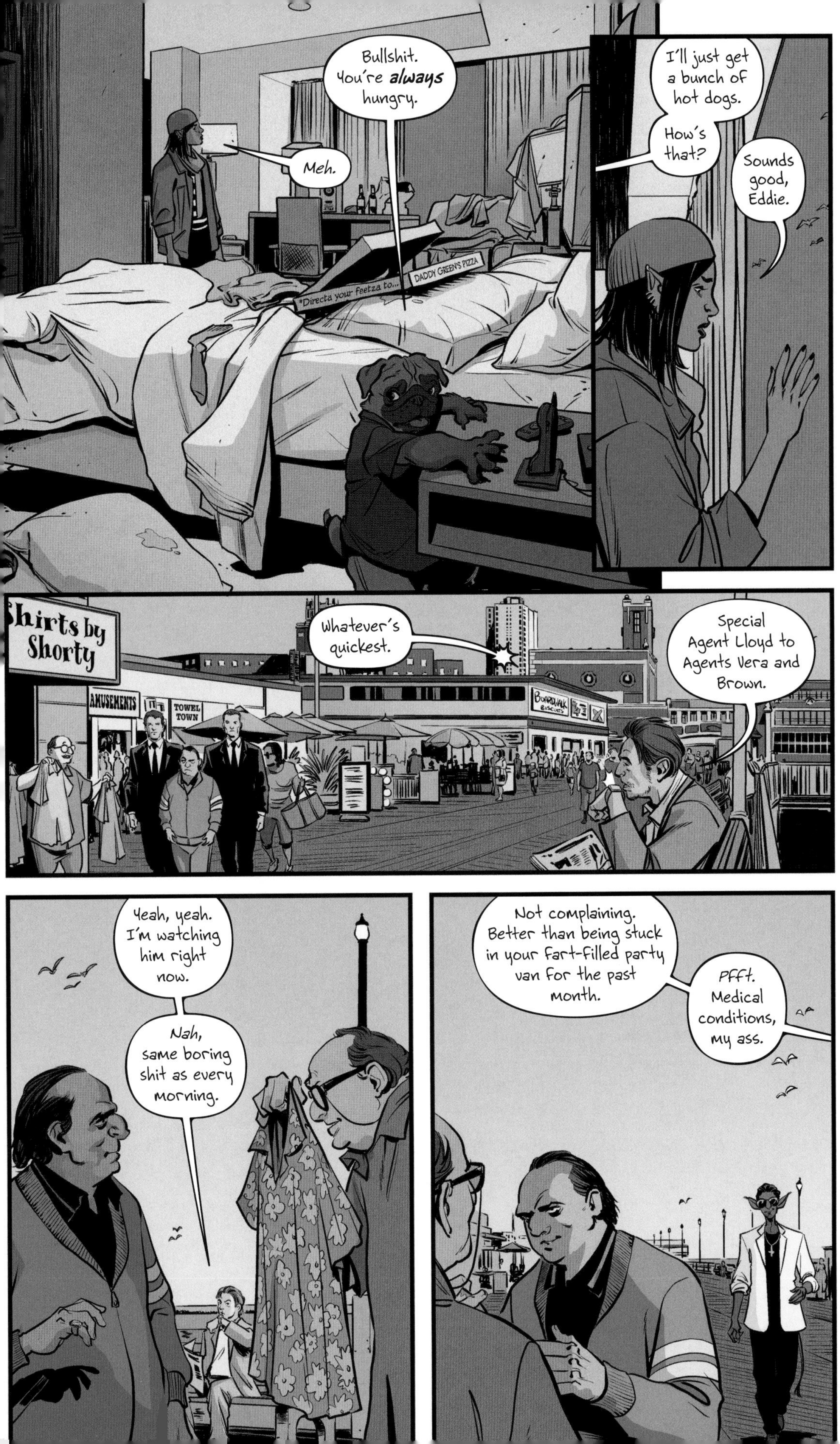
Bullshit. You're *always* hungry.
Meh.
"Directa your feetza to...
DADDY GREEN'S PIZZA
I'll just get a bunch of hot dogs.
How's that?
Sounds good, Eddie.
Shirts by Shorty
AMUSEMENTS
TOWEL TOWN
BOARDWALK BISCUITS
Whatever's quickest.
Special Agent Lloyd to Agents Vera and Brown.
Yeah, yeah. I'm watching him right now.
Nah, same boring shit as every morning.
Not complaining. Better than being stuck in your fart-filled party van for the past month.
Pfft. Medical conditions, my ass.

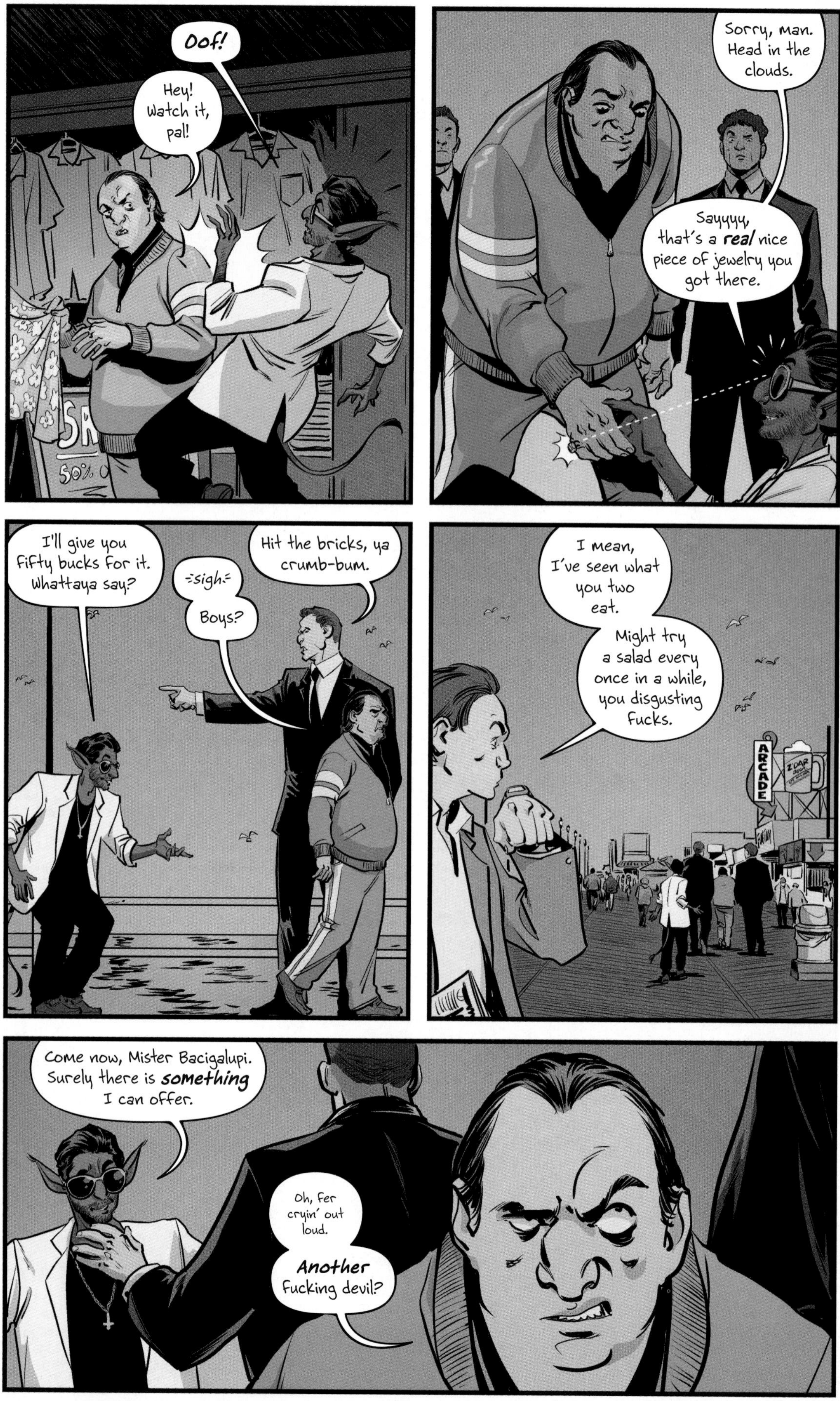
Oof!
Hey! Watch it, pal!
Sorry, man. Head in the clouds.
Sayyyy, that's a **real** nice piece of jewelry you got there.
I'll give you fifty bucks for it. Whattaya say?
-sigh-
Boys?
Hit the bricks, ya crumb-bum.
I mean, I've seen what you two eat.
Might try a salad every once in a while, you disgusting fucks.
ARCADE
Come now, Mister Bacigalupi. Surely there is **something** I can offer.
Oh, fer cryin' out loud.
Another fucking devil?

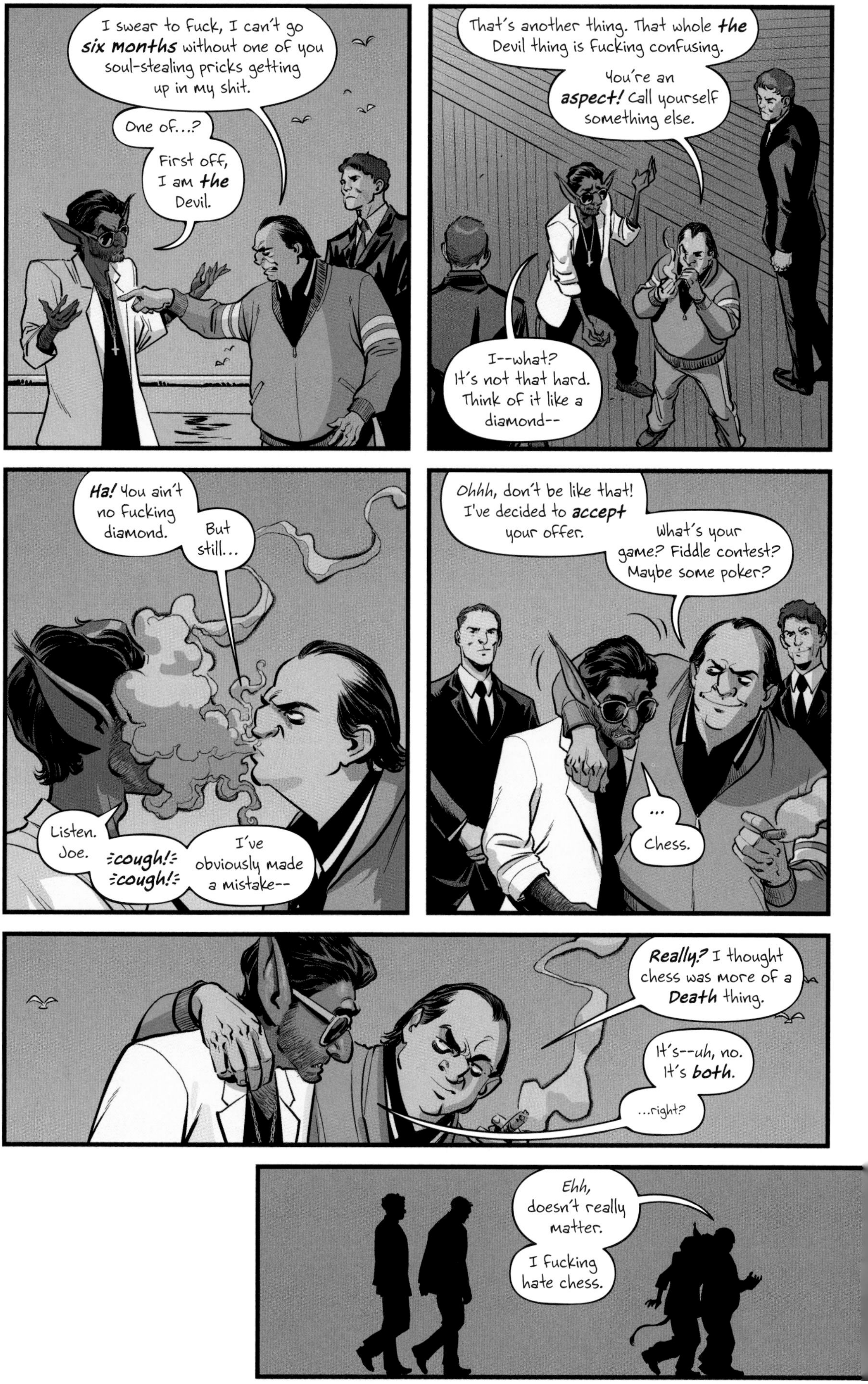
I swear to fuck, I can't go **six months** without one of you soul-stealing pricks getting up in my shit.
One of...?
First off, I am **the** Devil.
That's another thing. That whole **the** Devil thing is fucking confusing.
You're an **aspect!** Call yourself something else.
I--what? It's not that hard. Think of it like a diamond--
Ha! You ain't no fucking diamond.
But still...
Listen. Joe.
cough! cough!
I've obviously made a mistake--
Ohhh, don't be like that! I've decided to **accept** your offer.
What's your game? Fiddle contest? Maybe some poker?
...
Chess.
Really? I thought chess was more of a **Death** thing.
It's--uh, no. It's **both**.
...right?
Ehh, doesn't really matter.
I fucking hate chess.

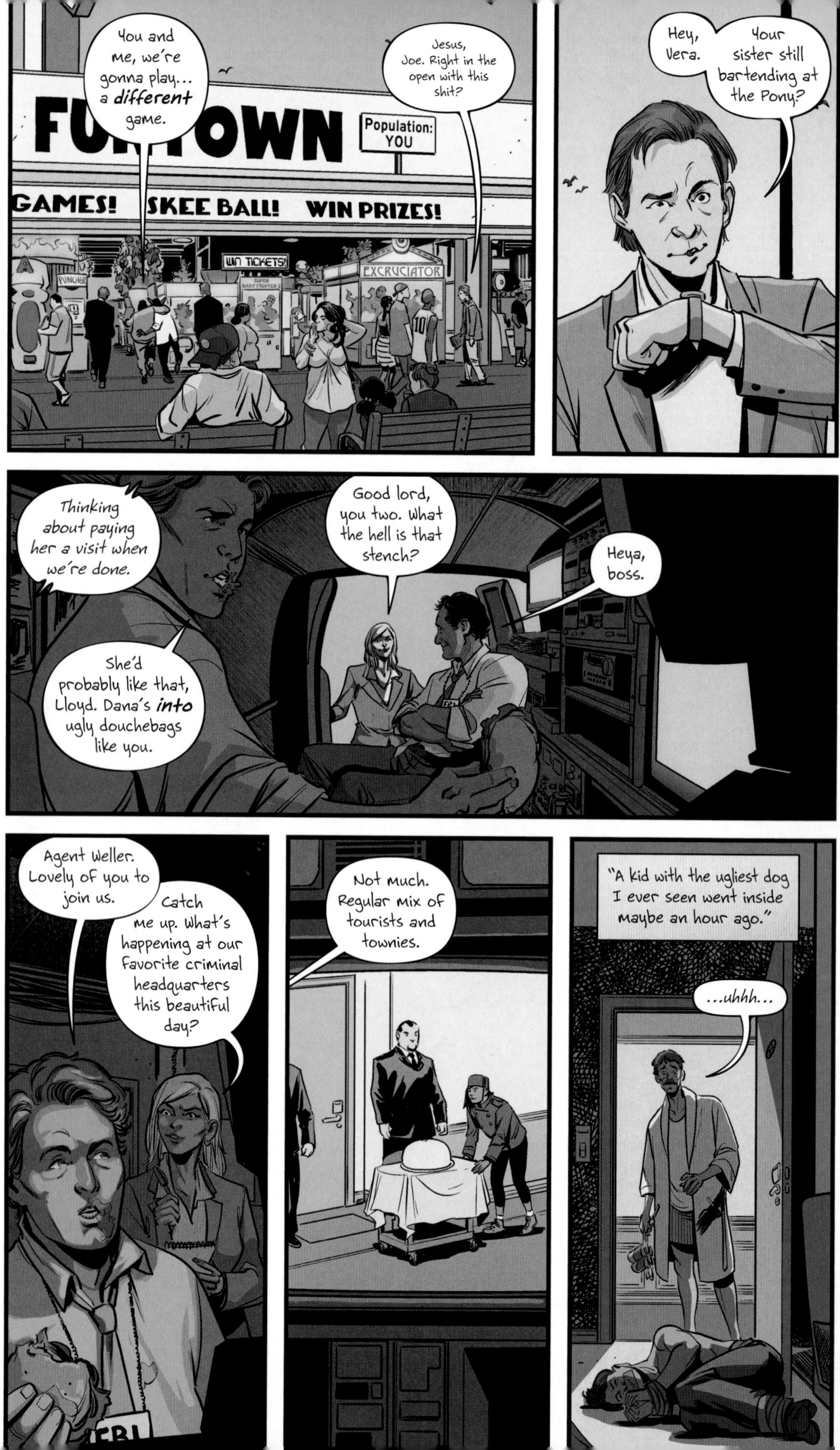
FUNTOWN
Population: YOU
GAMES!
SKEE BALL!
WIN PRIZES!
WIN TICKETS!
PUNCHER
SUPER BABY FIGHTER 2
EXCRUCIATOR
You and me, we're gonna play... a *different* game.
Jesus, Joe. Right in the open with this shit?
Hey, Vera.
Your sister still bartending at the Pony?
Thinking about paying her a visit when we're done.
She'd probably like that, Lloyd. Dana's *into* ugly douchebags like you.
Good lord, you two. What the hell is that stench?
Heya, boss.
Agent Weller. Lovely of you to join us.
Catch me up. What's happening at our favorite criminal headquarters this beautiful day?
Not much. Regular mix of tourists and townies.
"A kid with the ugliest dog I ever seen went inside maybe an hour ago."
...uhhh...
FBI

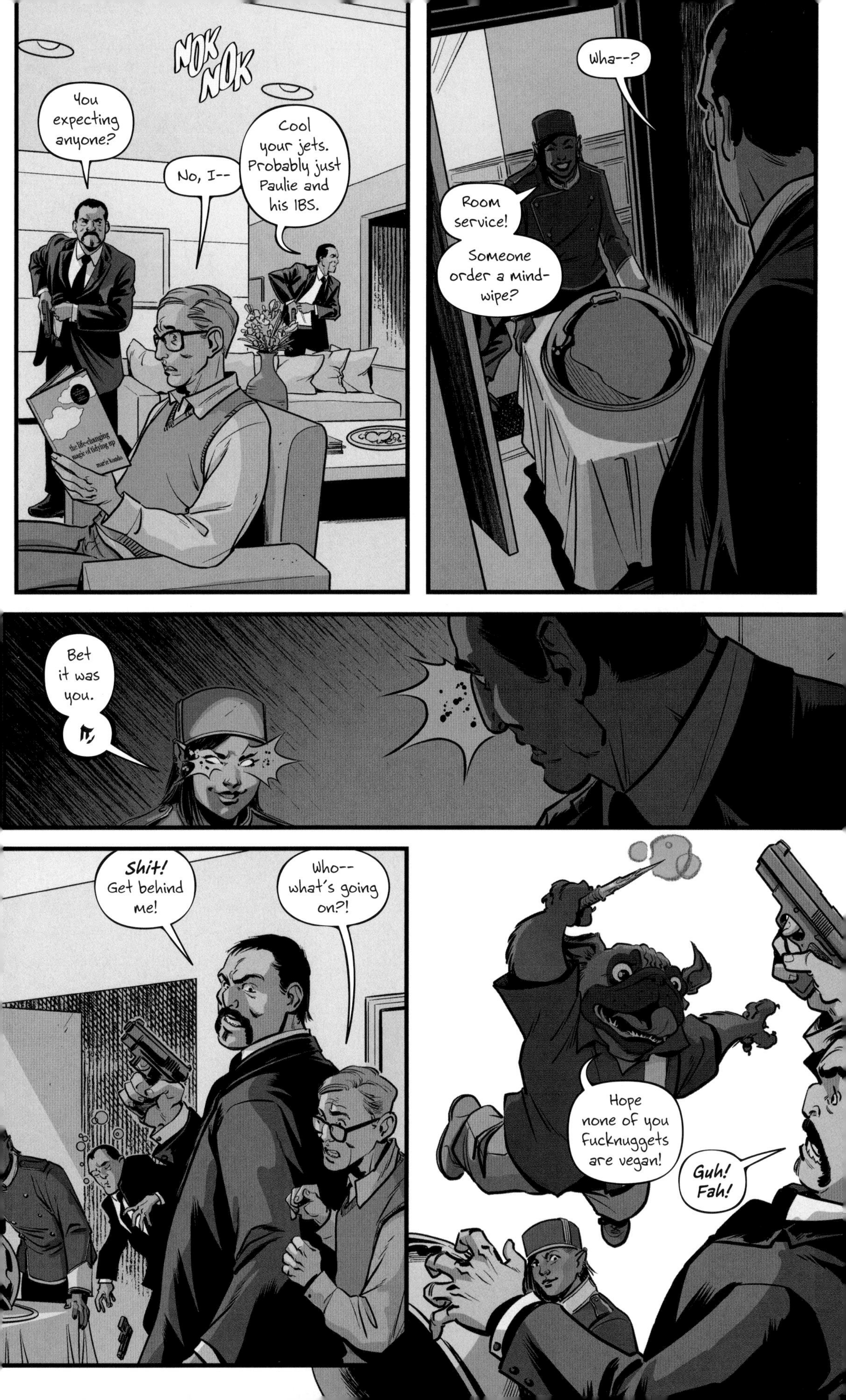
NOK NOK
You expecting anyone?
No, I--
Cool your jets. Probably just Paulie and his IBS.
the life-changing magic of tidying up
marie kondo
Wha--?
Room service!
Someone order a mind-wipe?
Bet it was you.
Shit! Get behind me!
Who-- what's going on?!
Hope none of you Fucknuggets are vegan!
Guh! Fah!

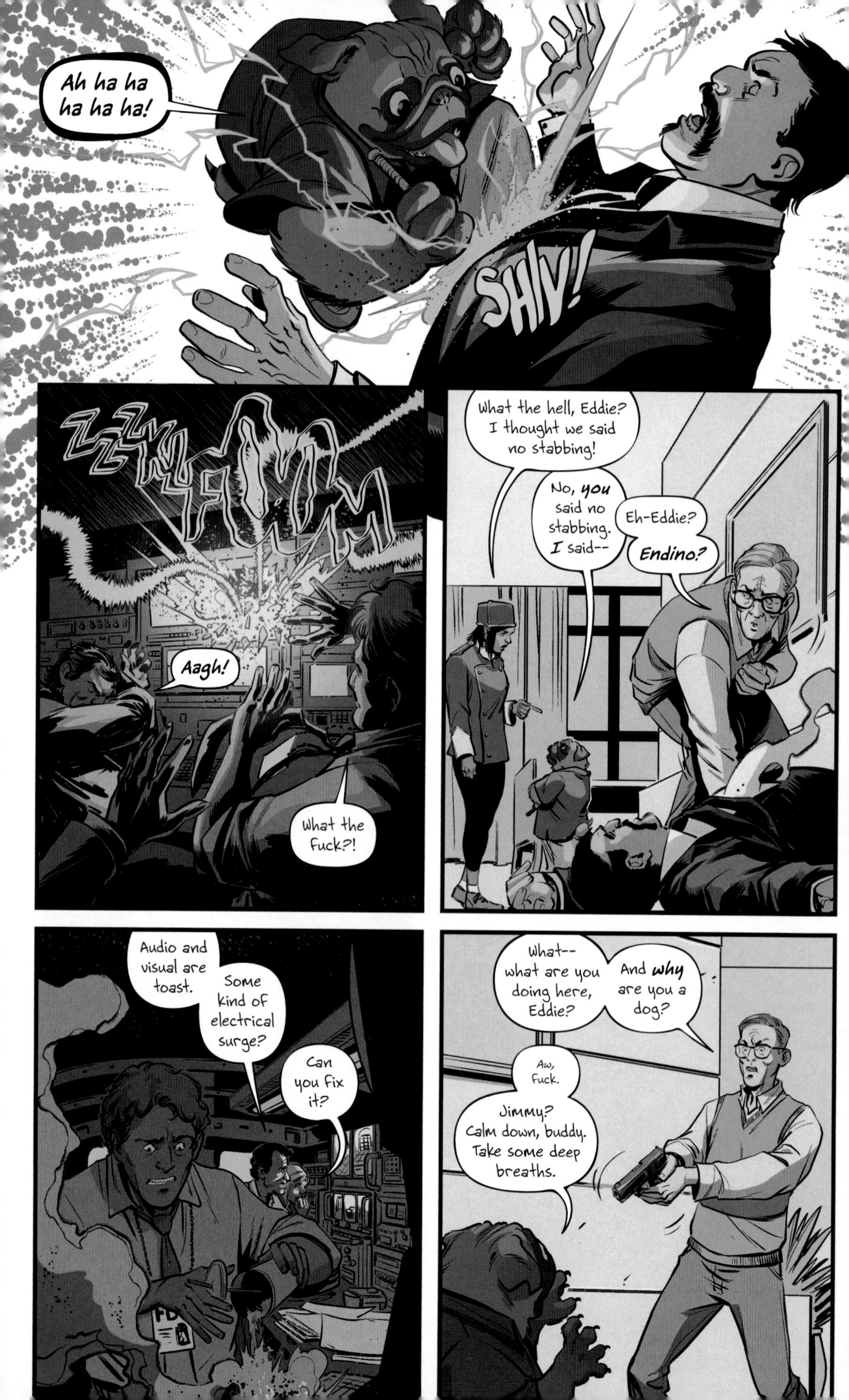

Ah ha ha ha ha ha!
SHIV!
ZZZWHOOM
Aagh!
What the Fuck?!
What the hell, Eddie? I thought we said no stabbing!
No, **you** said no stabbing. *I* said--
Eh-Eddie?
Endino?
Audio and visual are toast.
Some kind of electrical surge?
Can you fix it?
What--what are you doing here, Eddie?
And **why** are you a dog?
Aw, Fuck.
Jimmy? Calm down, buddy. Take some deep breaths.

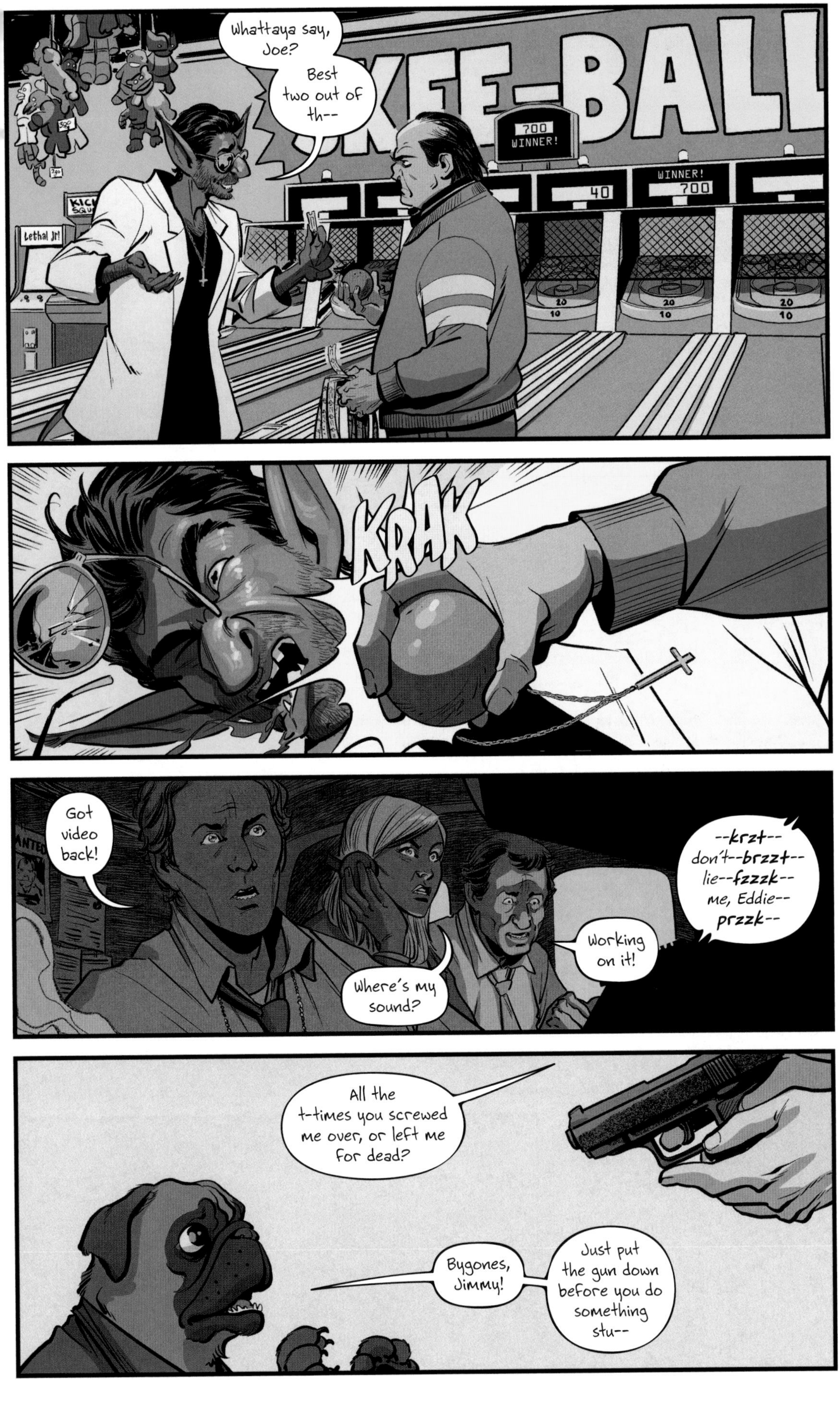
Whattaya say, Joe?
Best two out of th--
700 WINNER!
WINNER! 700
40
Lethal Jr!
KRAK
Got video back!
Where's my sound?
Working on it!
--krzt-- don't--brzzt-- lie--fzzzk-- me, Eddie-- przzk--
All the t-times you screwed me over, or left me for dead?
Bygones, Jimmy!
Just put the gun down before you do something stu--

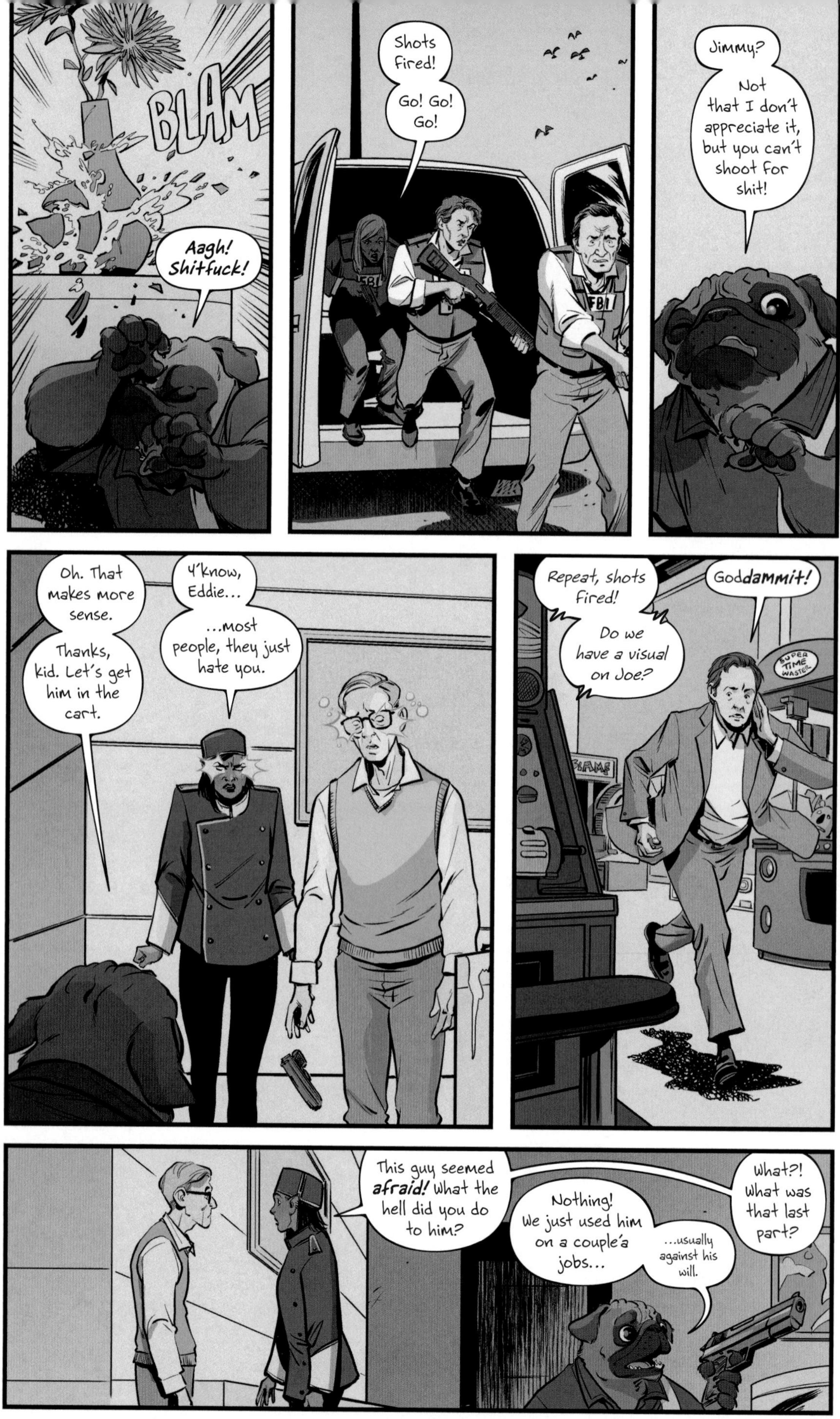
BLAM
Aagh! Shitfuck!
Shots fired!
Go! Go! Go!
FBI
FBI
Jimmy?
Not that I don't appreciate it, but you can't shoot for shit!
Oh. That makes more sense.
Thanks, kid. Let's get him in the cart.
Y'know, Eddie...
...most people, they just hate you.
Repeat, shots fired!
Do we have a visual on Joe?
Goddammit!
SUPER TIME WASTER
BLAM
This guy seemed afraid! What the hell did you do to him?
Nothing! We just used him on a couple'a jobs...
...usually against his will.
What?! What was that last part?

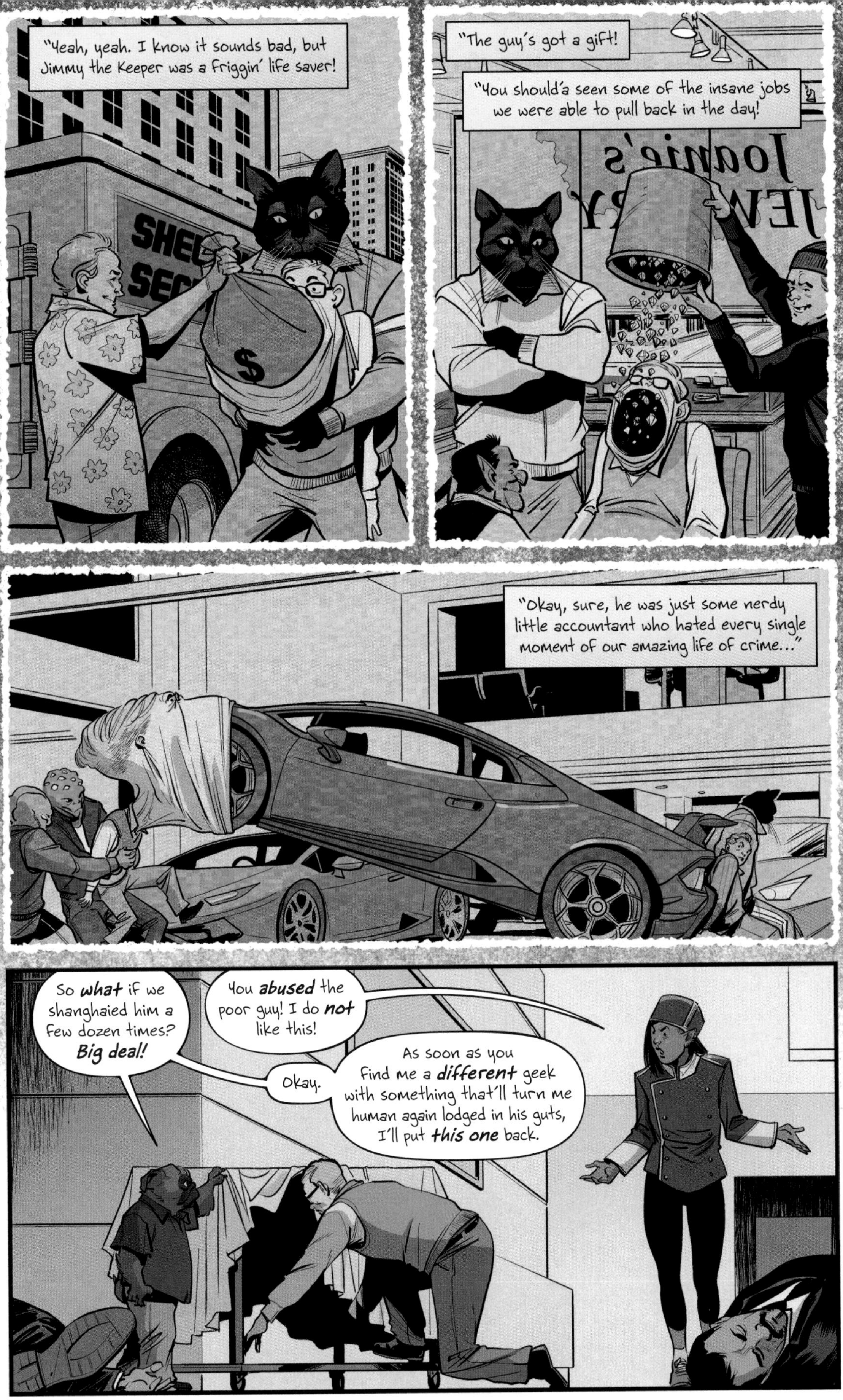

"Yeah, yeah. I know it sounds bad, but Jimmy the Keeper was a friggin' life saver!
SHE
SEC
$
"The guy's got a gift!
"You should'a seen some of the insane jobs we were able to pull back in the day!
Joanie's
JEW
"Okay, sure, he was just some nerdy little accountant who hated every single moment of our amazing life of crime..."
So what if we shanghaied him a few dozen times? Big deal!
You abused the poor guy! I do not like this!
Okay.
As soon as you find me a different geek with something that'll turn me human again lodged in his guts, I'll put this one back.

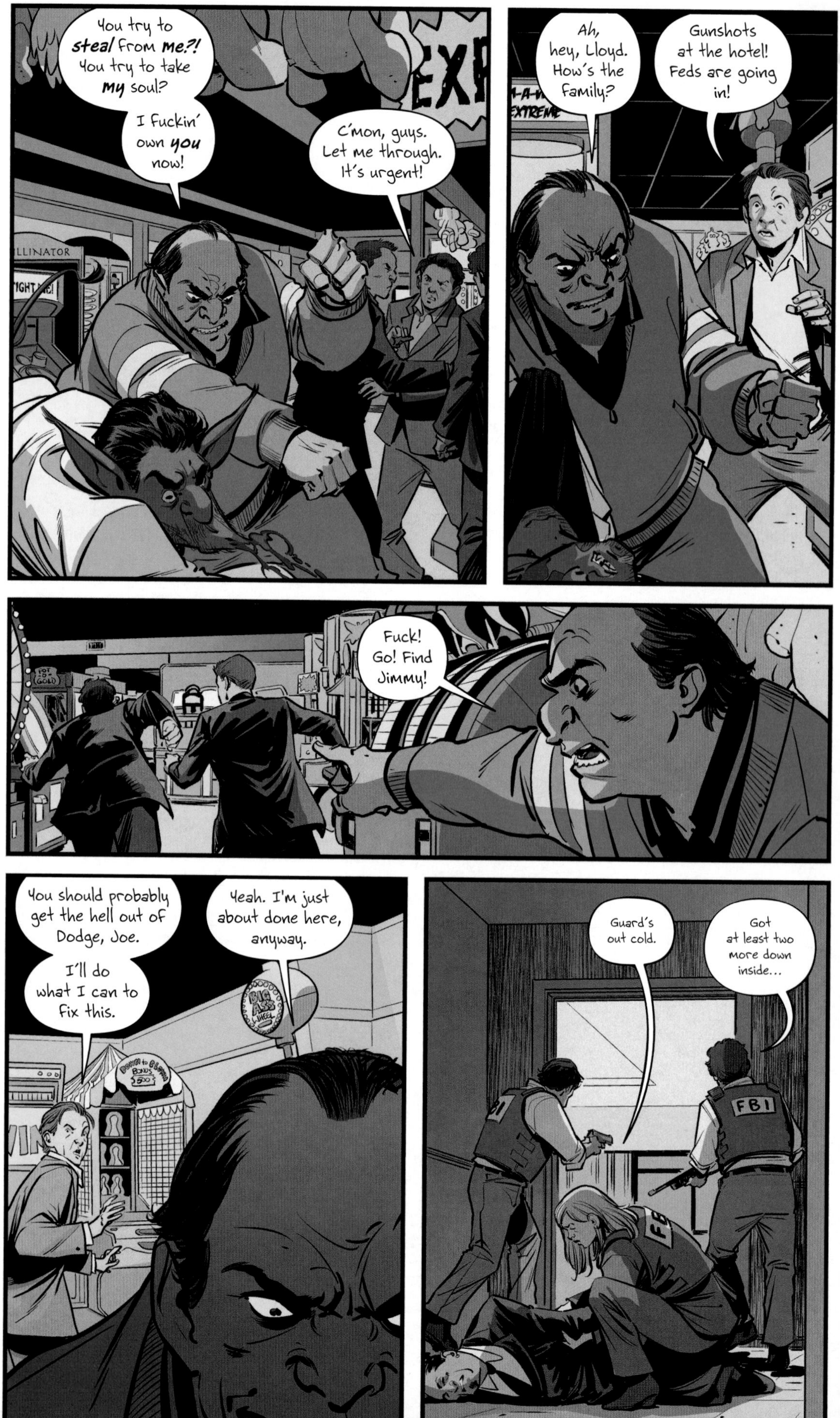
You try to steal from me?! You try to take my soul?
I fuckin' own you now!
C'mon, guys. Let me through. It's urgent!
Ah, hey, Lloyd. How's the family?
Gunshots at the hotel! Feds are going in!
Fuck! Go! Find Jimmy!
You should probably get the hell out of Dodge, Joe.
I'll do what I can to fix this.
Yeah. I'm just about done here, anyway.
Guard's out cold.
Got at least two more down inside...

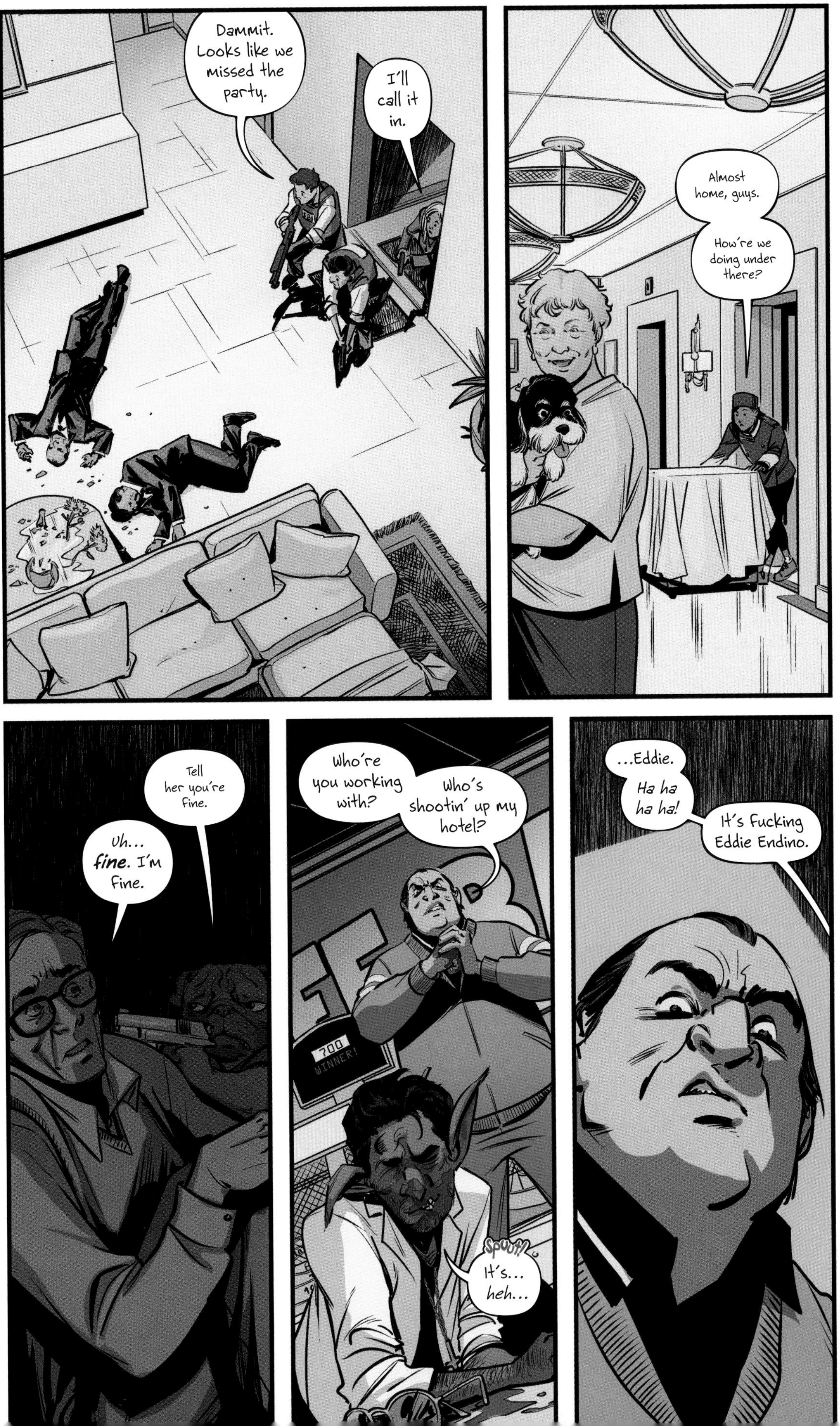

Dammit. Looks like we missed the party.
I'll call it in.
Almost home, guys.
How're we doing under there?
Tell her you're fine.
Uh... fine. I'm fine.
Who're you working with?
Who's shootin' up my hotel?
700
WINNER!
Spuuf!
It's... heh...
...Eddie.
Ha ha ha ha!
It's fucking Eddie Endino.

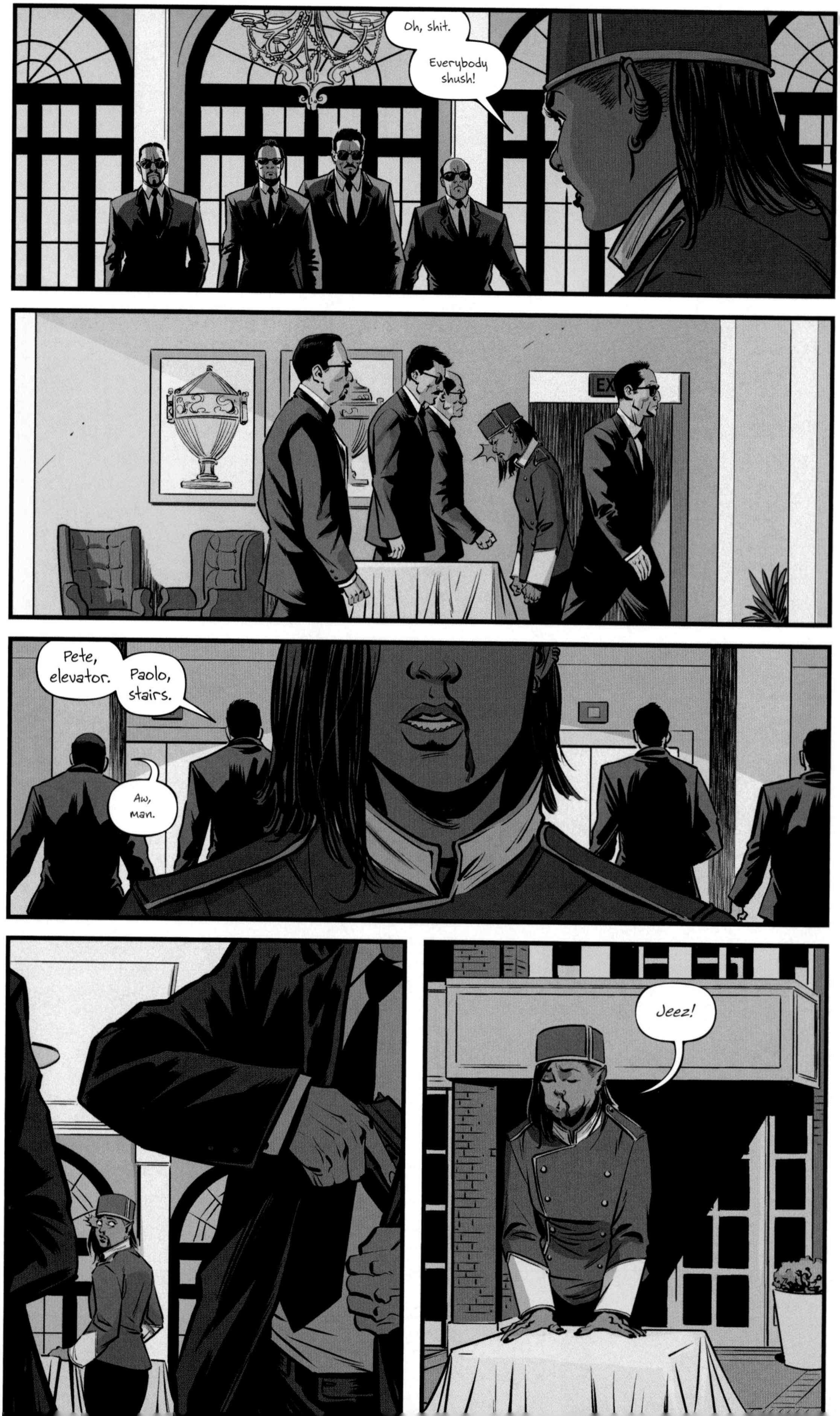
Oh, shit.
Everybody shush!
Pete, elevator.
Paolo, stairs.
Aw, man.
Jeez!

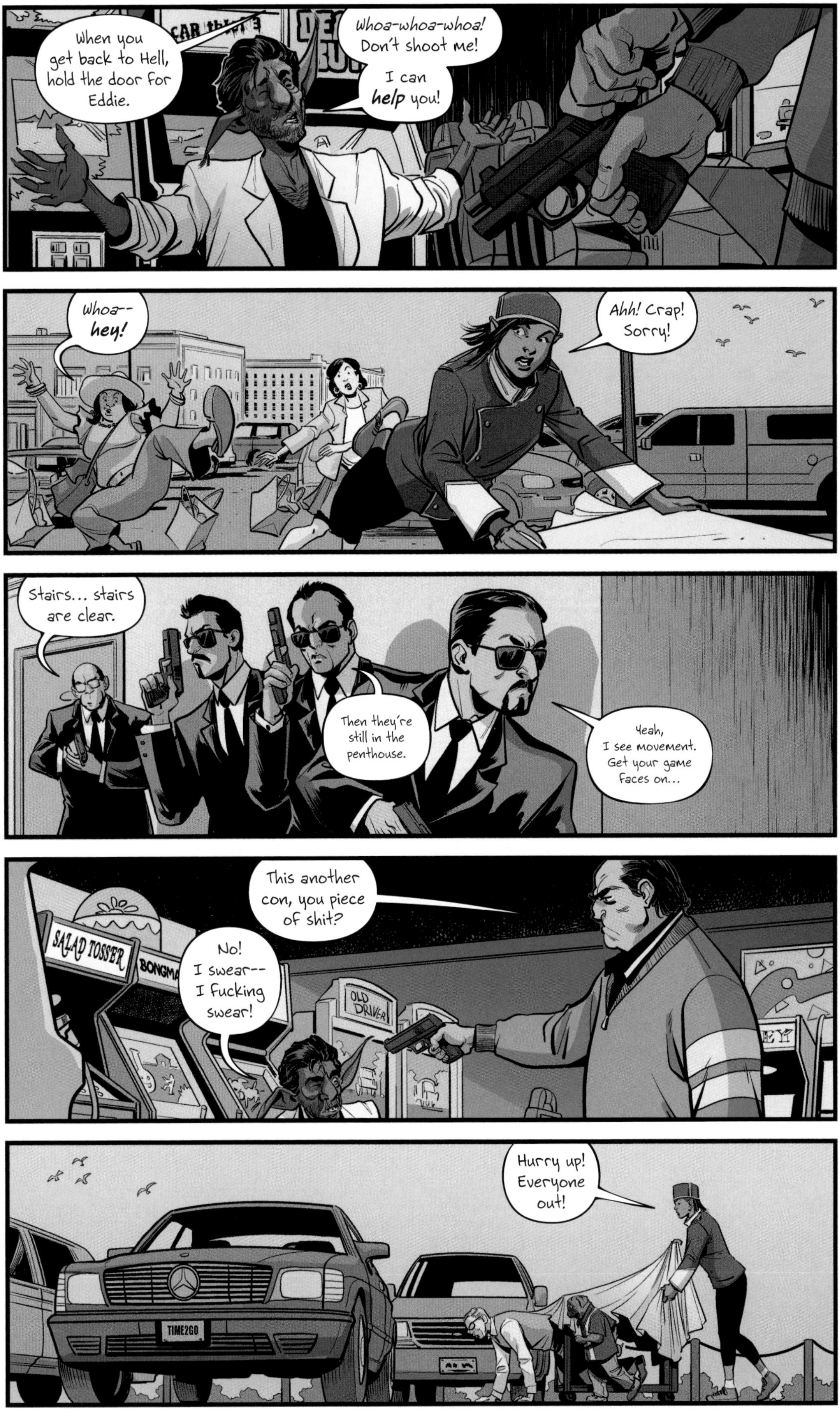

When you get back to Hell, hold the door for Eddie.
Whoa-whoa-whoa! Don't shoot me!
I can **help** you!
Whoa-- **hey!**
Ahh! Crap! Sorry!
Stairs... stairs are clear.
Then they're still in the penthouse.
Yeah, I see movement. Get your game faces on...
This another con, you piece of shit?
No! I swear-- I fucking swear!
SALAD TOSSER
OLD DRIVER
Hurry up! Everyone out!
TIME2GO

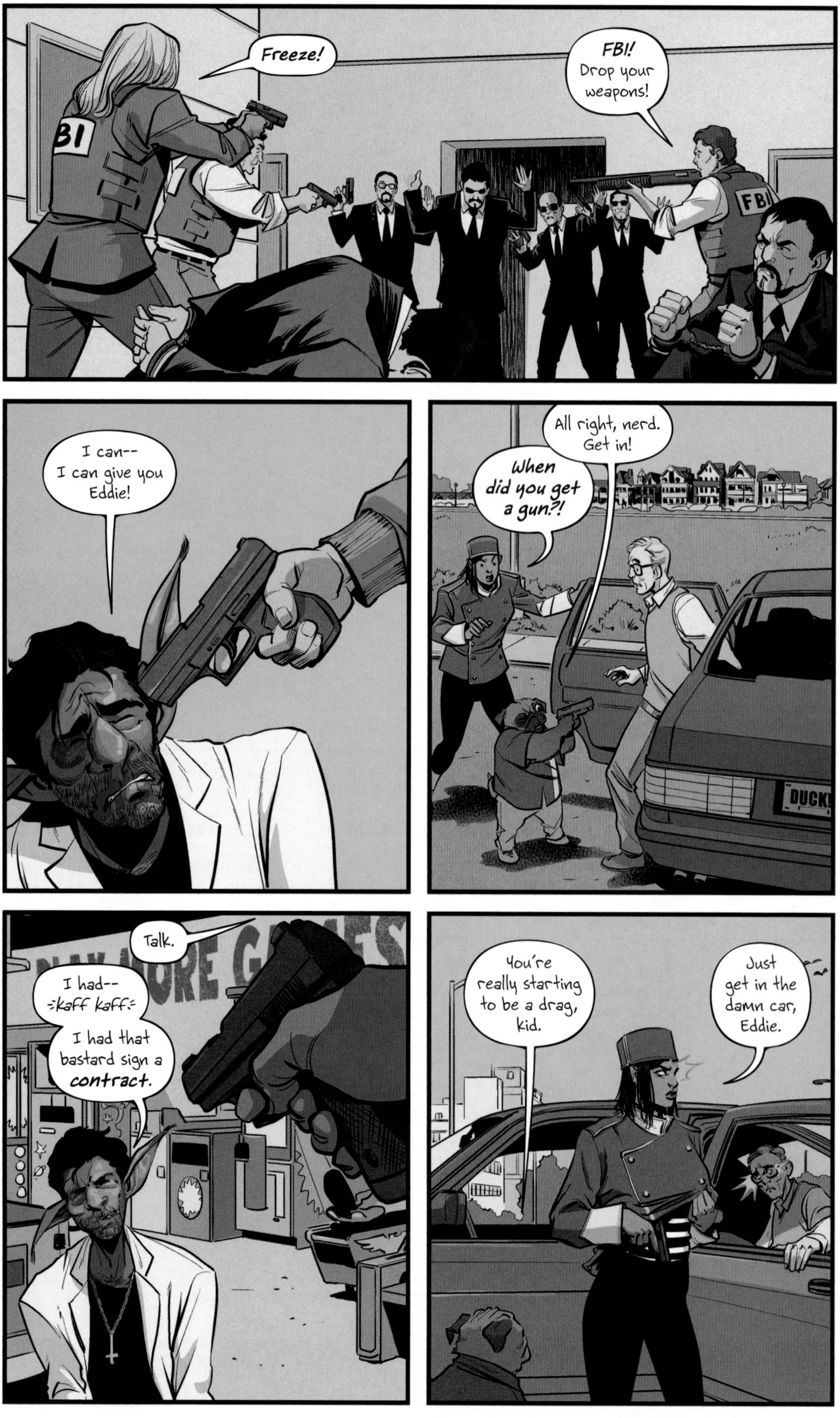

Freeze!
FBI! Drop your weapons!
I can-- I can give you Eddie!
All right, nerd. Get in!
When did you get a gun?!
Talk.
I had-- -kaff kaff-
I had that bastard sign a contract.
You're really starting to be a drag, kid.
Just get in the damn car, Eddie.

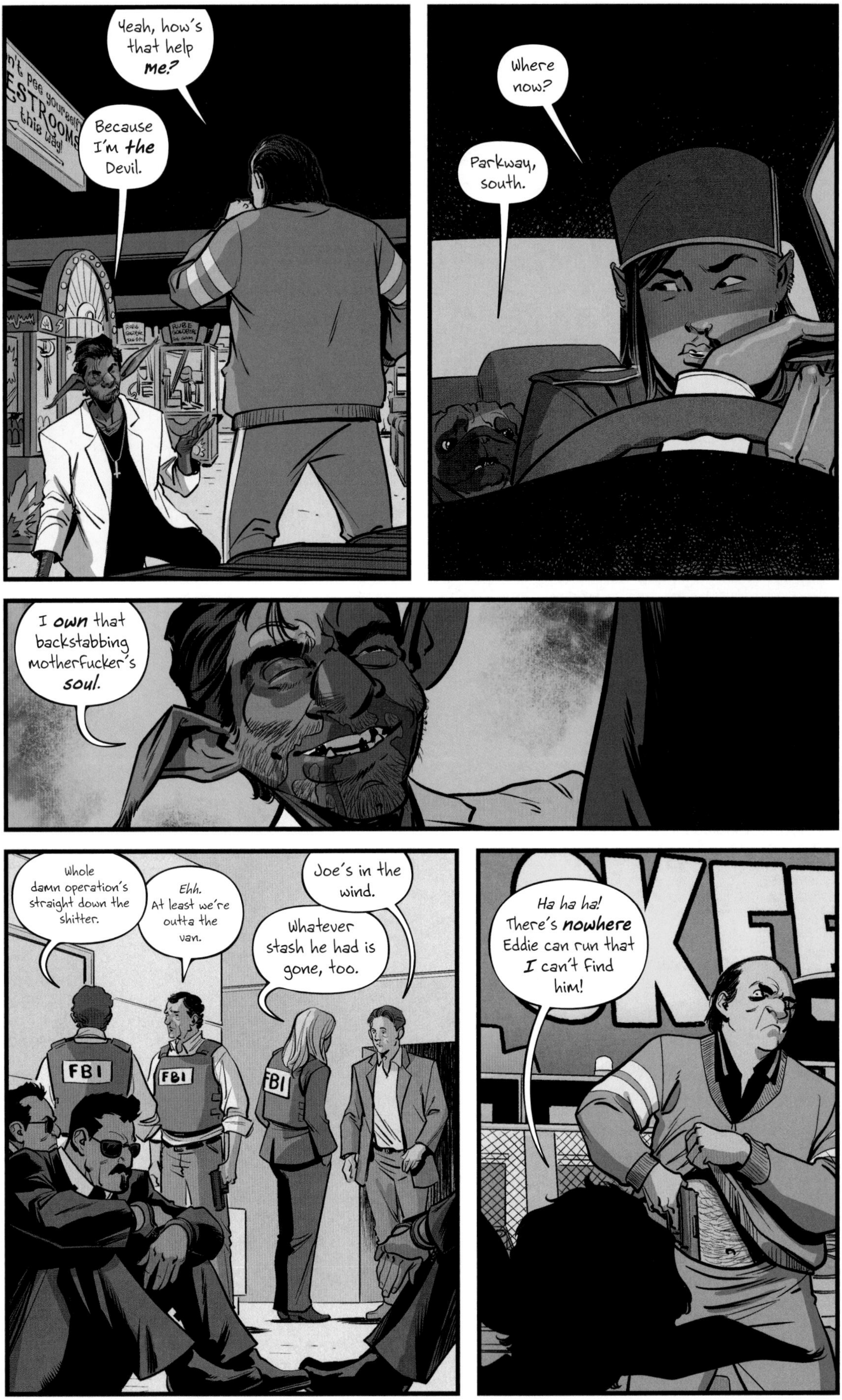
Yeah, how's that help me?
Because I'm the Devil.
Where now?
Parkway, south.
I own that backstabbing motherfucker's soul.
Whole damn operation's straight down the shitter.
Ehh. At least we're outta the van.
Joe's in the wind.
Whatever stash he had is gone, too.
FBI
FBI
FBI
Ha ha ha! There's nowhere Eddie can run that I can't find him!

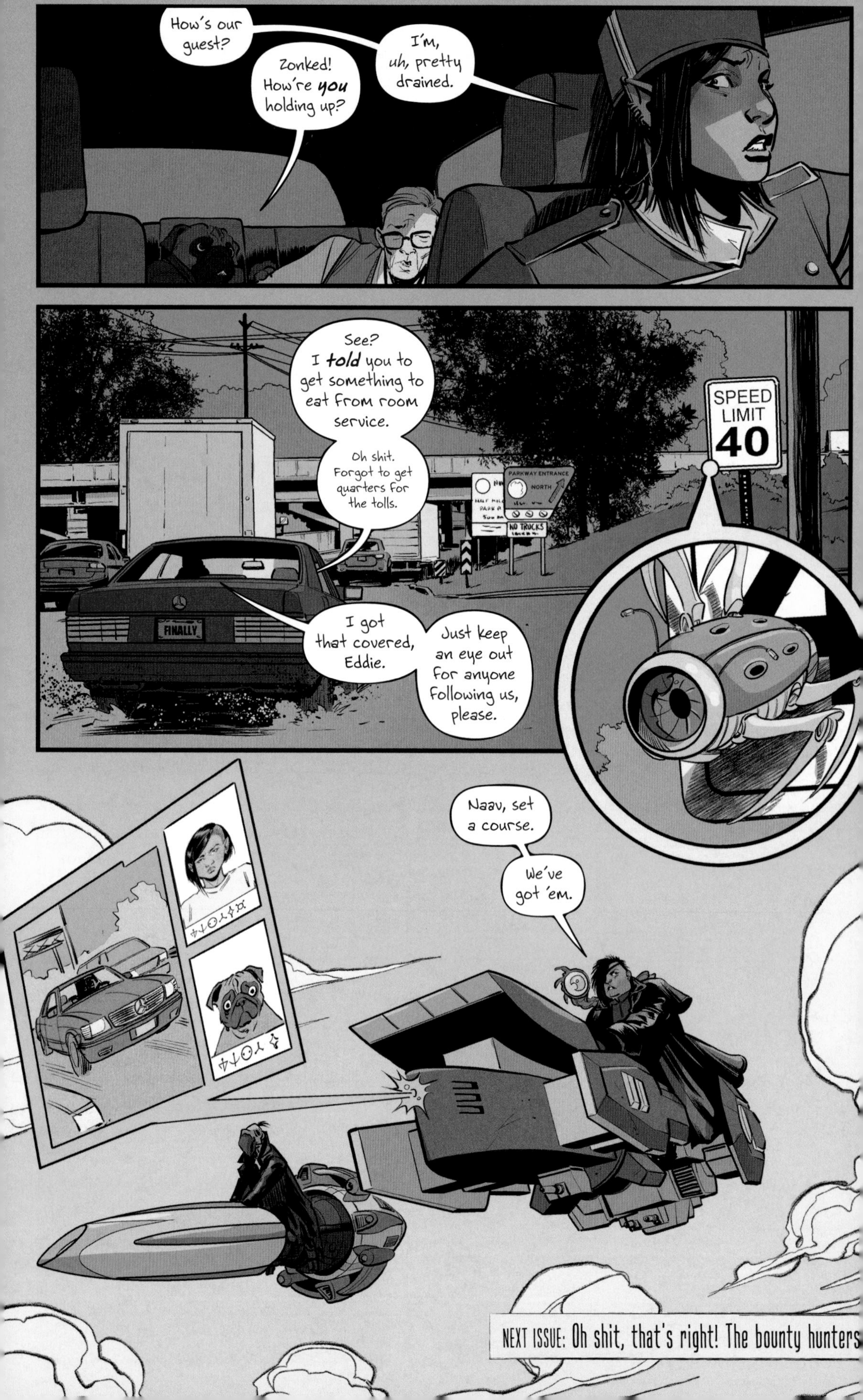

How's our guest?
I'm, uh, pretty drained.
Zonked! How're *you* holding up?
See? I **told** you to get something to eat from room service.
Oh shit. Forgot to get quarters for the tolls.
PARKWAY ENTRANCE
NORTH
NO TRUCKS
SPEED LIMIT 40
FINALLY
I got that covered, Eddie.
Just keep an eye out for anyone following us, please.
Naav, set a course.
We've got 'em.
NEXT ISSUE: Oh shit, that's right! The bounty hunters

BOOK THREE

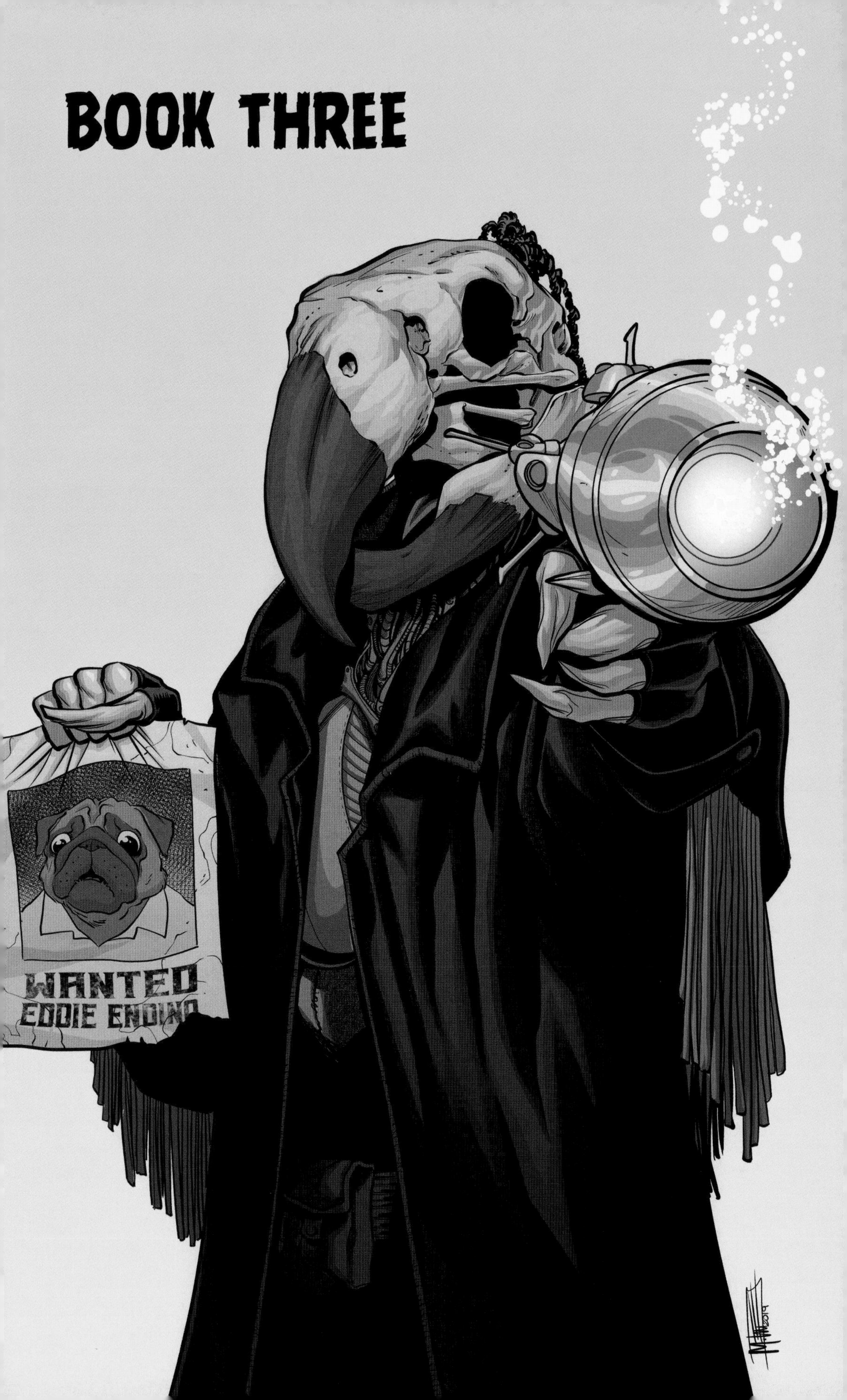
WANTED
EDDIE ENDING

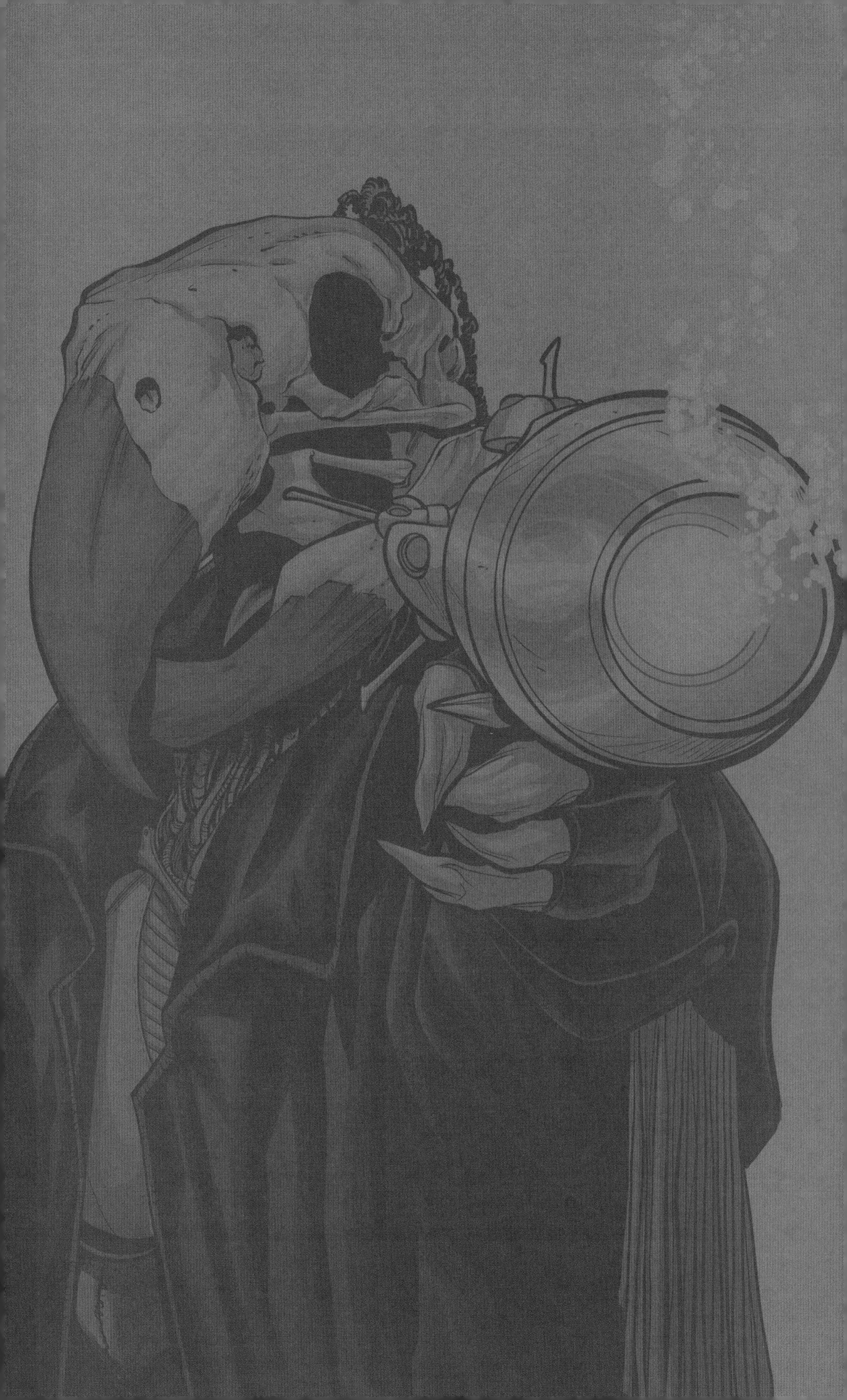

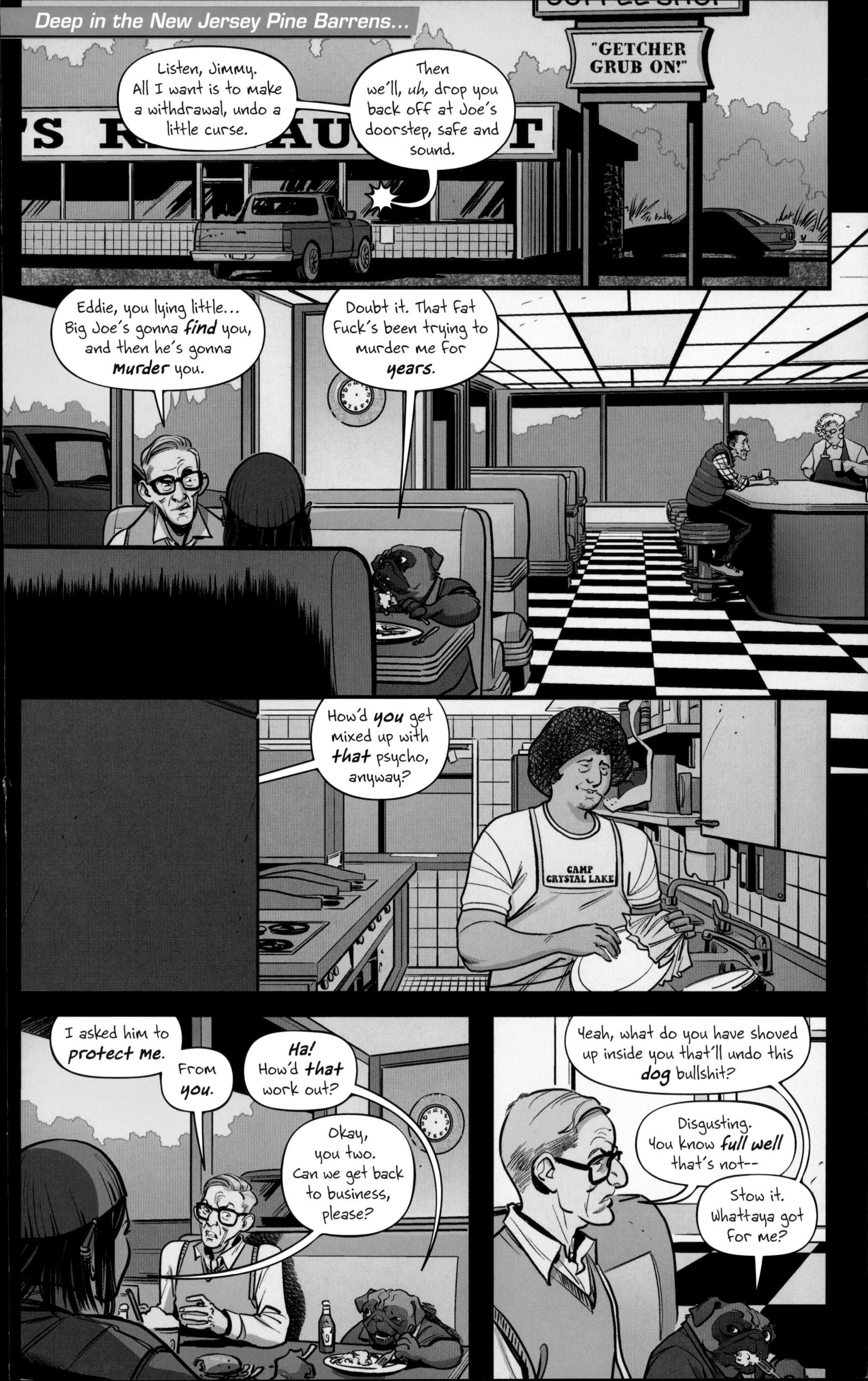

Deep in the New Jersey Pine Barrens...
"GETCHER GRUB ON!"
Listen, Jimmy. All I want is to make a withdrawal, undo a little curse.
Then we'll, uh, drop you back off at Joe's doorstep, safe and sound.
Eddie, you lying little... Big Joe's gonna *find* you, and then he's gonna **murder** you.
Doubt it. That fat fuck's been trying to murder me for ***years.***
How'd ***you*** get mixed up with ***that*** psycho, anyway?
CAMP CRYSTAL LAKE
I asked him to ***protect me.***
From ***you.***
Ha! How'd ***that*** work out?
Okay, you two. Can we get back to business, please?
Yeah, what do you have shoved up inside you that'll undo this ***dog*** bullshit?
Disgusting. You know ***full well*** that's not--
Stow it. Whattaya got for me?

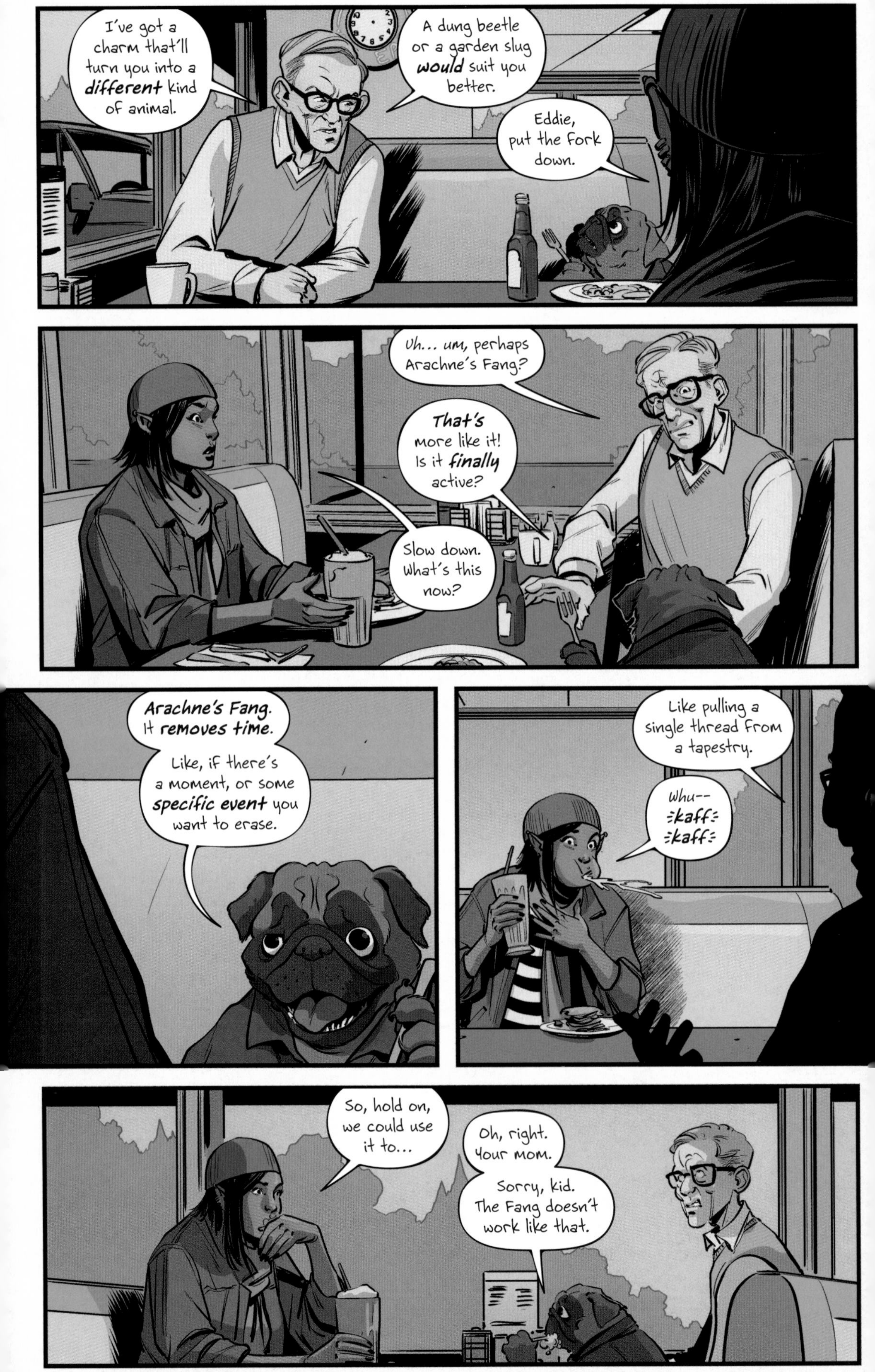
I've got a charm that'll turn you into a **different** kind of animal.
A dung beetle or a garden slug **would** suit you better.
Eddie, put the fork down.
Uh... um, perhaps Arachne's Fang?
That's more like it! Is it **finally** active?
Slow down. What's this now?
Arachne's Fang. It **removes time.**
Like, if there's a moment, or some **specific event** you want to erase.
Like pulling a single thread from a tapestry.
Whu-- kaff kaff
So, hold on, we could use it to...
Oh, right. Your mom.
Sorry, kid. The Fang doesn't work like that.

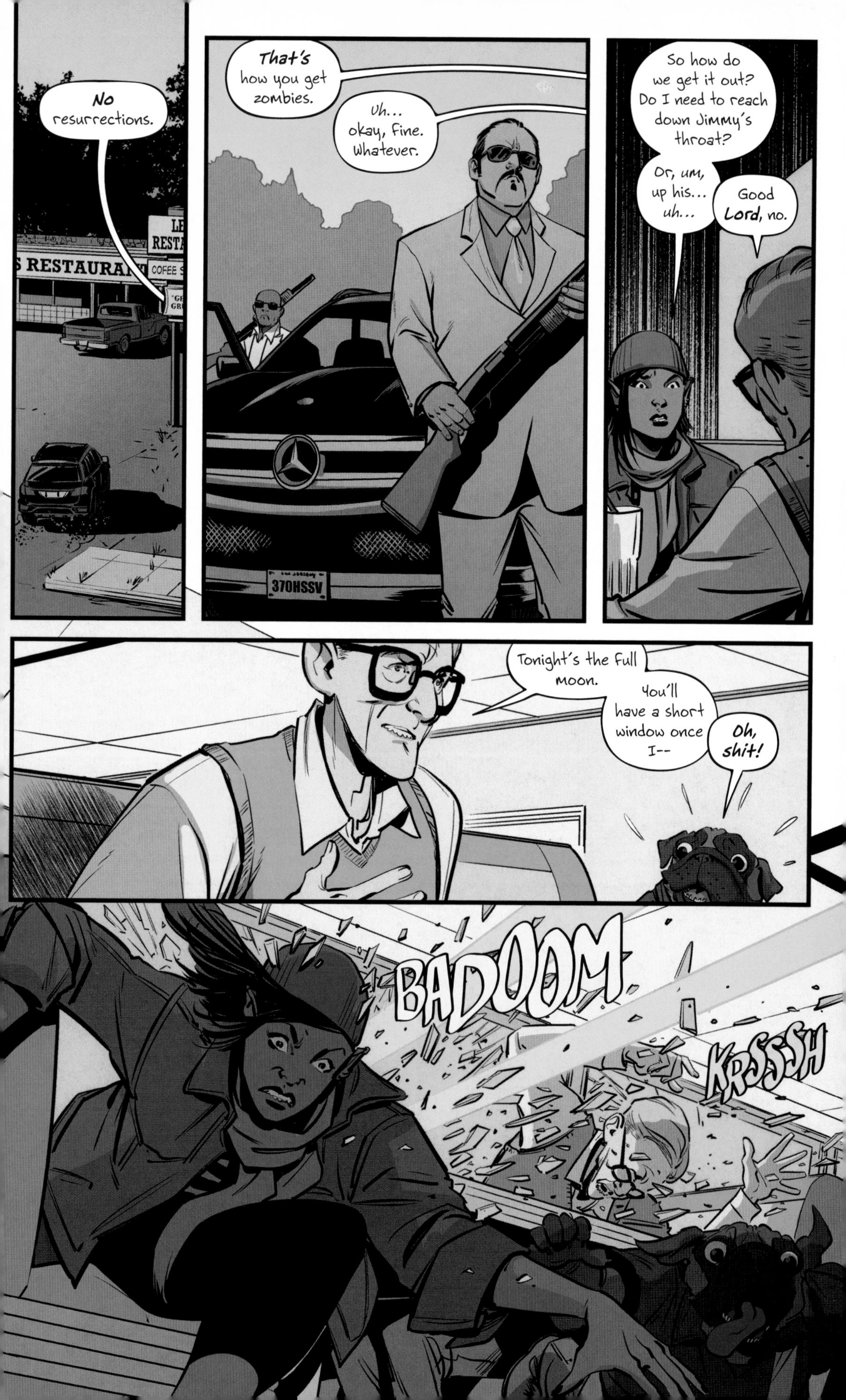
No resurrections.
That's how you get zombies.
Uh... okay, fine. Whatever.
370HSSV
So how do we get it out? Do I need to reach down Jimmy's throat?
Or, um, up his... uh...
Good Lord, no.
Tonight's the full moon.
You'll have a short window once I--
Oh, shit!
BADOOM
KRSSSH

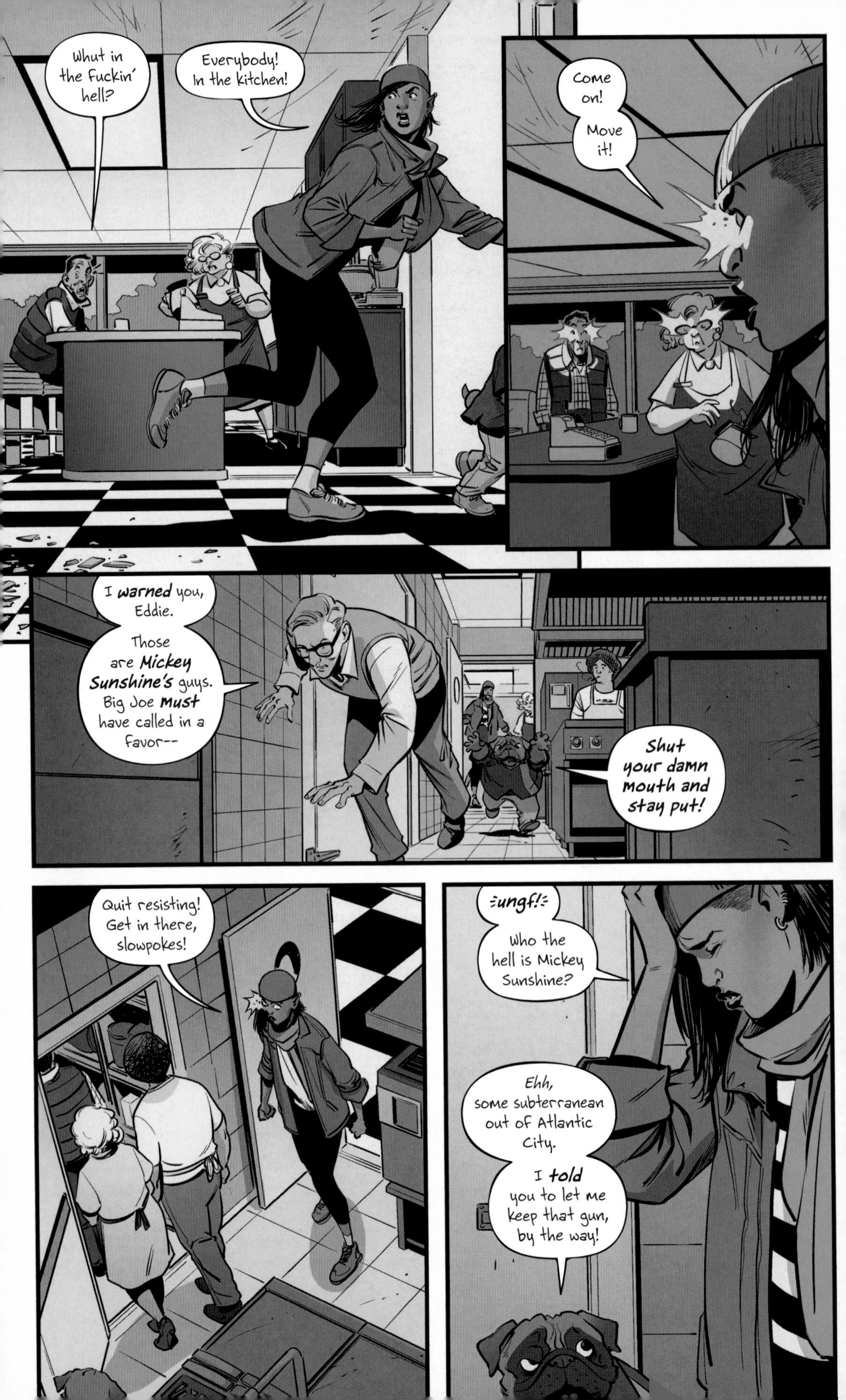
Whut in the Fuckin' hell?
Everybody! In the kitchen!
Come on!
Move it!
I **warned** you, Eddie.
Those are **Mickey Sunshine's** guys. Big Joe **must** have called in a favor--
Shut your damn mouth and stay put!
Quit resisting! Get in there, slowpokes!
ungf!
Who the hell is Mickey Sunshine?
Ehh, some subterranean out of Atlantic City.
I **told** you to let me keep that gun, by the way!

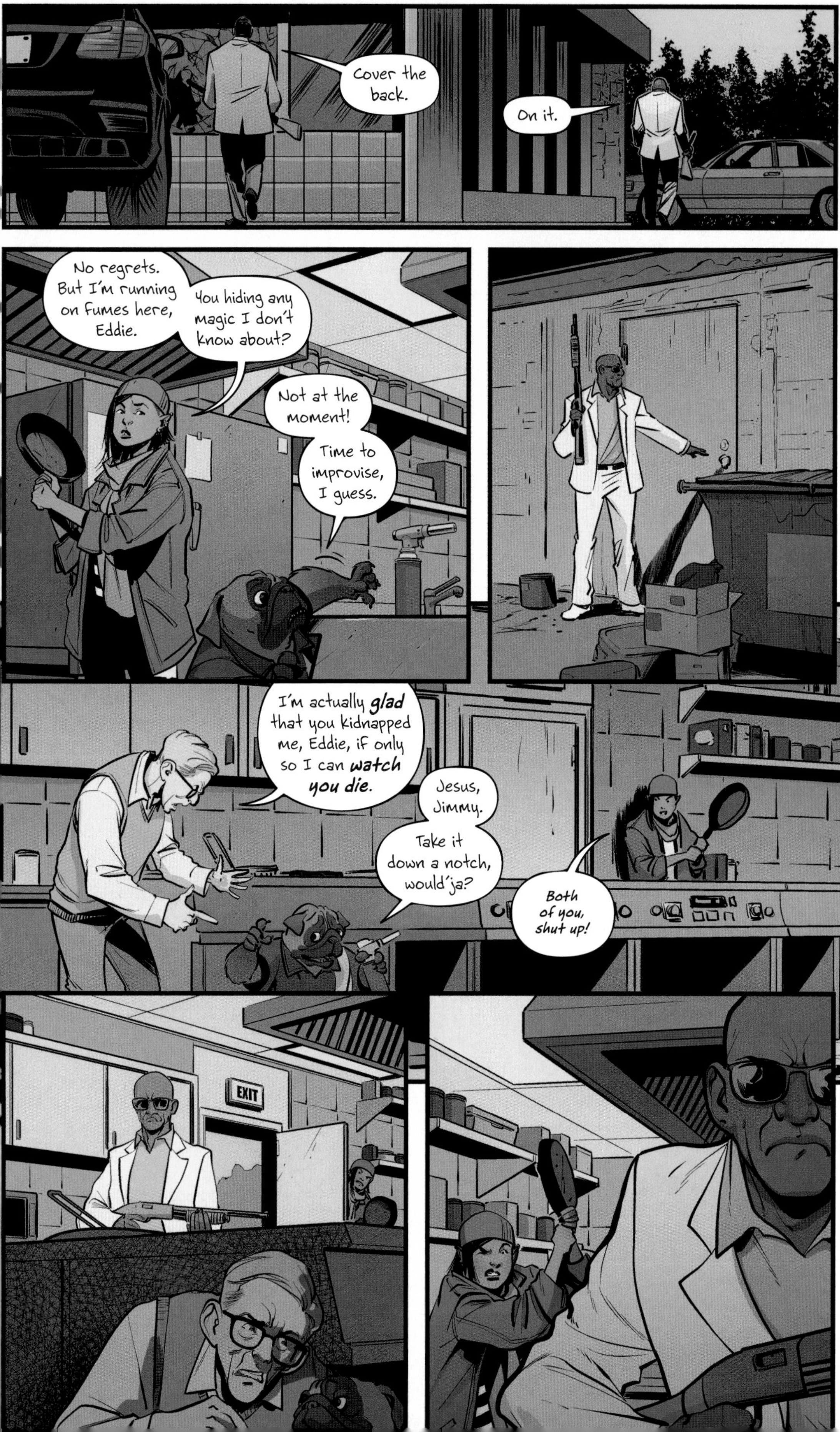
Cover the back.
On it.
No regrets. But I'm running on fumes here, Eddie.
You hiding any magic I don't know about?
Not at the moment!
Time to improvise, I guess.
I'm actually **glad** that you kidnapped me, Eddie, if only so I can **watch you die**.
Jesus, Jimmy.
Take it down a notch, would'ja?
Both of you, shut up!
EXIT

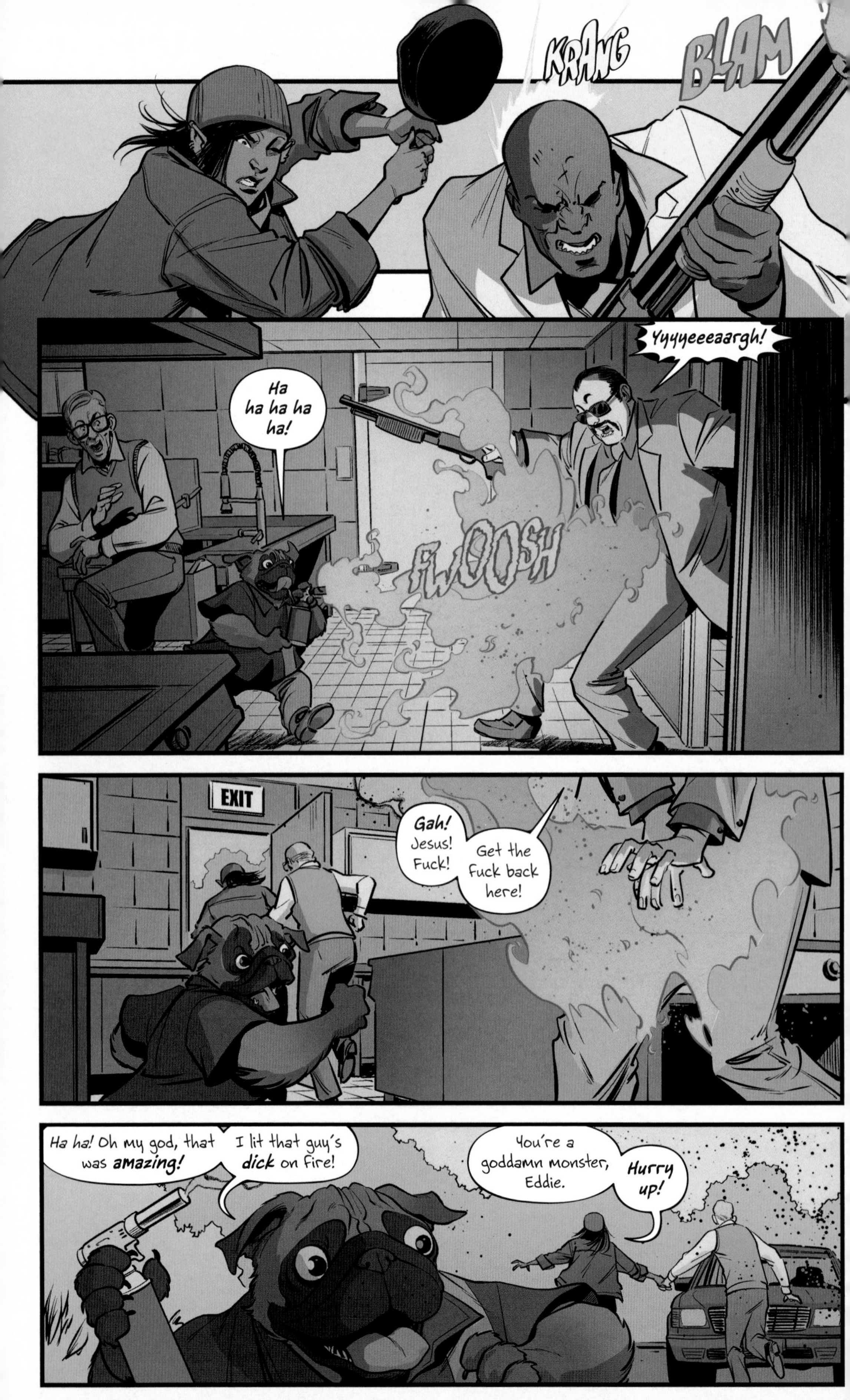
KRANG
BLAM
Yyyyeeeaargh!
Ha ha ha ha ha ha!
FWOOSH
EXIT
Gah! Jesus! Fuck!
Get the fuck back here!
Ha ha! Oh my god, that was **amazing!**
I lit that guy's **dick** on fire!
You're a goddamn monster, Eddie.
Hurry up!

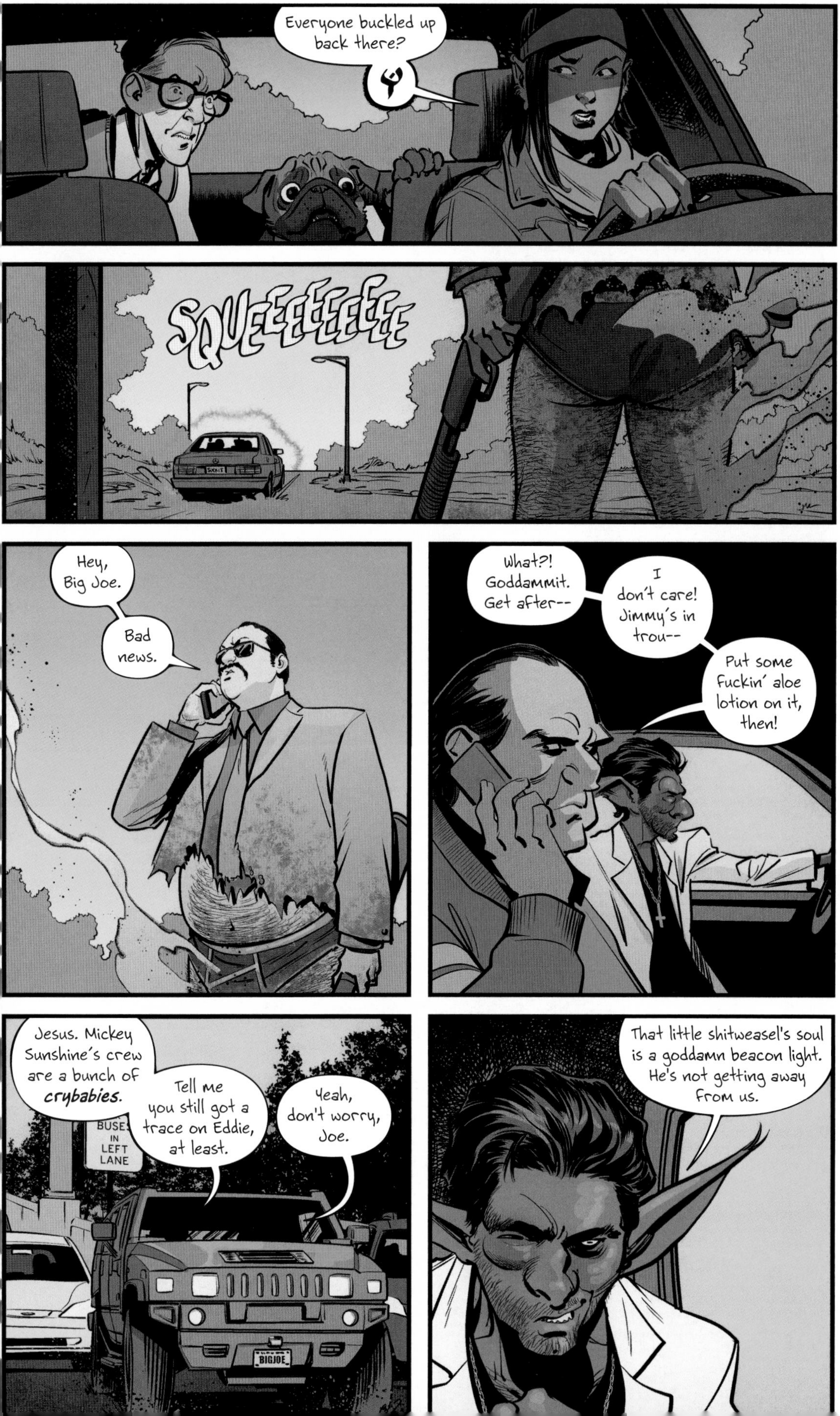
Everyone buckled up back there?
SQUEEEEEEEEE
SUCK-IT
Hey, Big Joe.
Bad news.
What?! Goddammit. Get after--
I don't care! Jimmy's in trou--
Put some fuckin' aloe lotion on it, then!
Jesus. Mickey Sunshine's crew are a bunch of *crybabies*.
Tell me you still got a trace on Eddie, at least.
Yeah, don't worry, Joe.
BUSES IN LEFT LANE
BIGJOE
That little shitweasel's soul is a goddamn beacon light. He's not getting away from us.

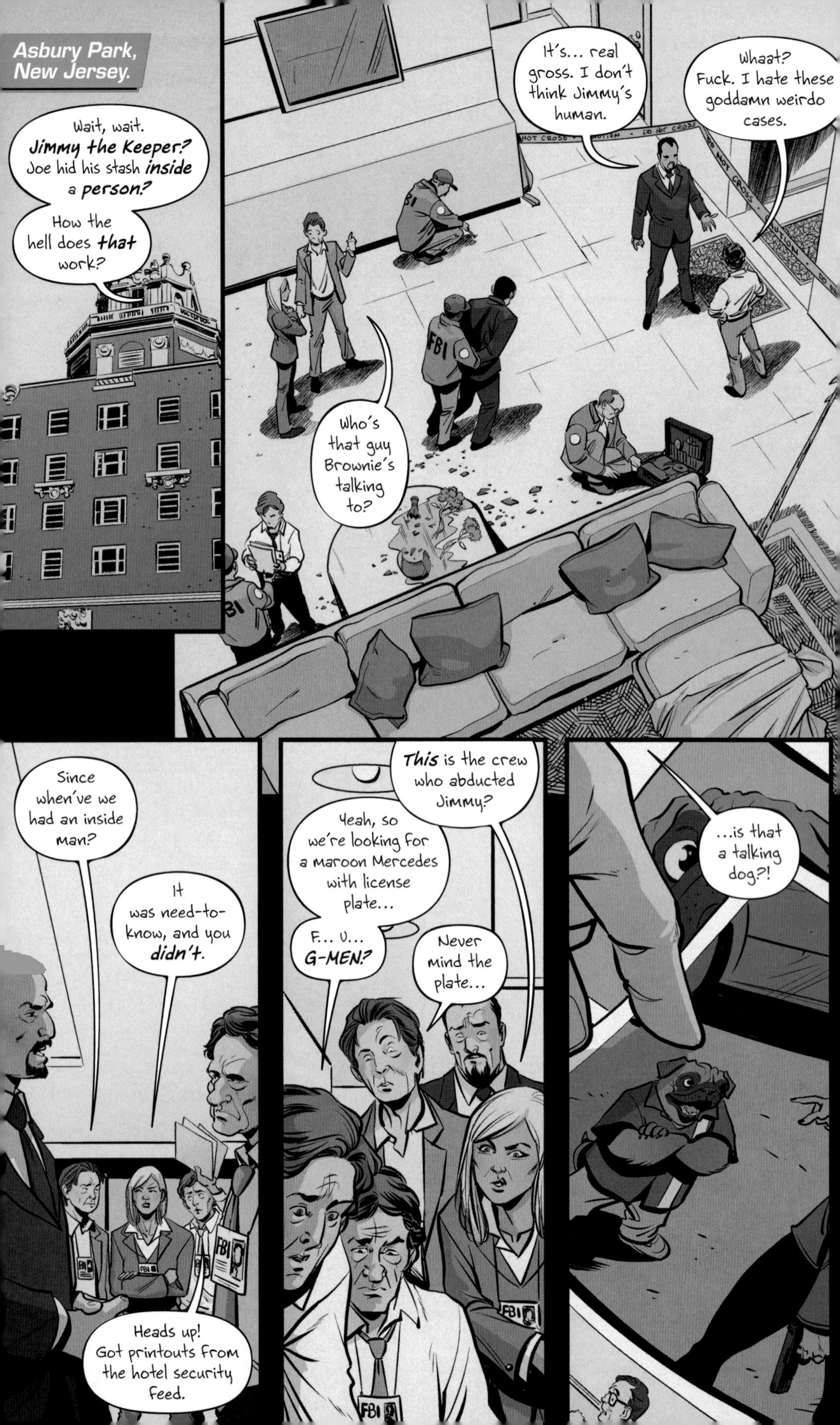

Asbury Park, New Jersey.
Wait, wait. Jimmy the Keeper? Joe hid his stash inside a person?
How the hell does that work?
It's... real gross. I don't think Jimmy's human.
Whaat? Fuck. I hate these goddamn weirdo cases.
Who's that guy Brownie's talking to?
Since when've we had an inside man?
It was need-to-know, and you didn't.
Heads up! Got printouts from the hotel security feed.
This is the crew who abducted Jimmy?
Yeah, so we're looking for a maroon Mercedes with license plate...
F... U... G-MEN?
Never mind the plate...
...is that a talking dog?!

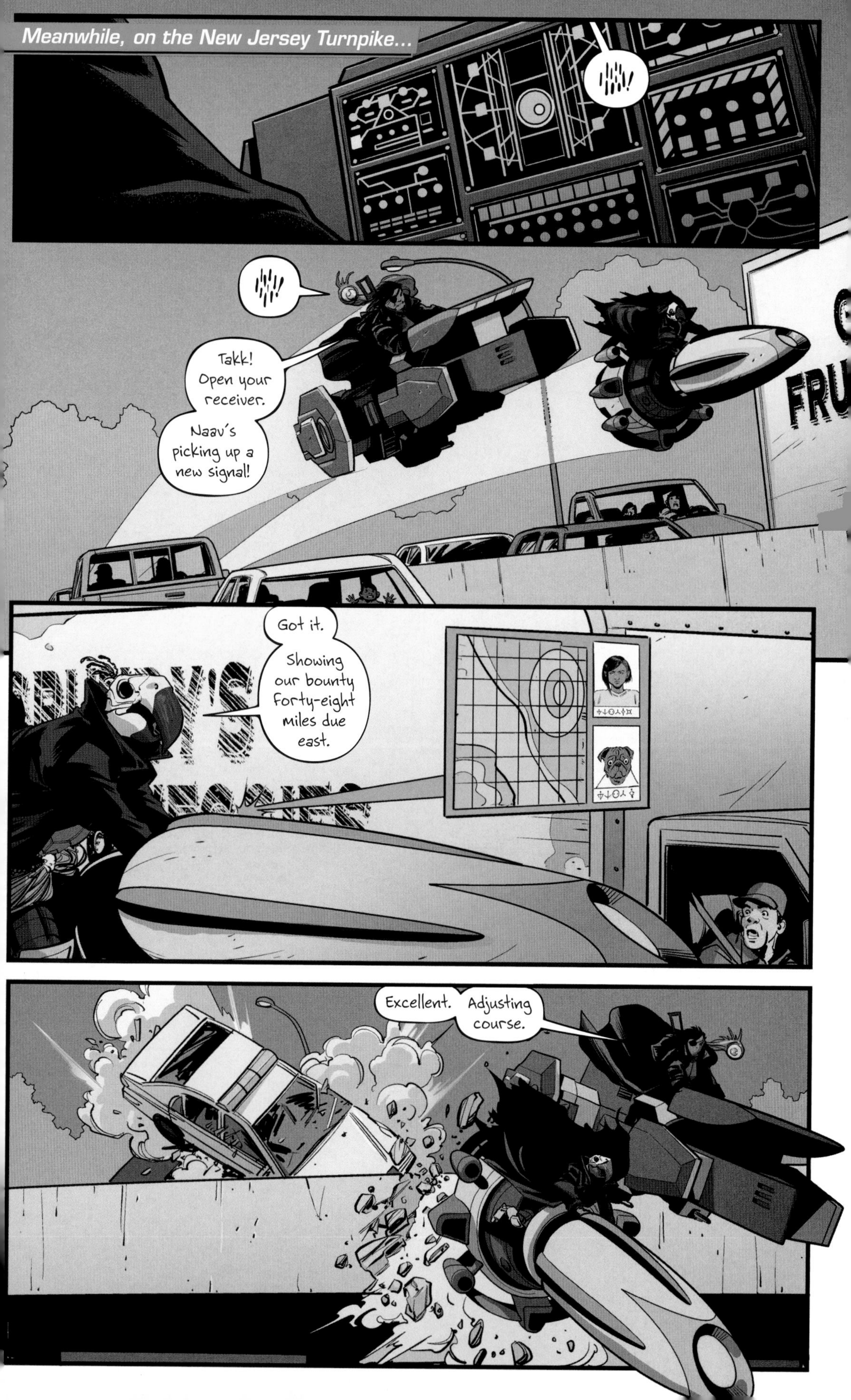

Meanwhile, on the New Jersey Turnpike...
Takk! Open your receiver.
Naav's picking up a new signal!
FRU
Got it.
Showing our bounty forty-eight miles due east.
Excellent. Adjusting course.

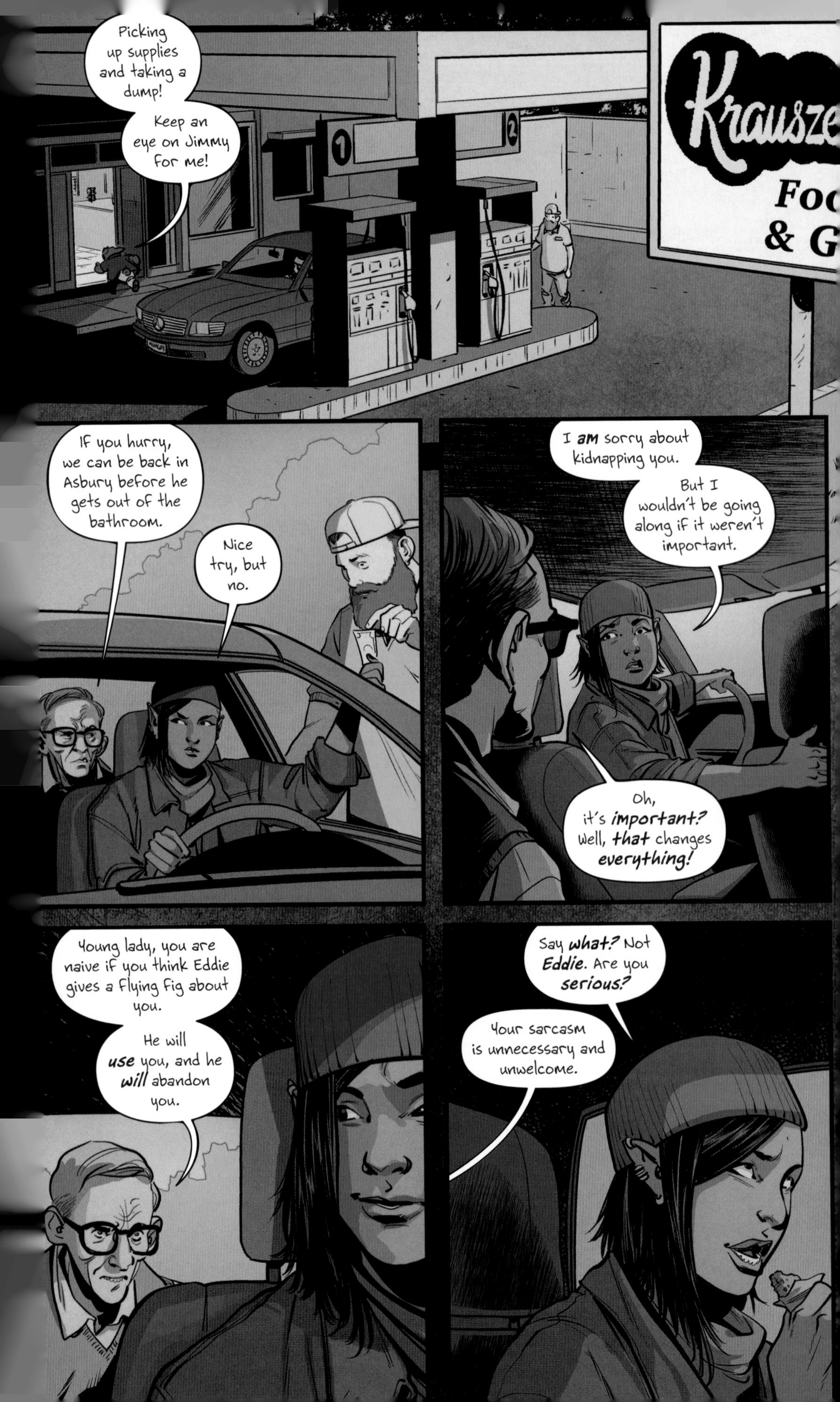
Picking up supplies and taking a dump!
Keep an eye on Jimmy for me!
Krausze
Foo
& G
If you hurry, we can be back in Asbury before he gets out of the bathroom.
Nice try, but no.
I am sorry about kidnapping you.
But I wouldn't be going along if it weren't important.
Oh, it's important? Well, that changes everything!
Young lady, you are naive if you think Eddie gives a flying fig about you.
He will use you, and he will abandon you.
Say what? Not Eddie. Are you serious?
Your sarcasm is unnecessary and unwelcome.

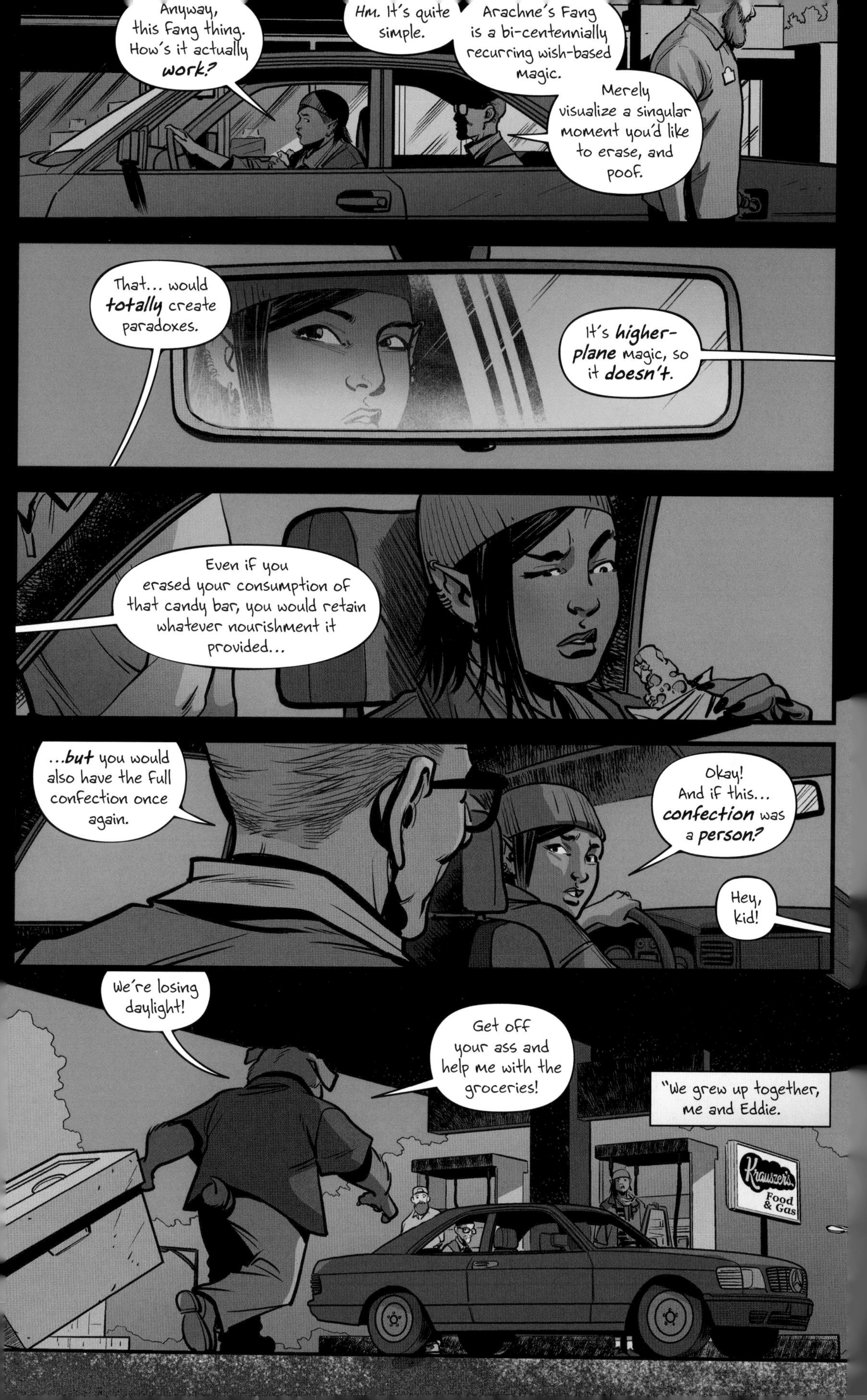

Anyway, this fang thing. How's it actually **work?**
Hm. It's quite simple.
Arachne's Fang is a bi-centennially recurring wish-based magic.
Merely visualize a singular moment you'd like to erase, and poof.
That... would **totally** create paradoxes.
It's **higher-plane** magic, so it **doesn't**.
Even if you erased your consumption of that candy bar, you would retain whatever nourishment it provided...
...**but** you would also have the full confection once again.
Okay! And if this... **confection** was a **person?**
Hey, kid!
We're losing daylight!
Get off your ass and help me with the groceries!
"We grew up together, me and Eddie.
Krauszer's
Food & Gas

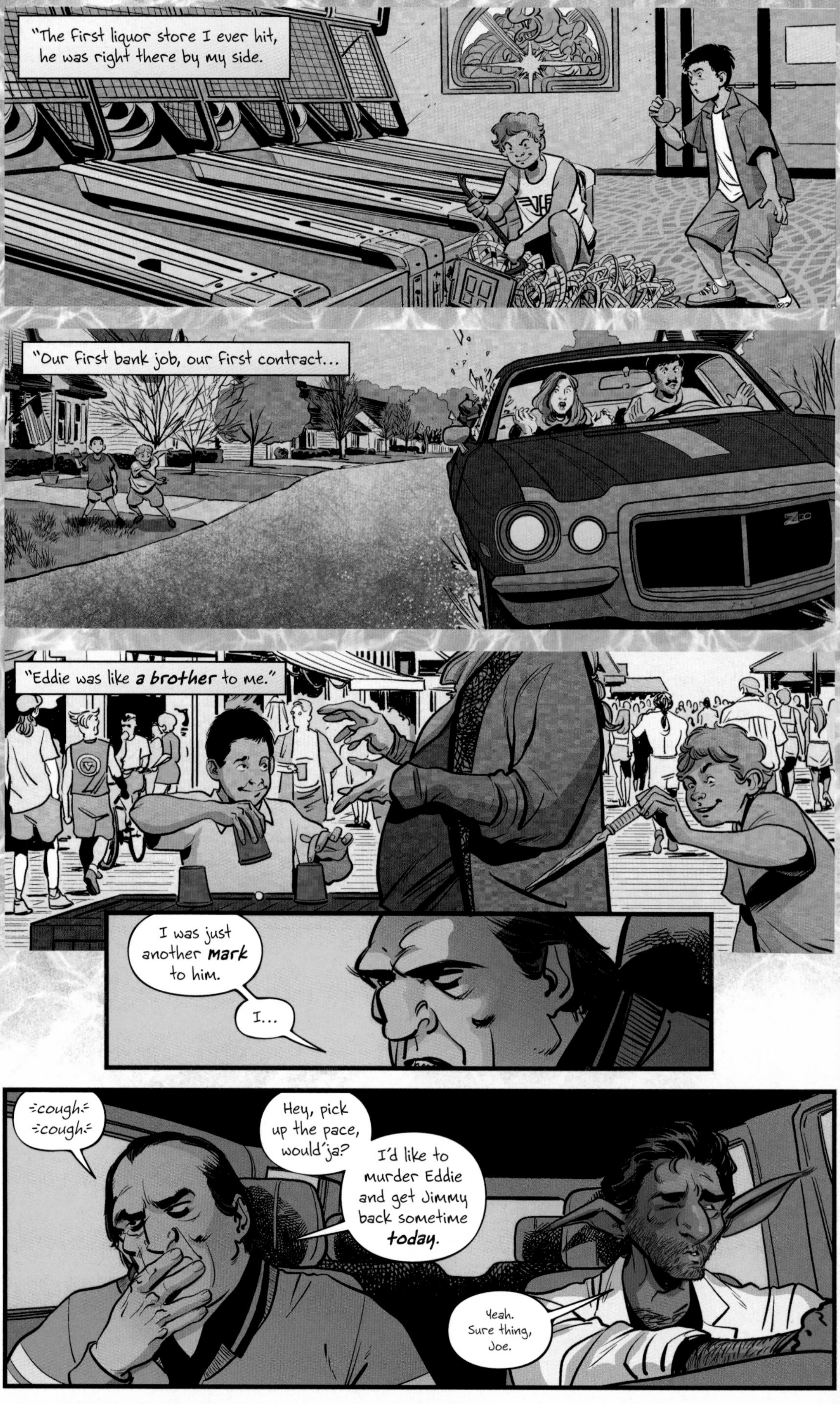
"The first liquor store I ever hit, he was right there by my side.
"Our first bank job, our first contract...
"Eddie was like **a brother** to me."
I was just another **mark** to him.
I...
=cough=
=cough=
Hey, pick up the pace, would'ja?
I'd like to murder Eddie and get Jimmy back sometime **today**.
Yeah. Sure thing, Joe.

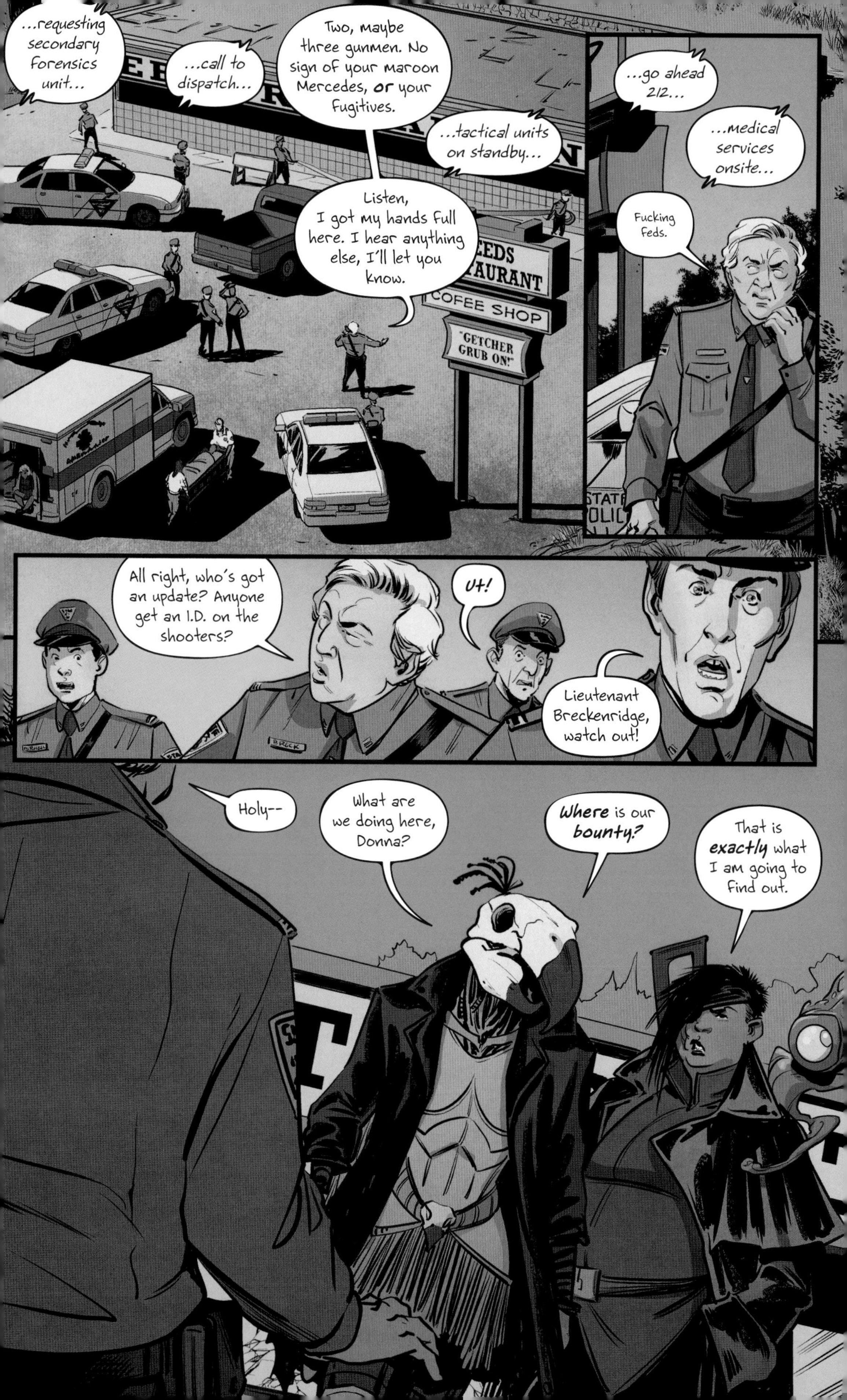

...requesting secondary forensics unit...
...call to dispatch...
Two, maybe three gunmen. No sign of your maroon Mercedes, or your Fugitives.
...tactical units on standby...
Listen, I got my hands full here. I hear anything else, I'll let you know.
COFEE SHOP
"GETCHER GRUB ON!"
...go ahead 212...
...medical services onsite...
Fucking Feds.
All right, who's got an update? Anyone get an I.D. on the shooters?
Ut!
Lieutenant Breckenridge, watch out!
Holy--
What are we doing here, Donna?
Where is our bounty?
That is exactly what I am going to find out.

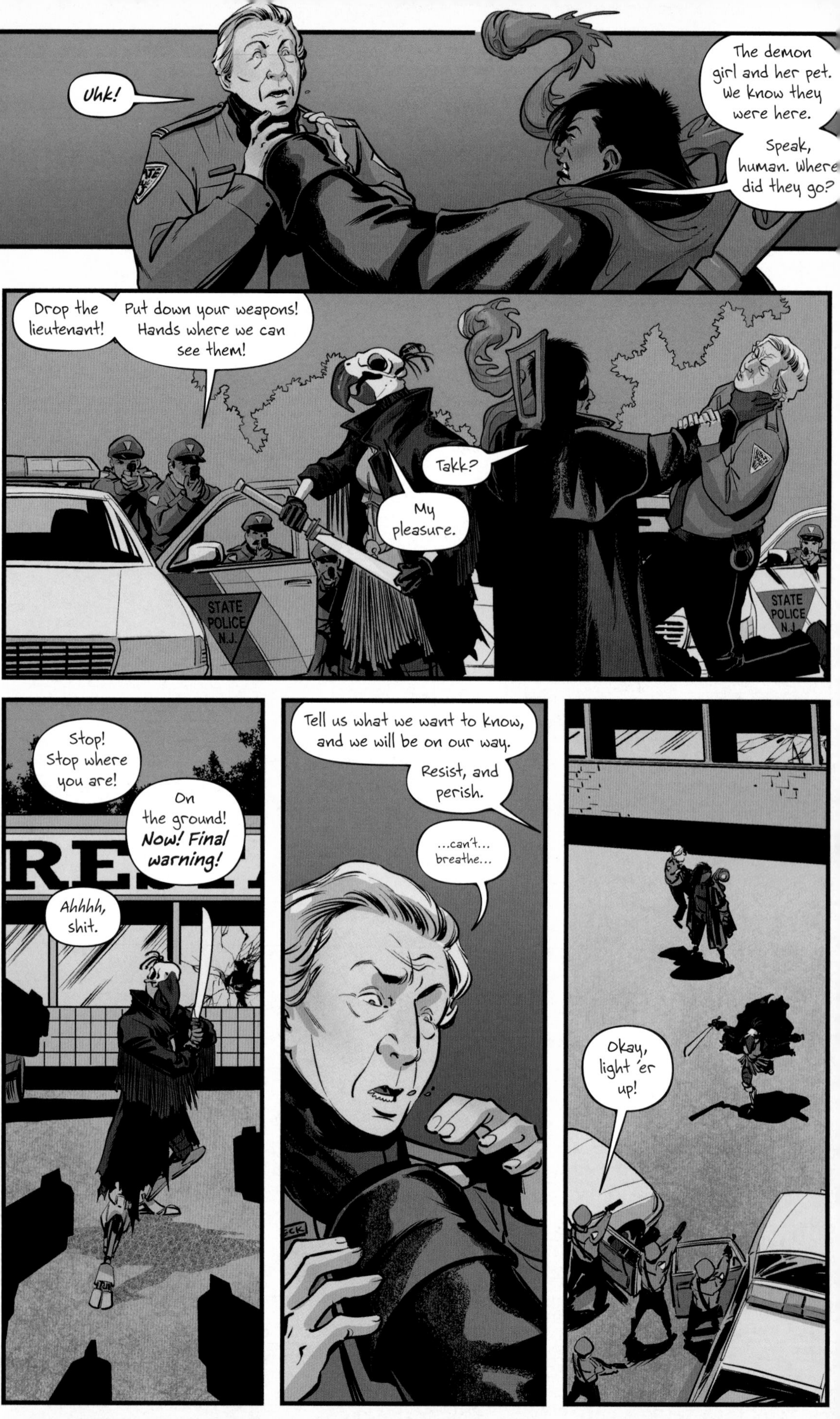
Uhk!
The demon girl and her pet. We know they were here.
Speak, human. Where did they go?
Drop the lieutenant!
Put down your weapons! Hands where we can see them!
Takk?
My pleasure.
STATE POLICE N.J.
STATE POLICE N.J.
Stop! Stop where you are!
On the ground! Now! Final warning!
Ahhhh, shit.
Tell us what we want to know, and we will be on our way.
Resist, and perish.
...can't... breathe...
Okay, light 'er up!

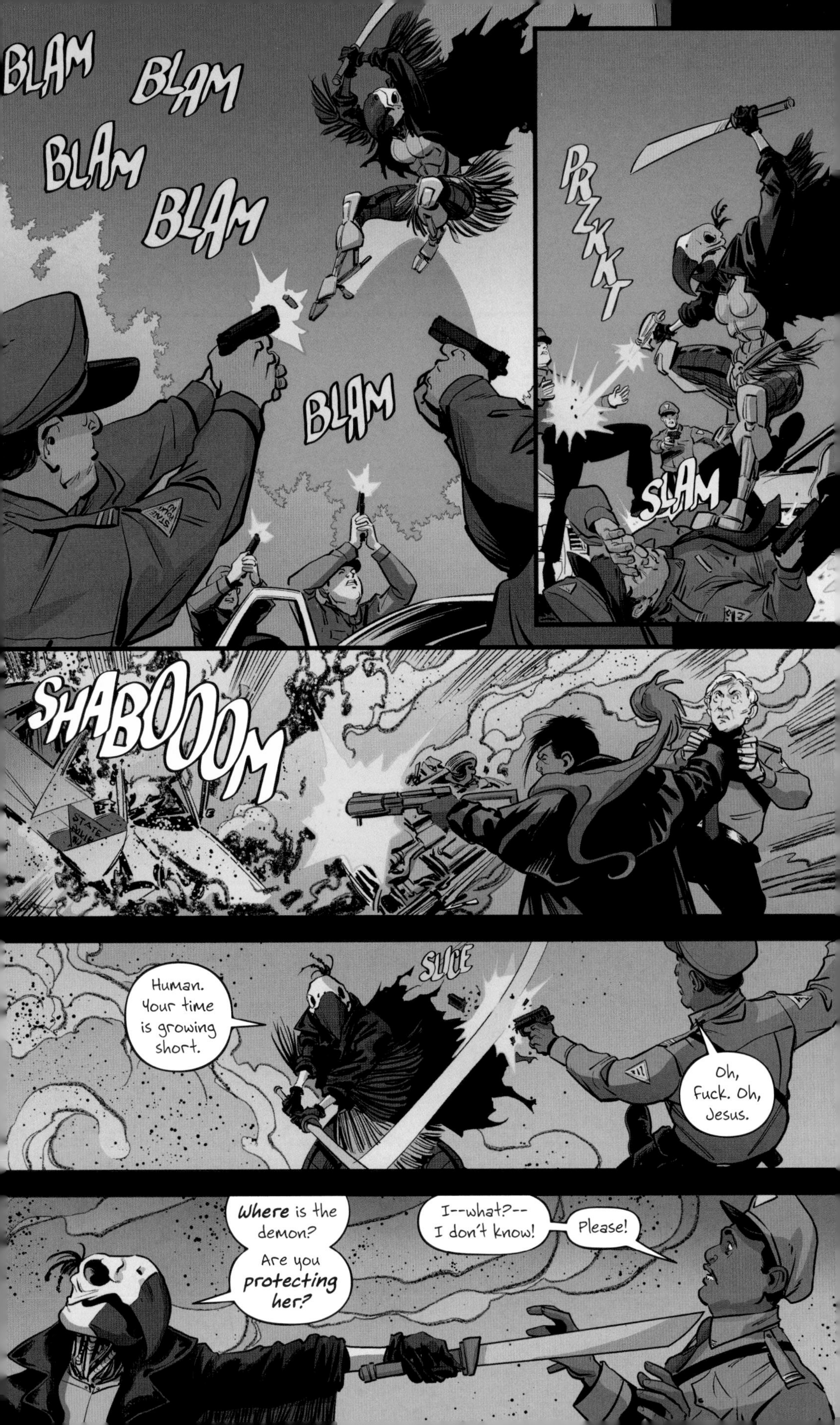
BLAM
BLAM
BLAM
BLAM
BLAM
PRZKKT
SLAM
SHABOOOM
STATE POLICE
Human. Your time is growing short.
SLICE
Oh, Fuck. Oh, Jesus.
Where is the demon?
Are you protecting her?
I--what?-- I don't know!
Please!

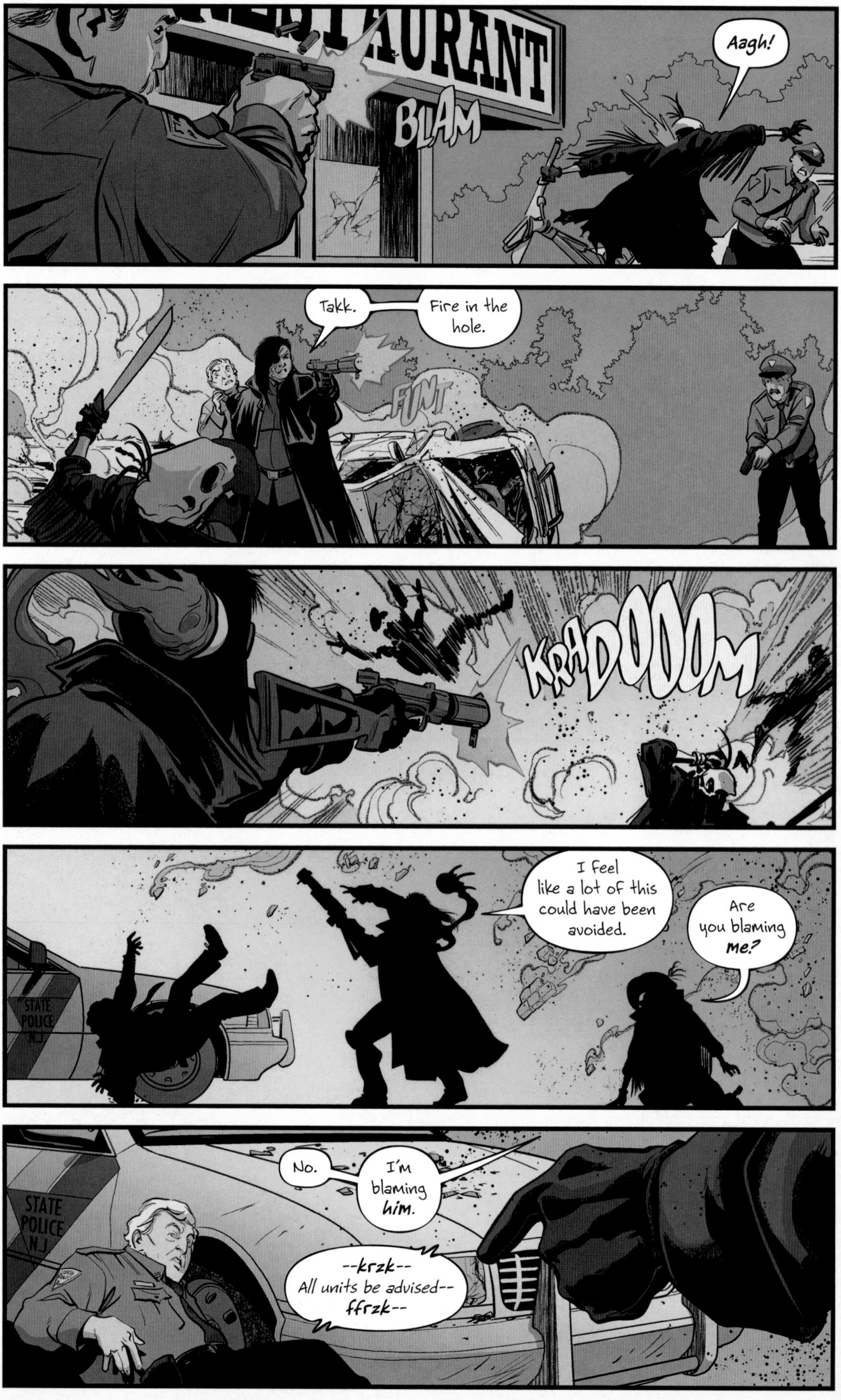
RESTAURANT
BLAM
Aagh!
Takk.
Fire in the hole.
FINT
KRADOOOM
STATE POLICE N.J.
I feel like a lot of this could have been avoided.
Are you blaming **me?**
STATE POLICE N.J.
No.
I'm blaming **him.**
--krzk--
All units be advised--
ffrzk--

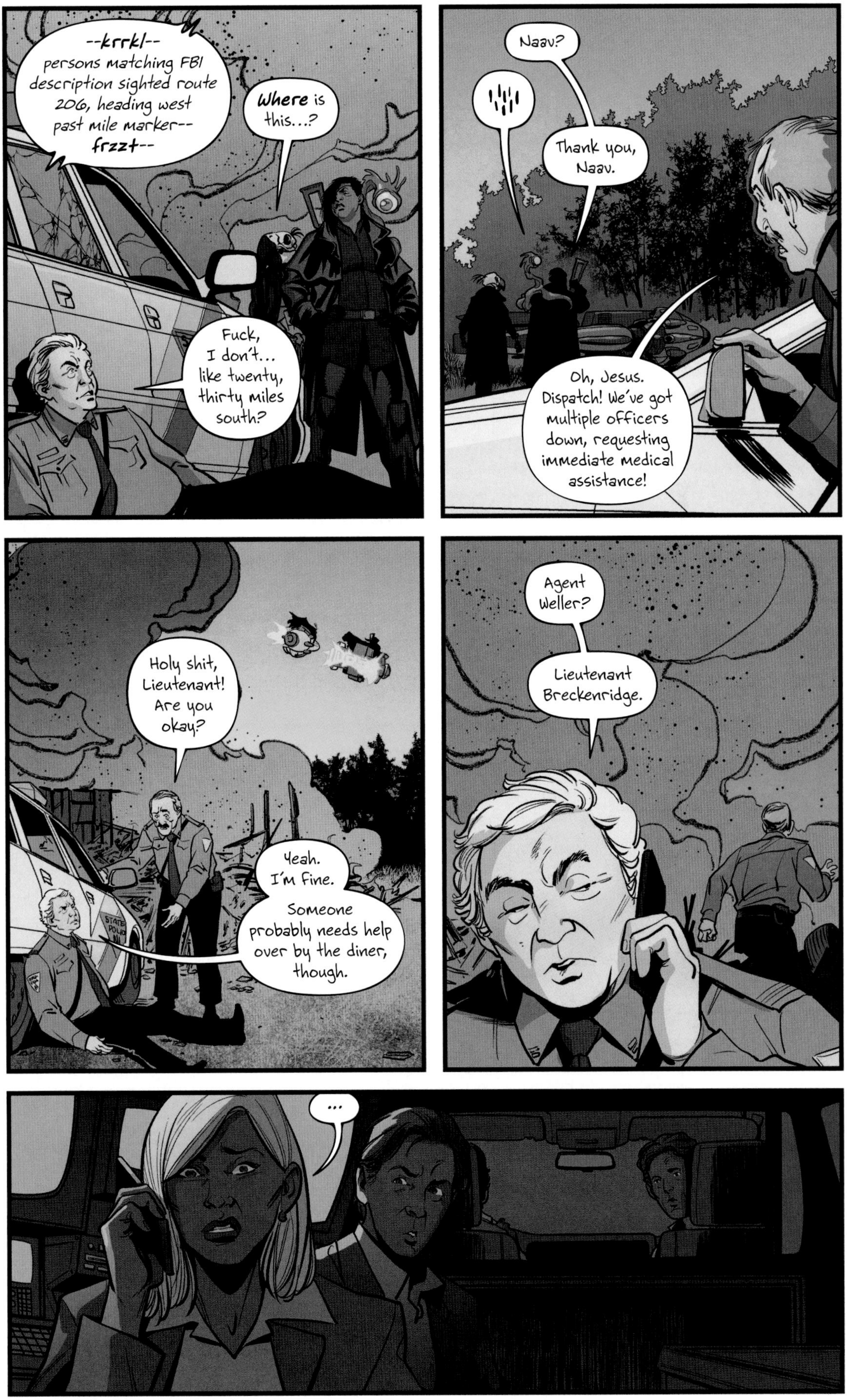
--krrkl-- persons matching FBI description sighted route 206, heading west past mile marker-- frzzt--
Where is this...?
Fuck, I don't... like twenty, thirty miles south?
Naav?
Thank you, Naav.
Oh, Jesus. Dispatch! We've got multiple officers down, requesting immediate medical assistance!
Holy shit, Lieutenant! Are you okay?
Yeah. I'm fine.
Someone probably needs help over by the diner, though.
Agent Weller?
Lieutenant Breckenridge.
...

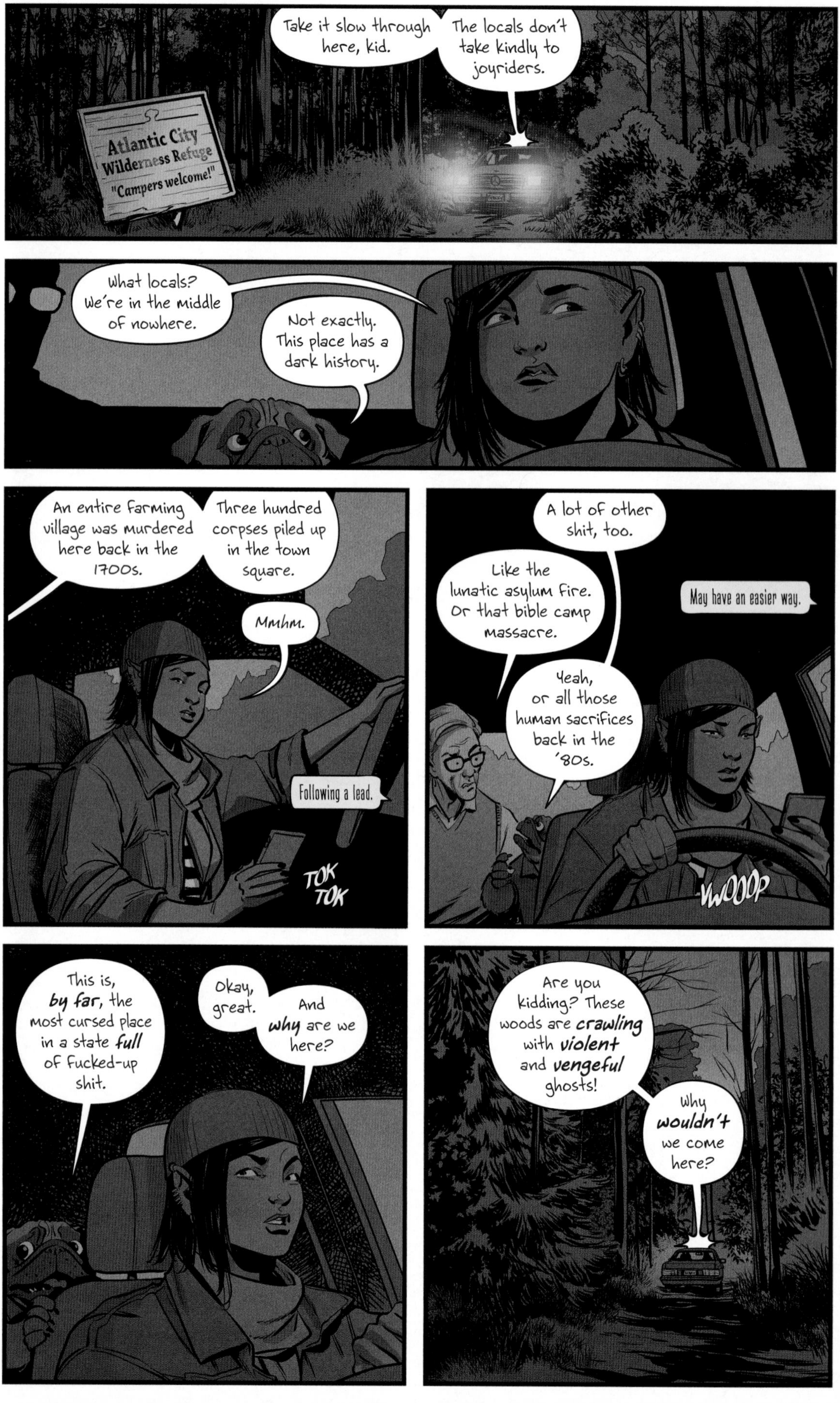
Take it slow through here, kid.
The locals don't take kindly to joyriders.
Atlantic City Wilderness Refuge "Campers welcome!"
What locals? We're in the middle of nowhere.
Not exactly. This place has a dark history.
An entire farming village was murdered here back in the 1700s.
Three hundred corpses piled up in the town square.
Mmhm.
Following a lead.
TOK TOK
A lot of other shit, too.
Like the lunatic asylum fire. Or that bible camp massacre.
May have an easier way.
Yeah, or all those human sacrifices back in the '80s.
VWOOOP
This is, **by far**, the most cursed place in a state **full** of fucked-up shit.
Okay, great.
And **why** are we here?
Are you kidding? These woods are **crawling** with **violent** and **vengeful** ghosts!
Why **wouldn't** we come here?

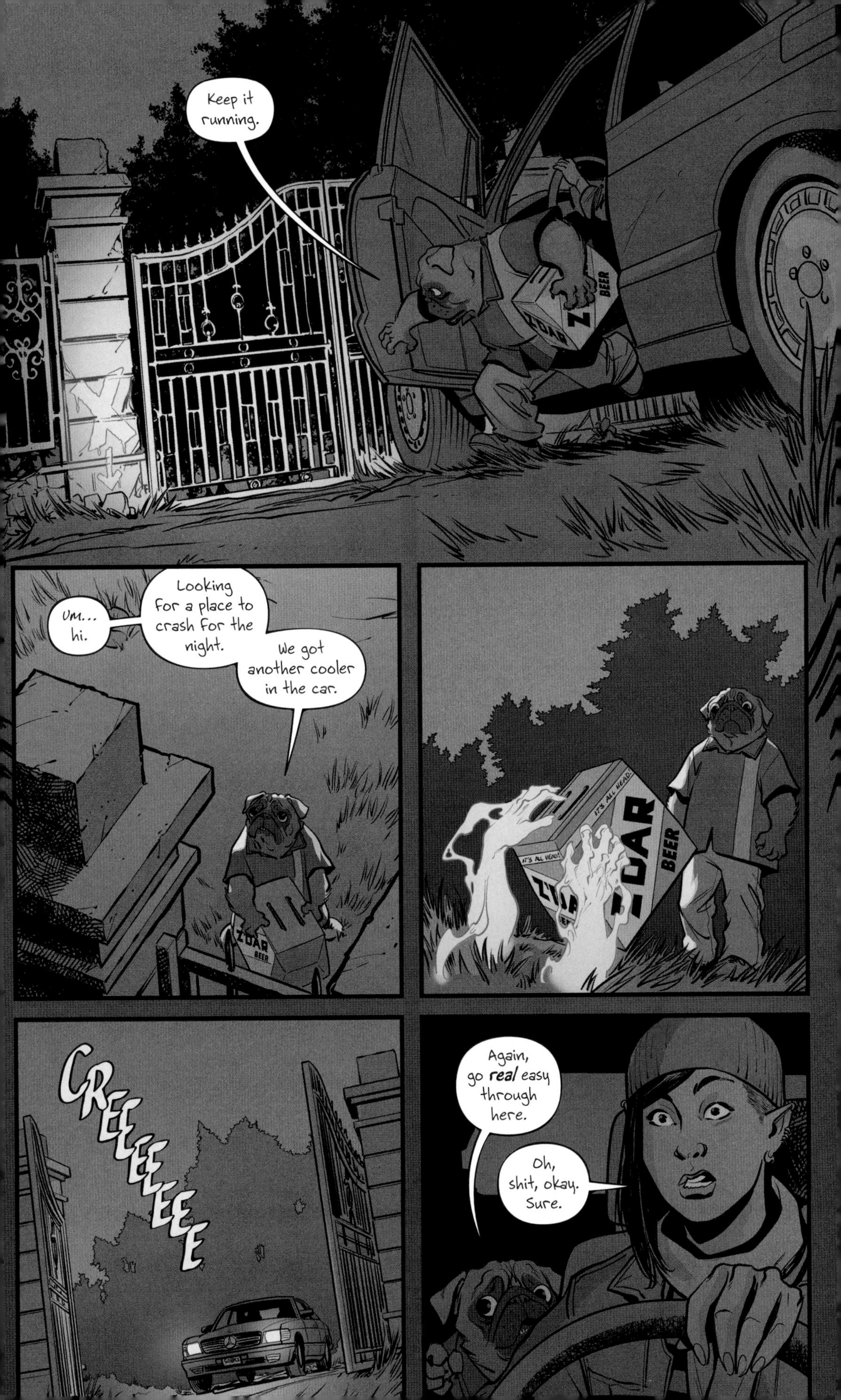

Keep it running.
ZOAR BEER
Um... hi.
Looking for a place to crash for the night.
We got another cooler in the car.
ZOAR BEER
IT'S ALL HEAD!
ZOAR BEER
CREEEEEEEE
Again, go **real** easy through here.
Oh, shit, okay. Sure.

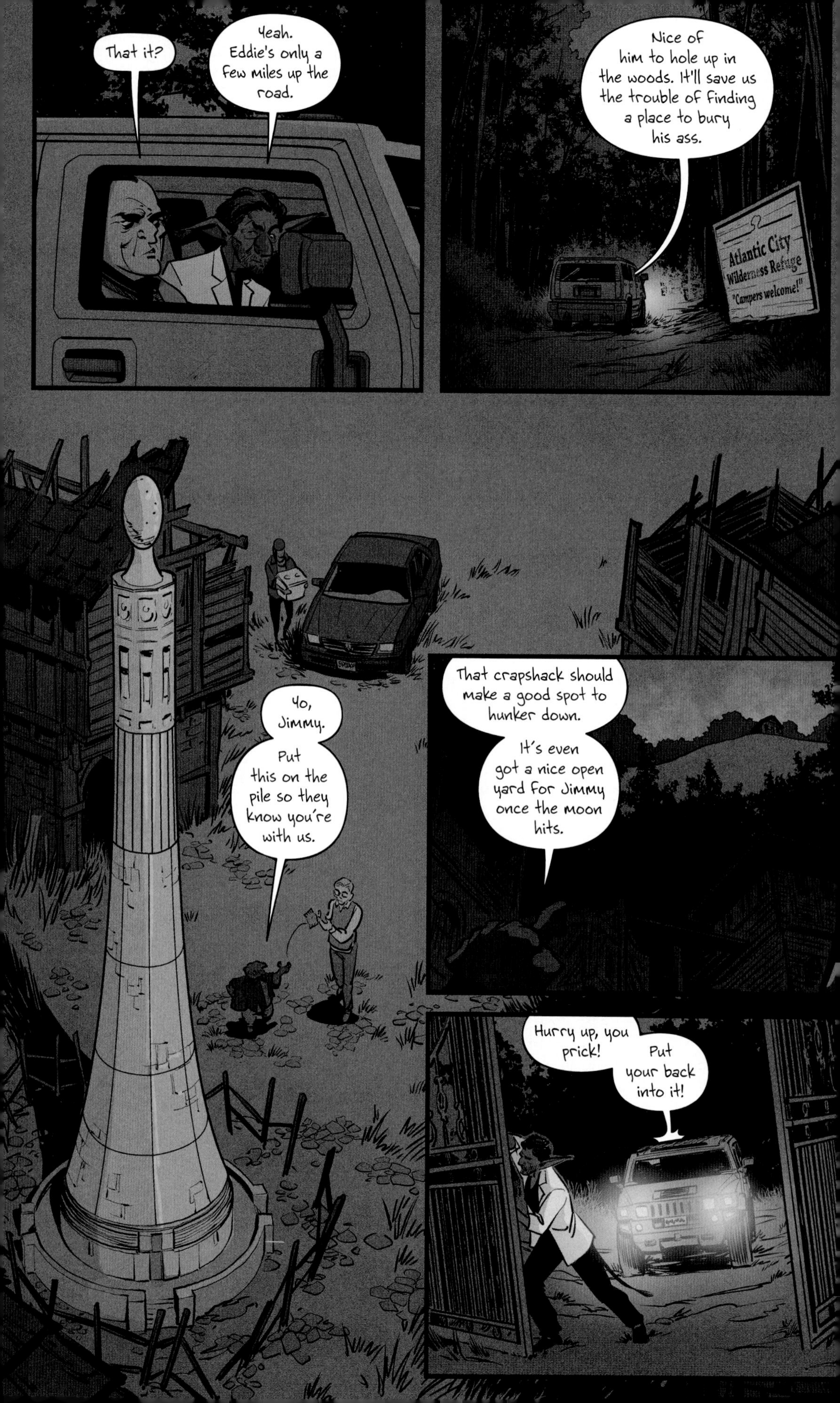
That it?
Yeah. Eddie's only a few miles up the road.
Nice of him to hole up in the woods. It'll save us the trouble of finding a place to bury his ass.
Atlantic City Wilderness Refuge "Campers welcome!"
Yo, Jimmy.
Put this on the pile so they know you're with us.
That crapshack should make a good spot to hunker down.
It's even got a nice open yard for Jimmy once the moon hits.
Hurry up, you prick!
Put your back into it!

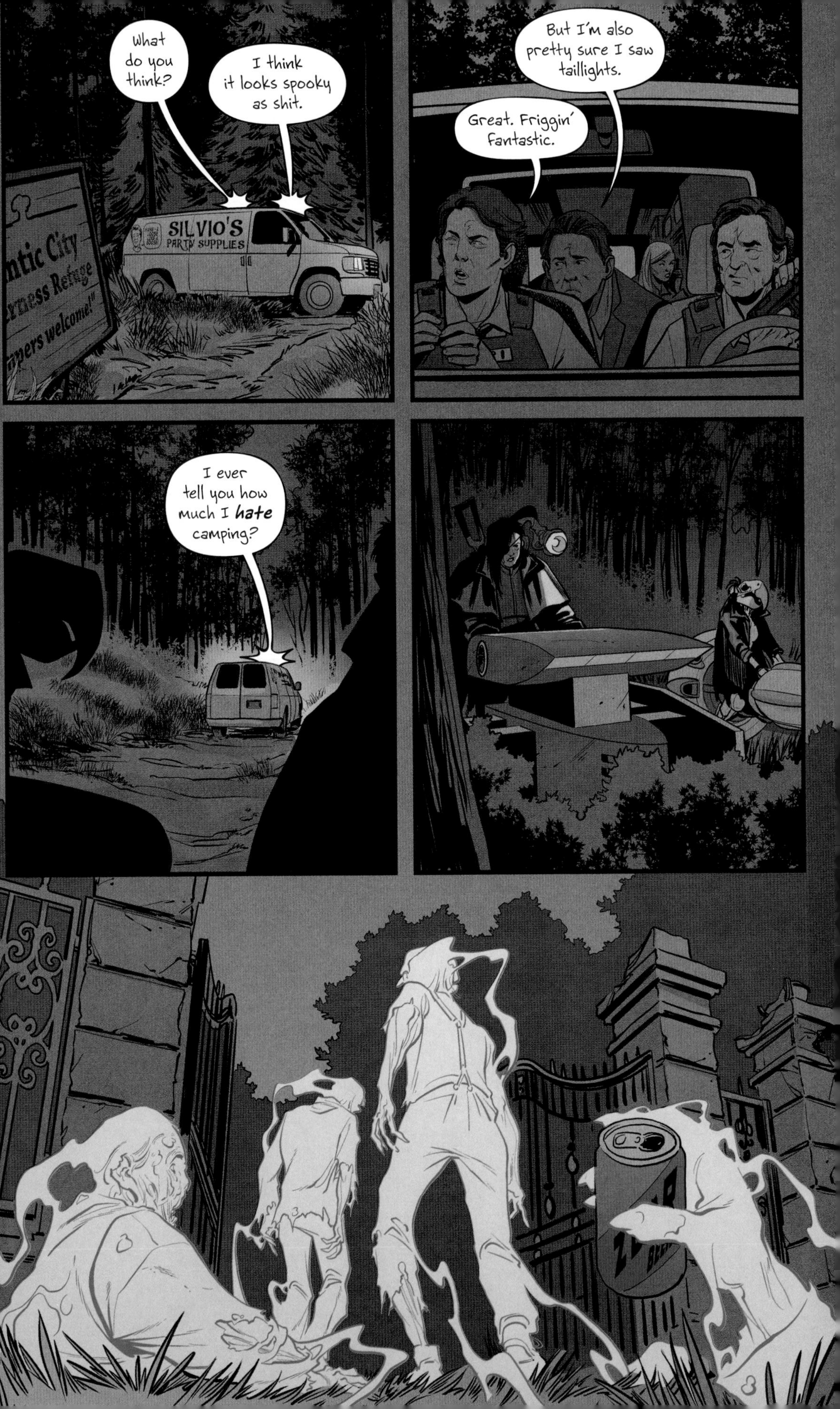
What do you think?
I think it looks spooky as shit.
SILVIO'S PARTY SUPPLIES
But I'm also pretty sure I saw taillights.
Great. Friggin' fantastic.
I ever tell you how much I *hate* camping?

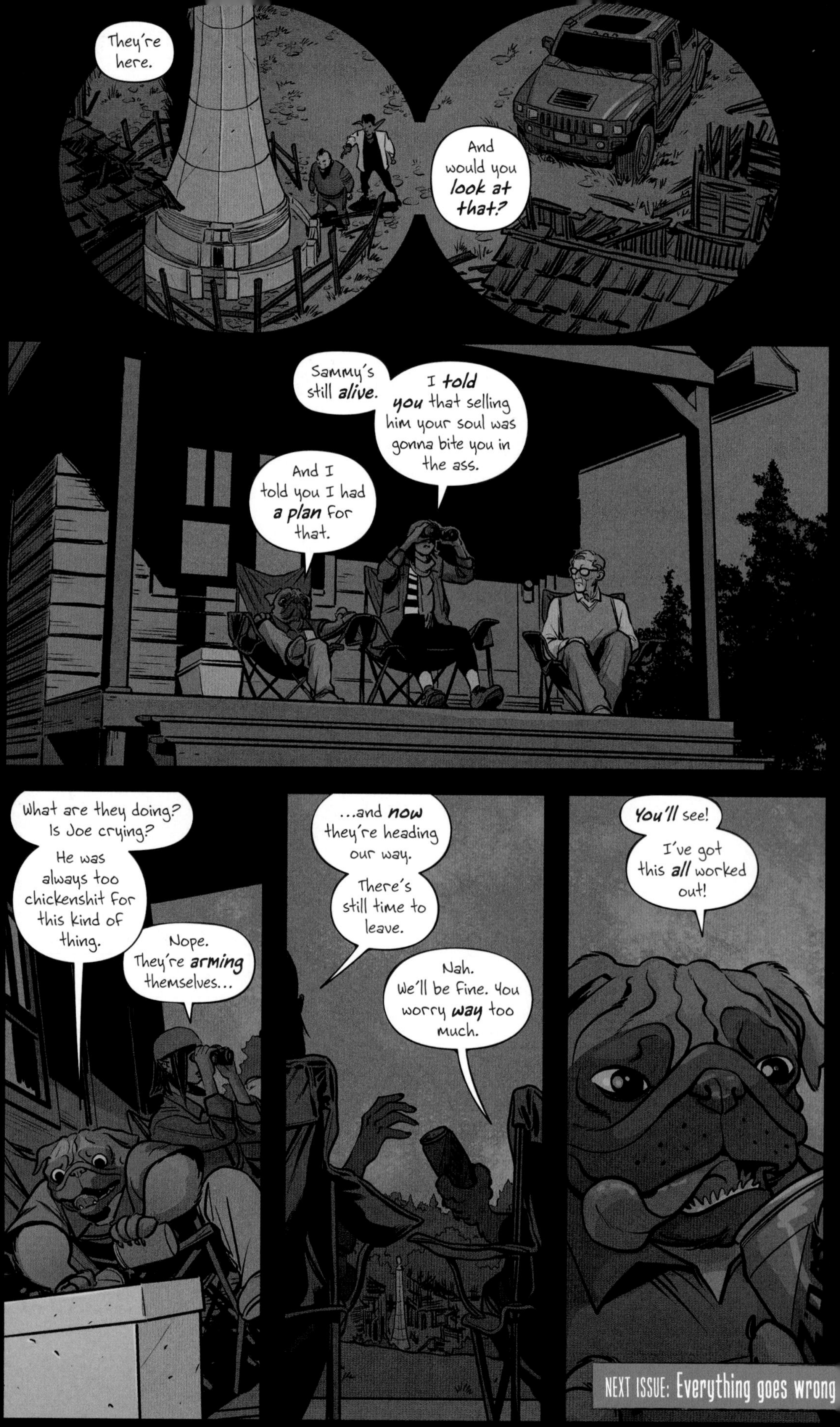
They're here.
And would you look at that?
Sammy's still alive.
I told you that selling him your soul was gonna bite you in the ass.
And I told you I had a plan for that.
What are they doing? Is Joe crying?
He was always too chickenshit for this kind of thing.
Nope. They're arming themselves...
...and now they're heading our way.
There's still time to leave.
Nah. We'll be fine. You worry way too much.
You'll see!
I've got this all worked out!
NEXT ISSUE: Everything goes wrong

BOOK FOUR

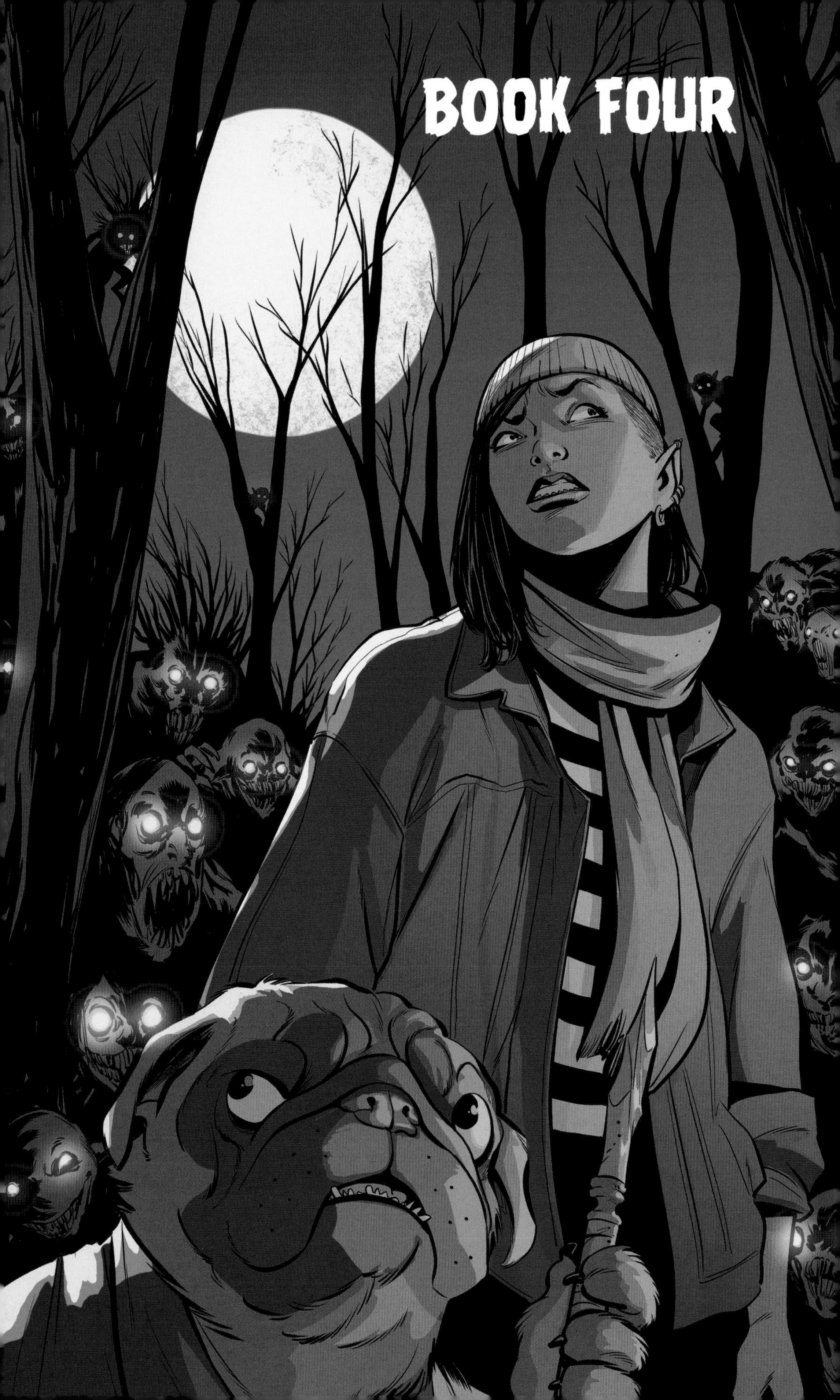

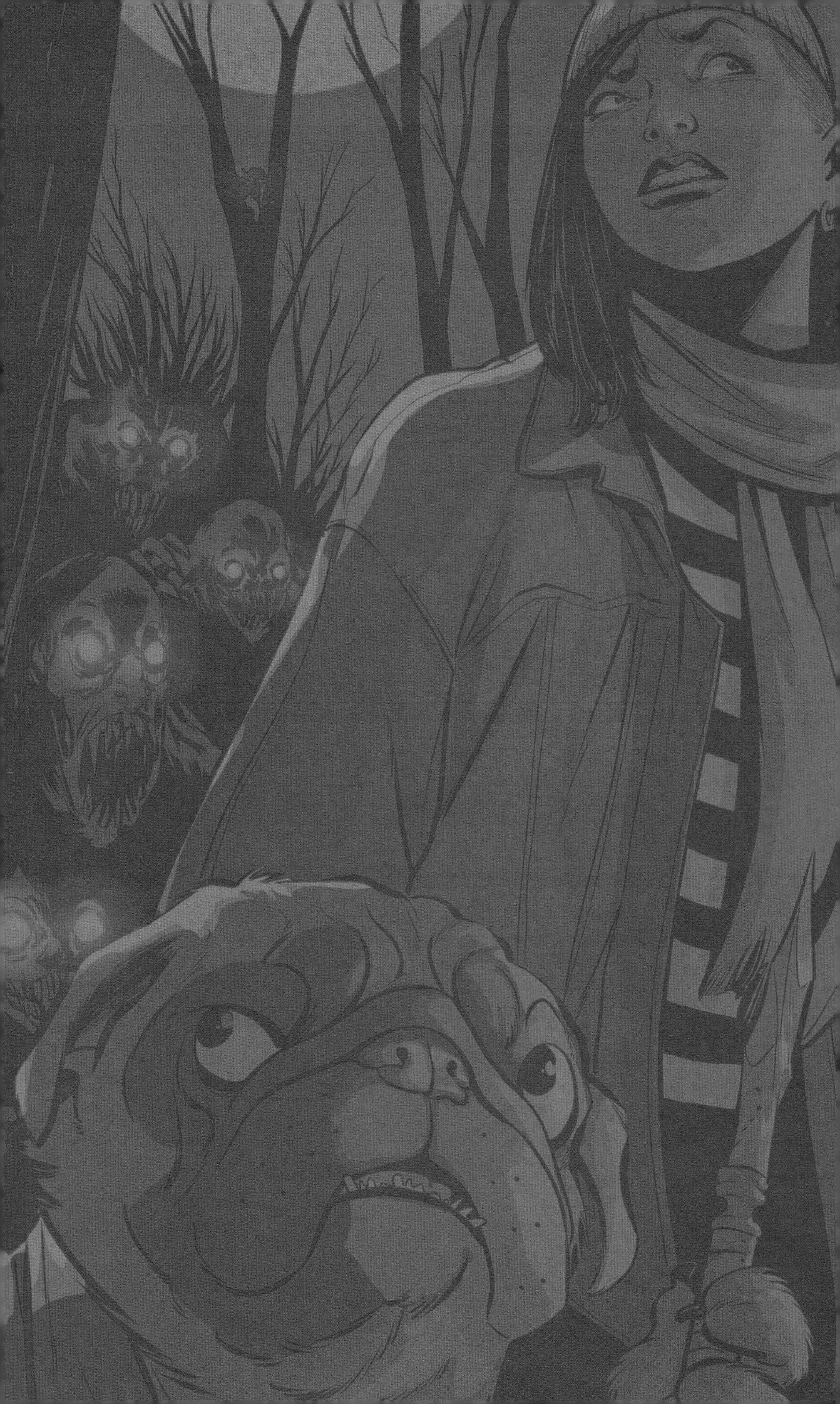

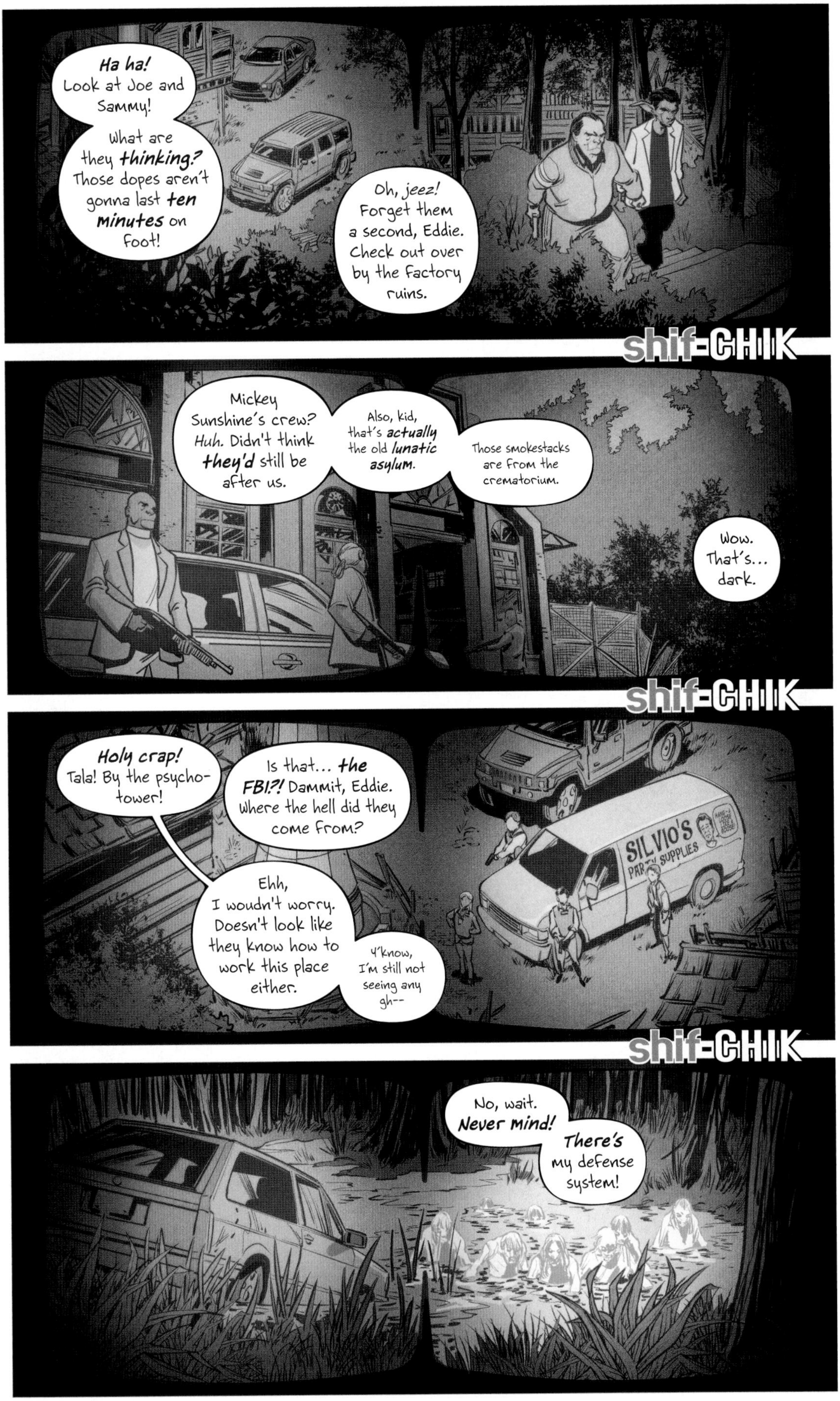
Ha ha! Look at Joe and Sammy!
What are they thinking? Those dopes aren't gonna last ten minutes on foot!
Oh, jeez! Forget them a second, Eddie. Check out over by the factory ruins.
shif-CHIK
Mickey Sunshine's crew? Huh. Didn't think they'd still be after us.
Also, kid, that's actually the old lunatic asylum.
Those smokestacks are from the crematorium.
Wow. That's... dark.
shif-CHIK
Holy crap! Tala! By the psycho-tower!
Is that... the FBI?! Dammit, Eddie. Where the hell did they come from?
Ehh, I woudn't worry. Doesn't look like they know how to work this place either.
Y'know, I'm still not seeing any gh--
SILVIO'S PARTY SUPPLIES
shif-CHIK
No, wait. Never mind!
There's my defense system!

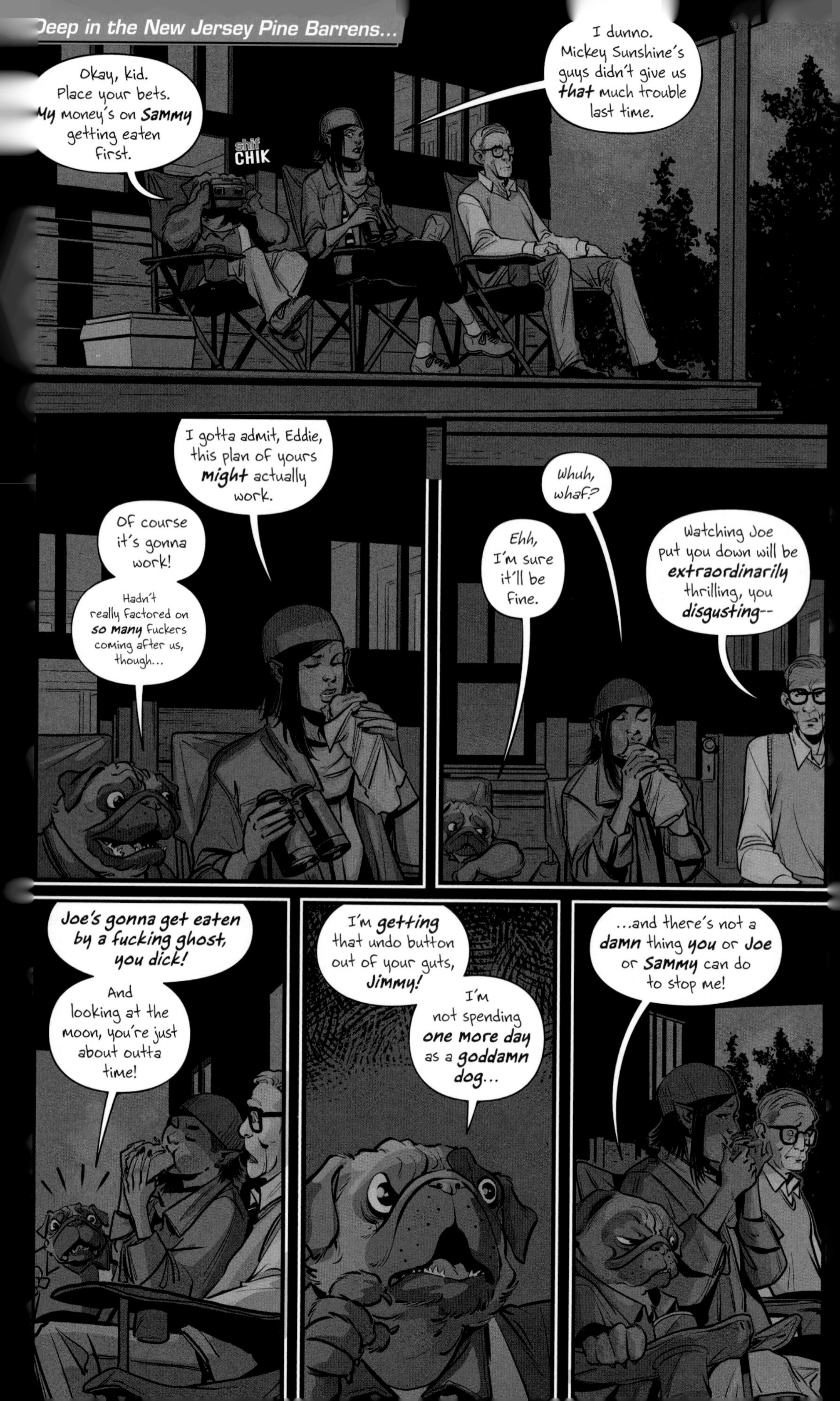

Deep in the New Jersey Pine Barrens...
Okay, kid. Place your bets. My money's on Sammy getting eaten first.
shif CHIK
I dunno. Mickey Sunshine's guys didn't give us that much trouble last time.
I gotta admit, Eddie, this plan of yours might actually work.
Of course it's gonna work!
Hadn't really factored on so many fuckers coming after us, though...
Whuh, whaf?
Ehh, I'm sure it'll be fine.
Watching Joe put you down will be extraordinarily thrilling, you disgusting--
Joe's gonna get eaten by a fucking ghost, you dick!
And looking at the moon, you're just about outta time!
I'm getting that undo button out of your guts, Jimmy!
I'm not spending one more day as a goddamn dog...
...and there's not a damn thing you or Joe or Sammy can do to stop me!

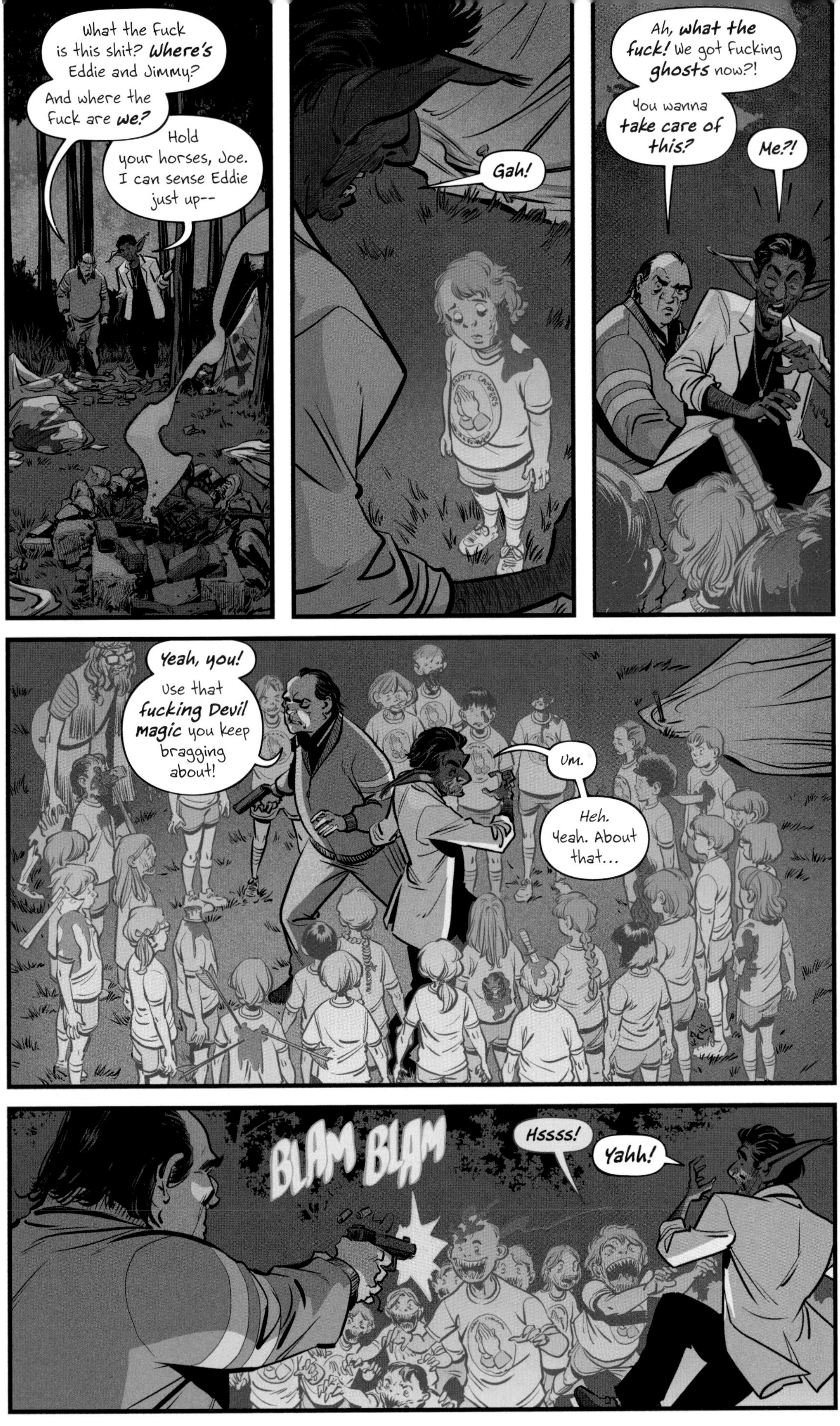
What the fuck is this shit? Where's Eddie and Jimmy?
And where the fuck are we?
Hold your horses, Joe. I can sense Eddie just up--
Gah!
Ah, what the fuck! We got fucking ghosts now?!
You wanna take care of this?
Me?!
Yeah, you!
Use that fucking Devil magic you keep bragging about!
Um.
Heh. Yeah. About that...
BLAM BLAM
Hssss!
Yahh!

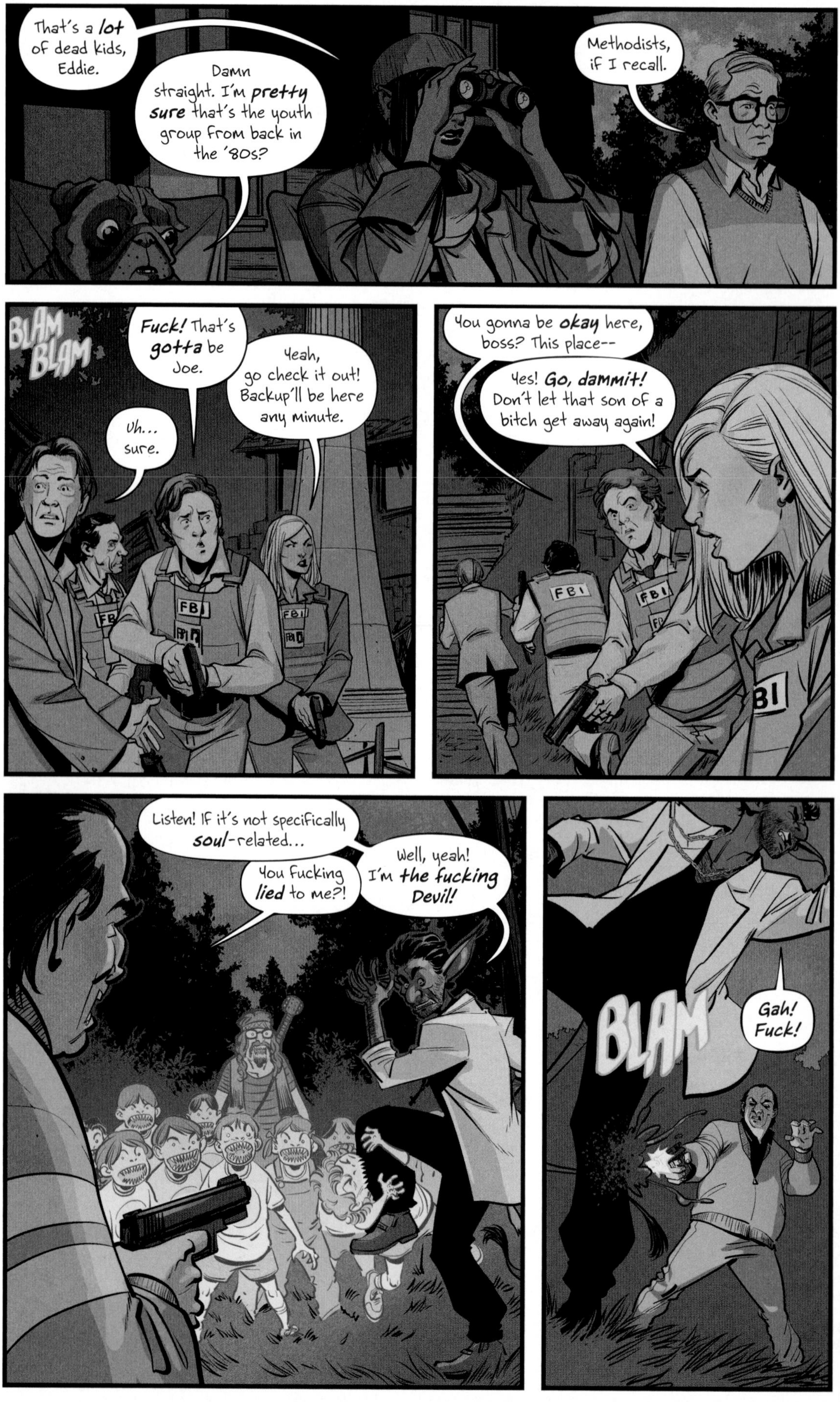
That's a lot of dead kids, Eddie.
Damn straight. I'm pretty sure that's the youth group from back in the '80s?
Methodists, if I recall.
BLAM BLAM
Fuck! That's gotta be Joe.
Yeah, go check it out! Backup'll be here any minute.
Uh... sure.
You gonna be okay here, boss? This place--
Yes! Go, dammit! Don't let that son of a bitch get away again!
Listen! If it's not specifically soul-related...
You fucking lied to me?!
Well, yeah! I'm the fucking Devil!
BLAM
Gah! Fuck!

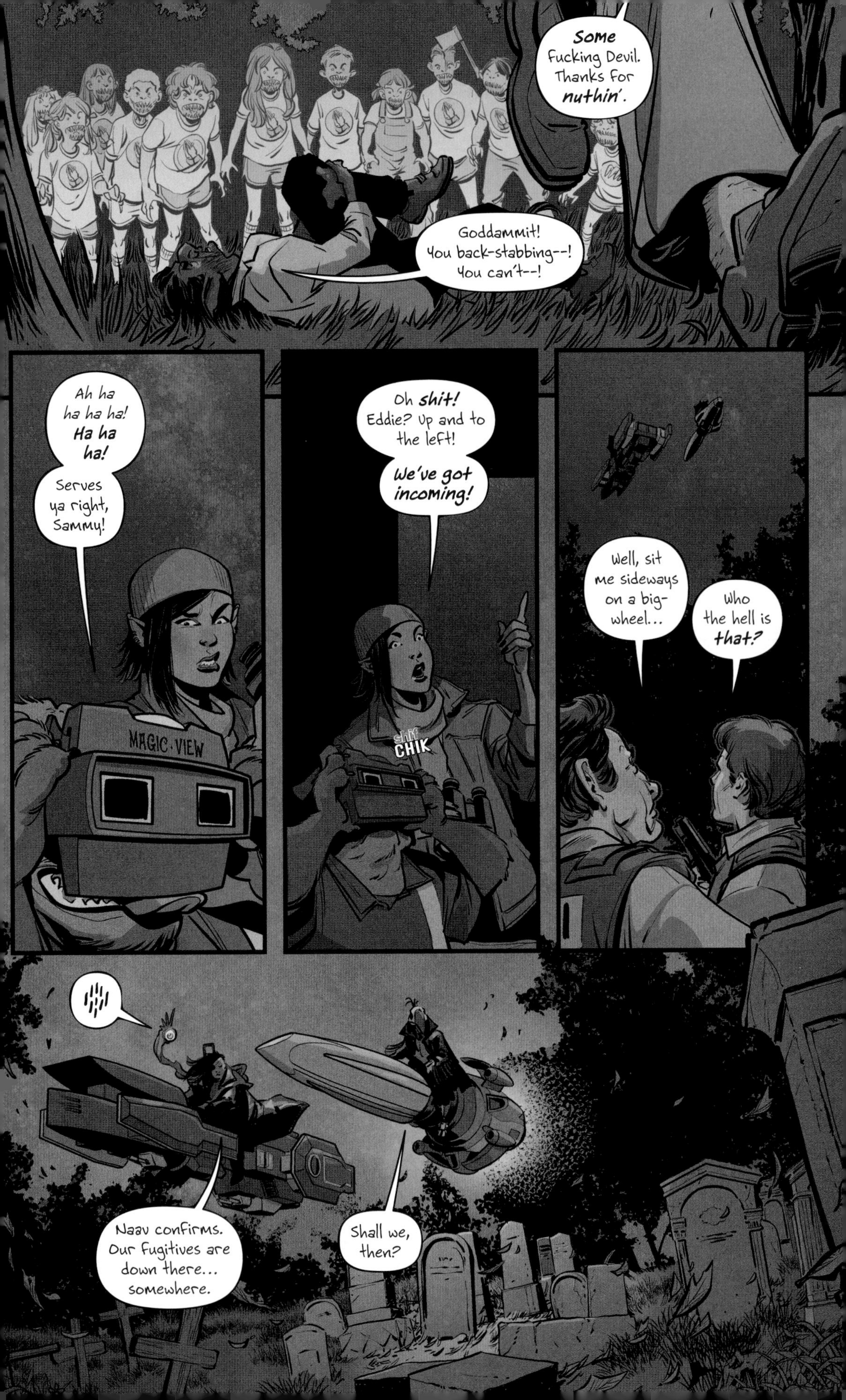

Some Fucking Devil. Thanks for nuthin'.
Goddammit! You back-stabbing--! You can't--!
Ah ha ha ha ha! Ha ha ha!
Serves ya right, Sammy!
MAGIC·VIEW
Oh shit! Eddie? Up and to the left!
We've got incoming!
CHIK
Well, sit me sideways on a big-wheel...
Who the hell is that?
Naav confirms. Our fugitives are down there... somewhere.
Shall we, then?

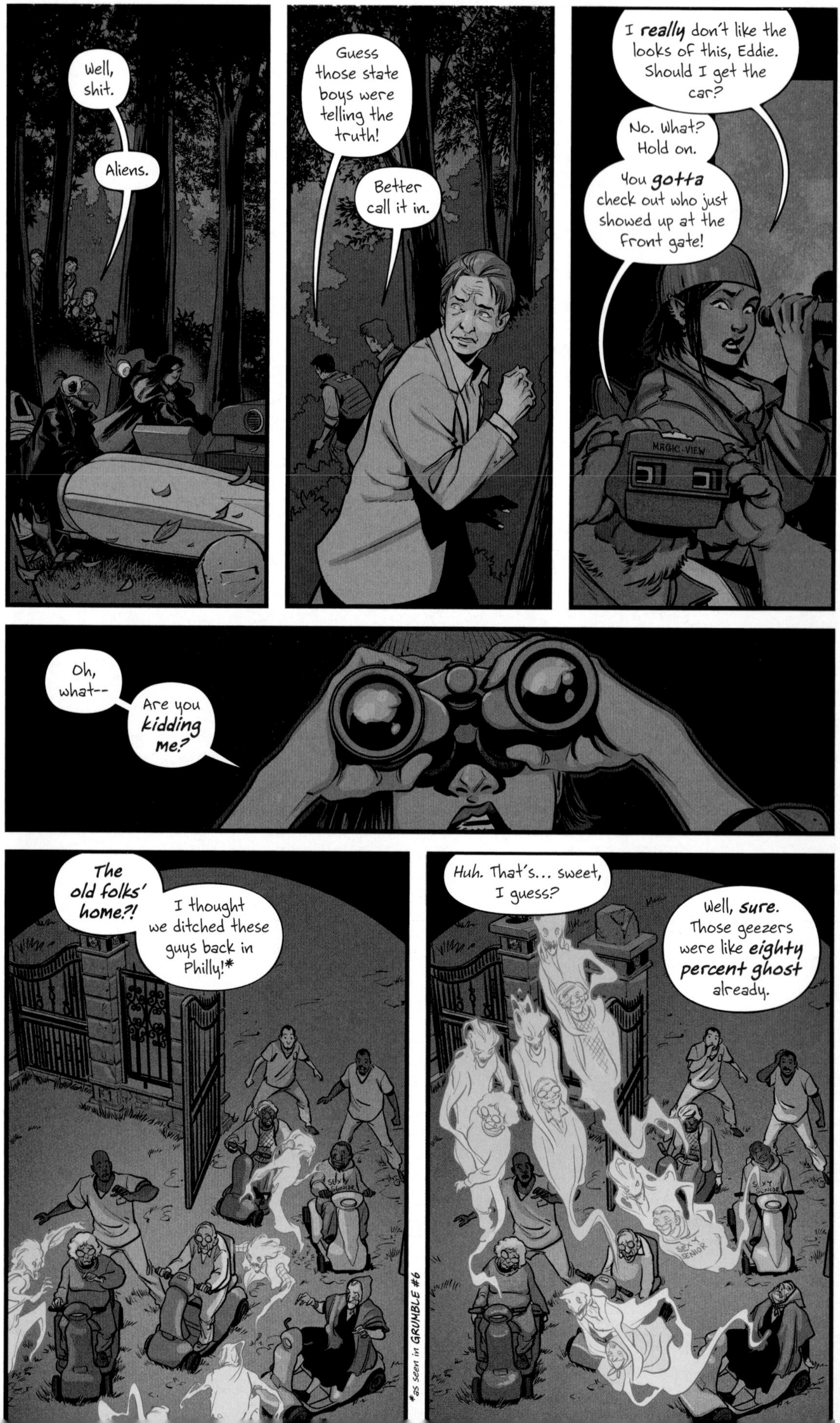
Well, shit.
Aliens.
Guess those state boys were telling the truth!
Better call it in.
I **really** don't like the looks of this, Eddie. Should I get the car?
No. What? Hold on.
You **gotta** check out who just showed up at the front gate!
MAGIC·VIEW
Oh, what--
Are you **kidding me?**
The old folks' home?!
I thought we ditched these guys back in Philly!*
SEXY SENIOR
*as seen in GRUMBLE #6
Huh. That's... sweet, I guess?
Well, **sure.** Those geezers were like **eighty percent ghost** already.
SEXY SENIOR

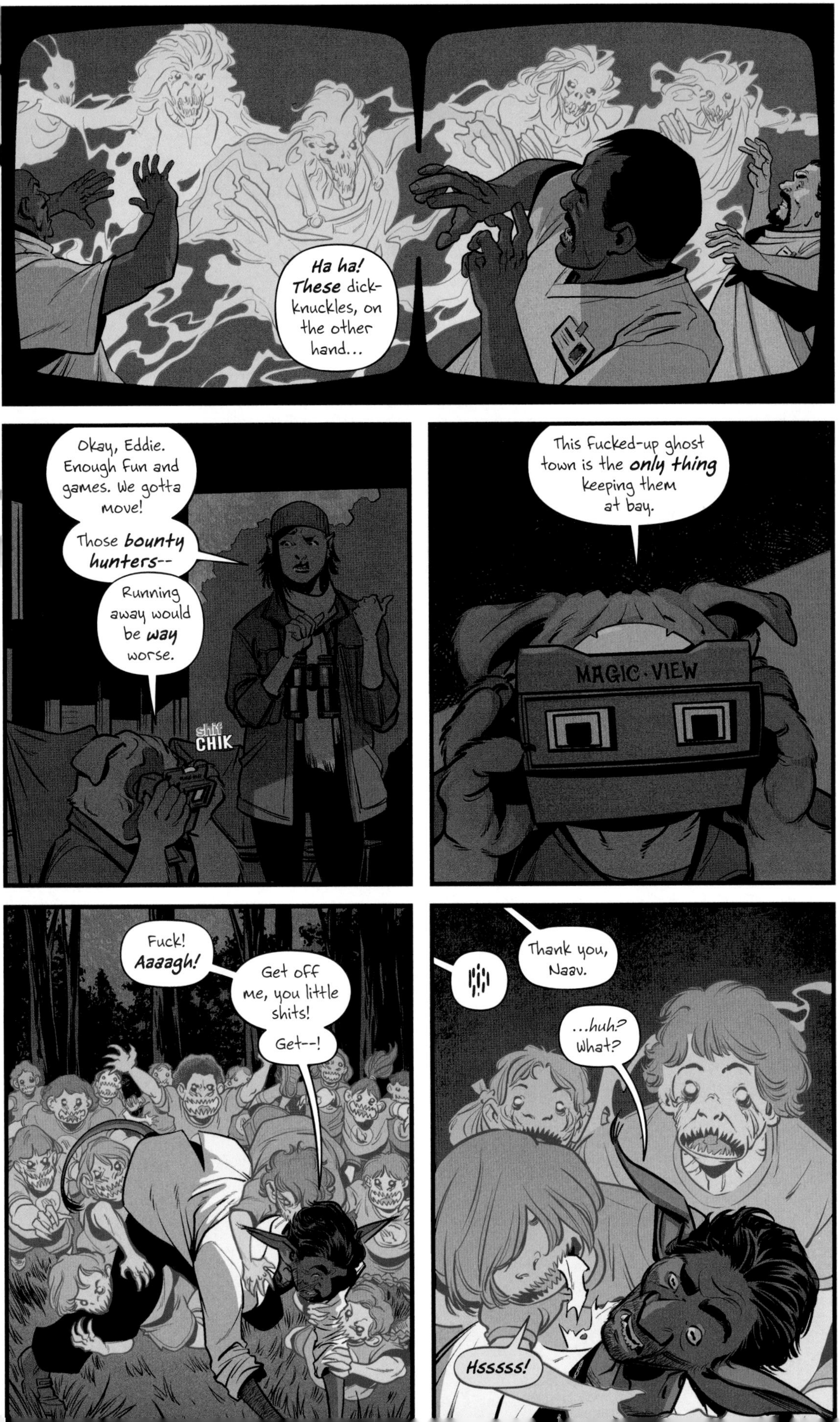
Ha ha! These dick-knuckles, on the other hand...
Okay, Eddie. Enough fun and games. We gotta move!
Those bounty hunters--
Running away would be way worse.
shif CHIK
This fucked-up ghost town is the only thing keeping them at bay.
MAGIC·VIEW
Fuck! Aaaagh!
Get off me, you little shits!
Get--!
Thank you, Naav.
...huh? What?
Hsssss!

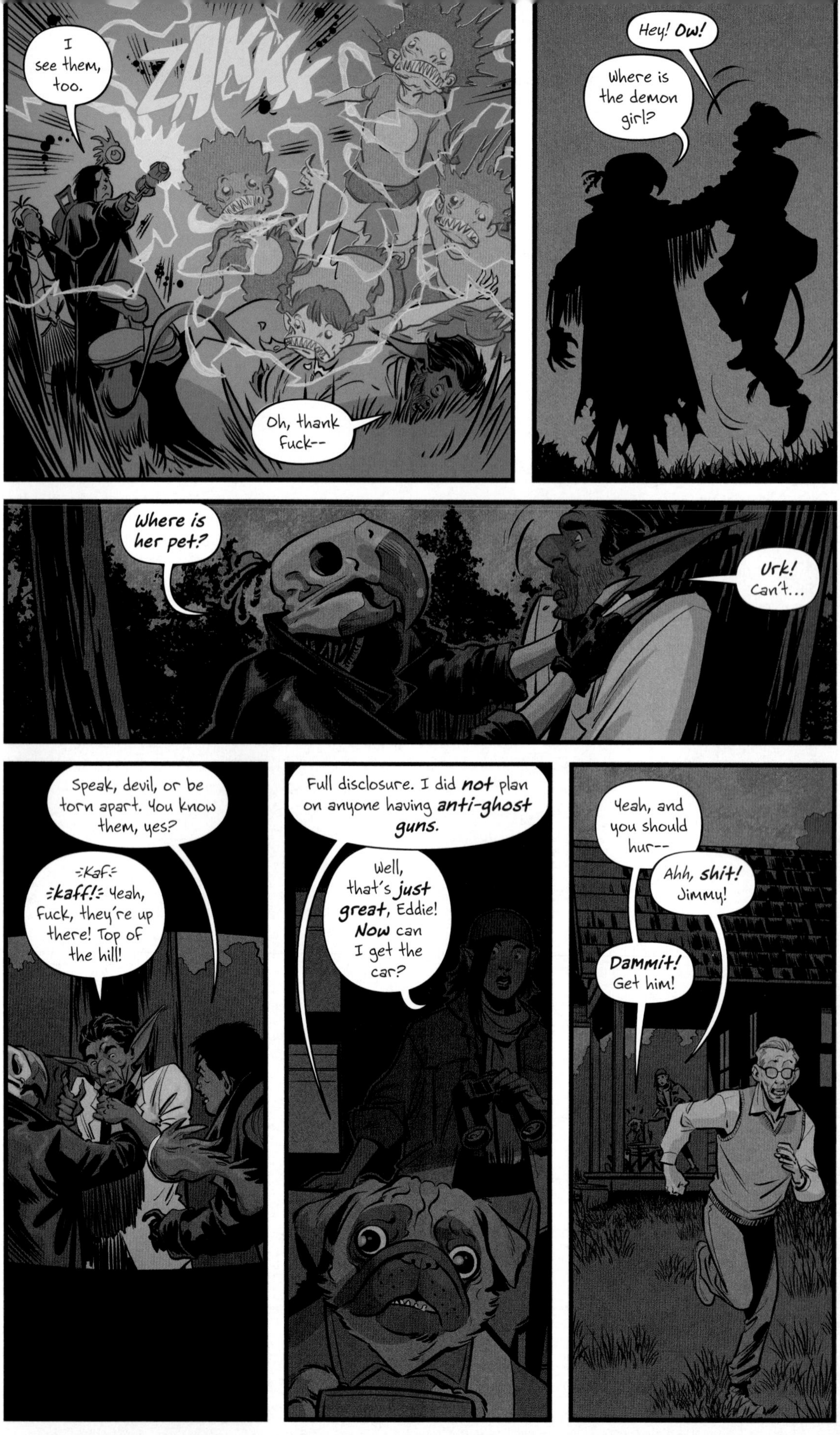
ZAKKK
I see them, too.
Oh, thank Fuck--
Hey! Ow!
Where is the demon girl?
Where is her pet?
Urk! Can't...
Speak, devil, or be torn apart. You know them, yes?
Kaf kaff! Yeah, fuck, they're up there! Top of the hill!
Full disclosure. I did not plan on anyone having anti-ghost guns.
Well, that's just great, Eddie! Now can I get the car?
Yeah, and you should hur--
Ahh, shit! Jimmy!
Dammit! Get him!

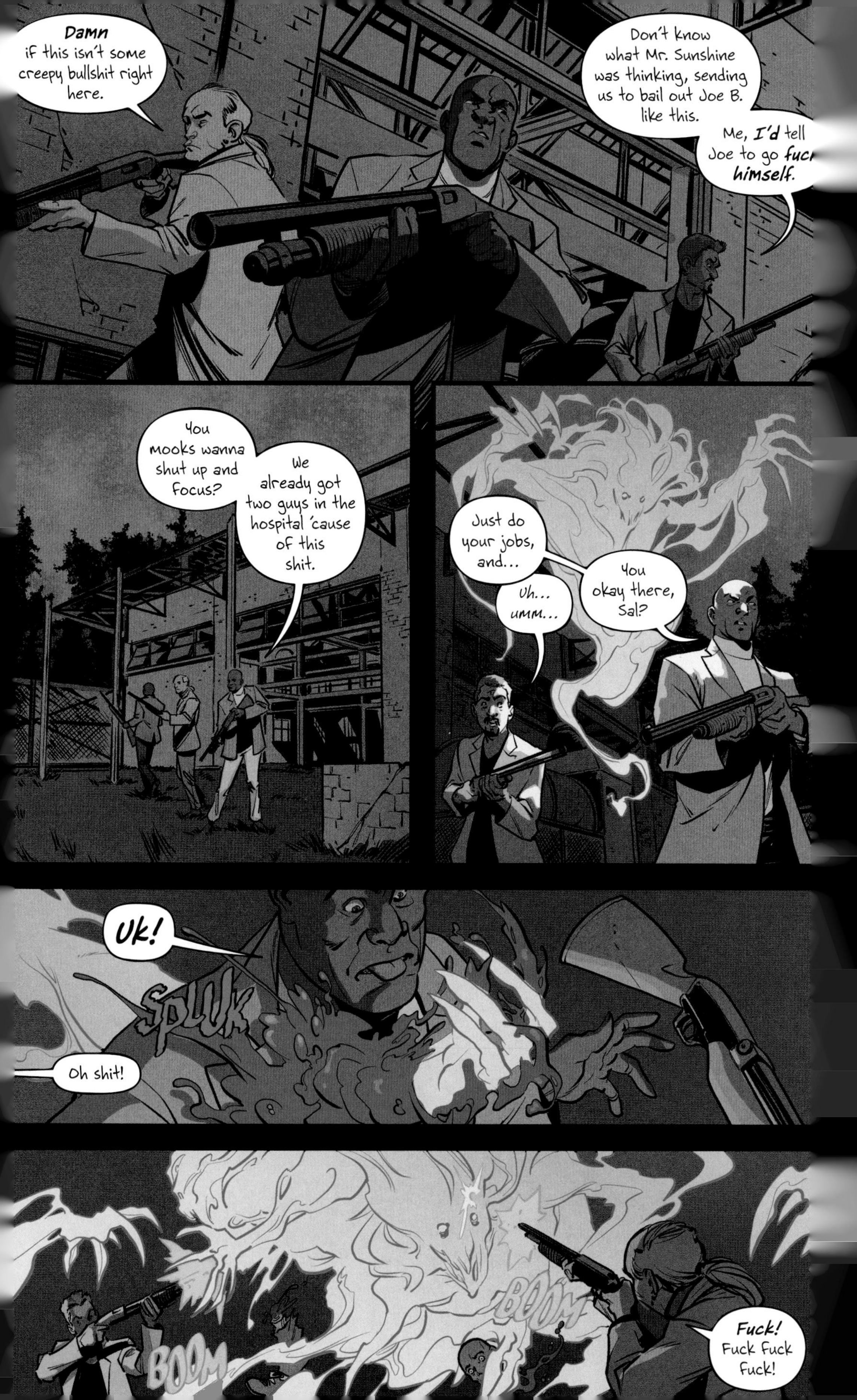
Damn if this isn't some creepy bullshit right here.
Don't know what Mr. Sunshine was thinking, sending us to bail out Joe B. like this.
Me, I'd tell Joe to go fuck himself.
You mooks wanna shut up and focus?
We already got two guys in the hospital 'cause of this shit.
Just do your jobs, and...
Uh... umm...
You okay there, Sal?
UK!
SPLUK
Oh shit!
BOOM
BOOM
Fuck! Fuck Fuck Fuck!

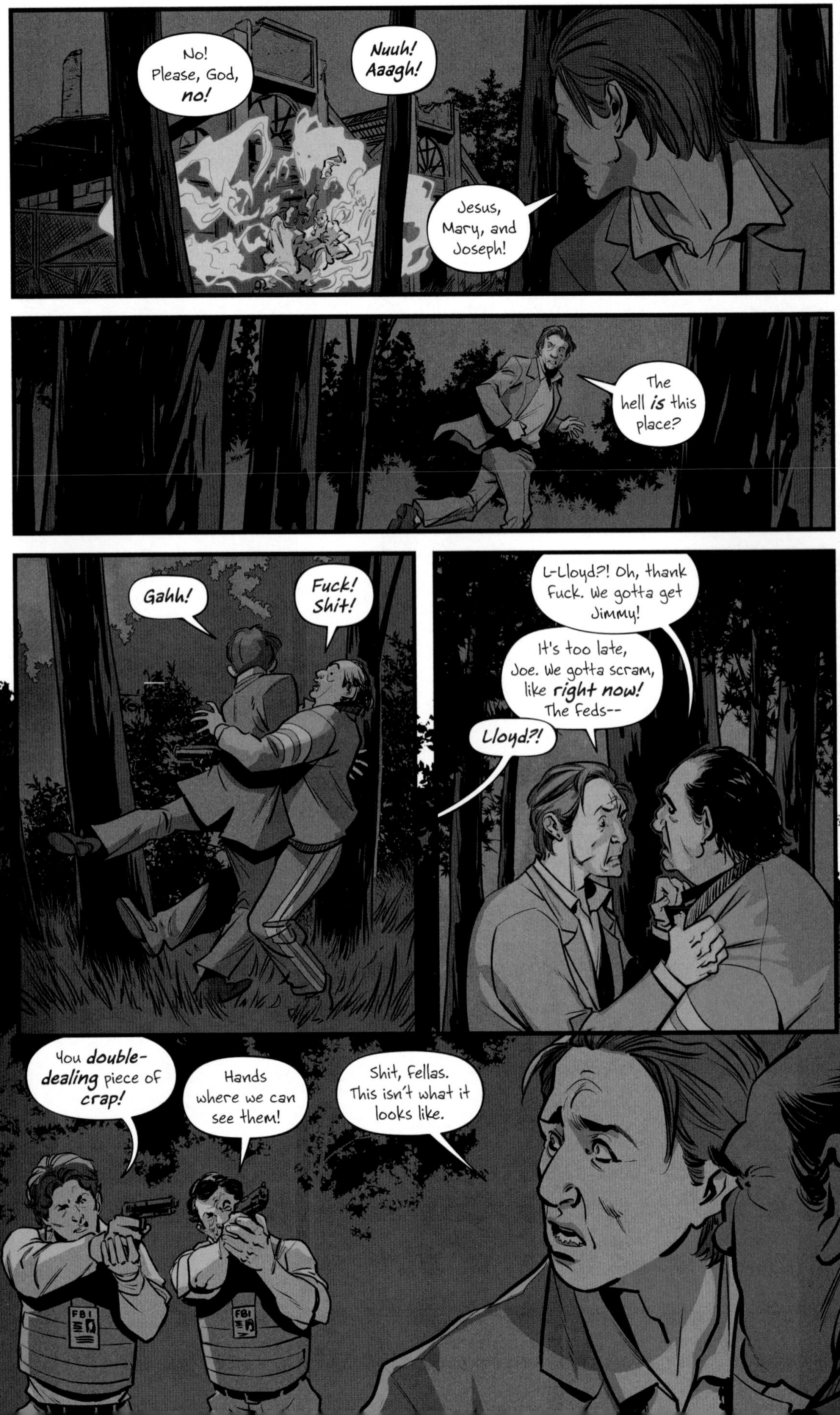
No! Please, God, no!
Nuuh! Aaagh!
Jesus, Mary, and Joseph!
The hell is this place?
Gahh!
Fuck! Shit!
L-Lloyd?! Oh, thank fuck. We gotta get Jimmy!
It's too late, Joe. We gotta scram, like right now! The feds--
Lloyd?!
You double-dealing piece of crap!
Hands where we can see them!
Shit, fellas. This isn't what it looks like.
FBI
FBI

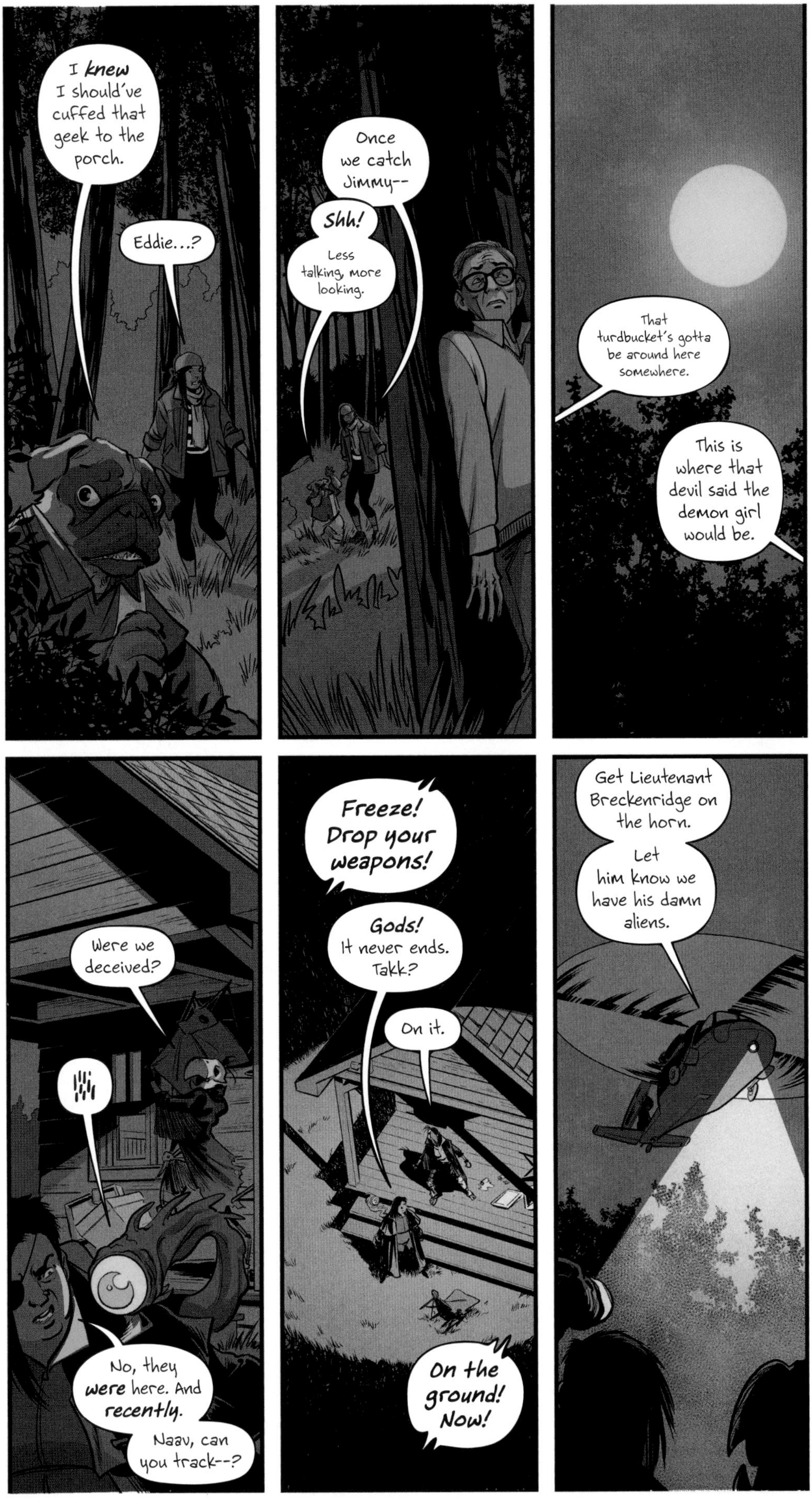
I knew I should've cuffed that geek to the porch.
Eddie...?
Once we catch Jimmy--
Shh!
Less talking, more looking.
That turdbucket's gotta be around here somewhere.
This is where that devil said the demon girl would be.
Were we deceived?
!!!
No, they were here. And recently.
Naav, can you track--?
Freeze! Drop your weapons!
Gods! It never ends. Takk?
On it.
On the ground! Now!
Get Lieutenant Breckenridge on the horn.
Let him know we have his damn aliens.

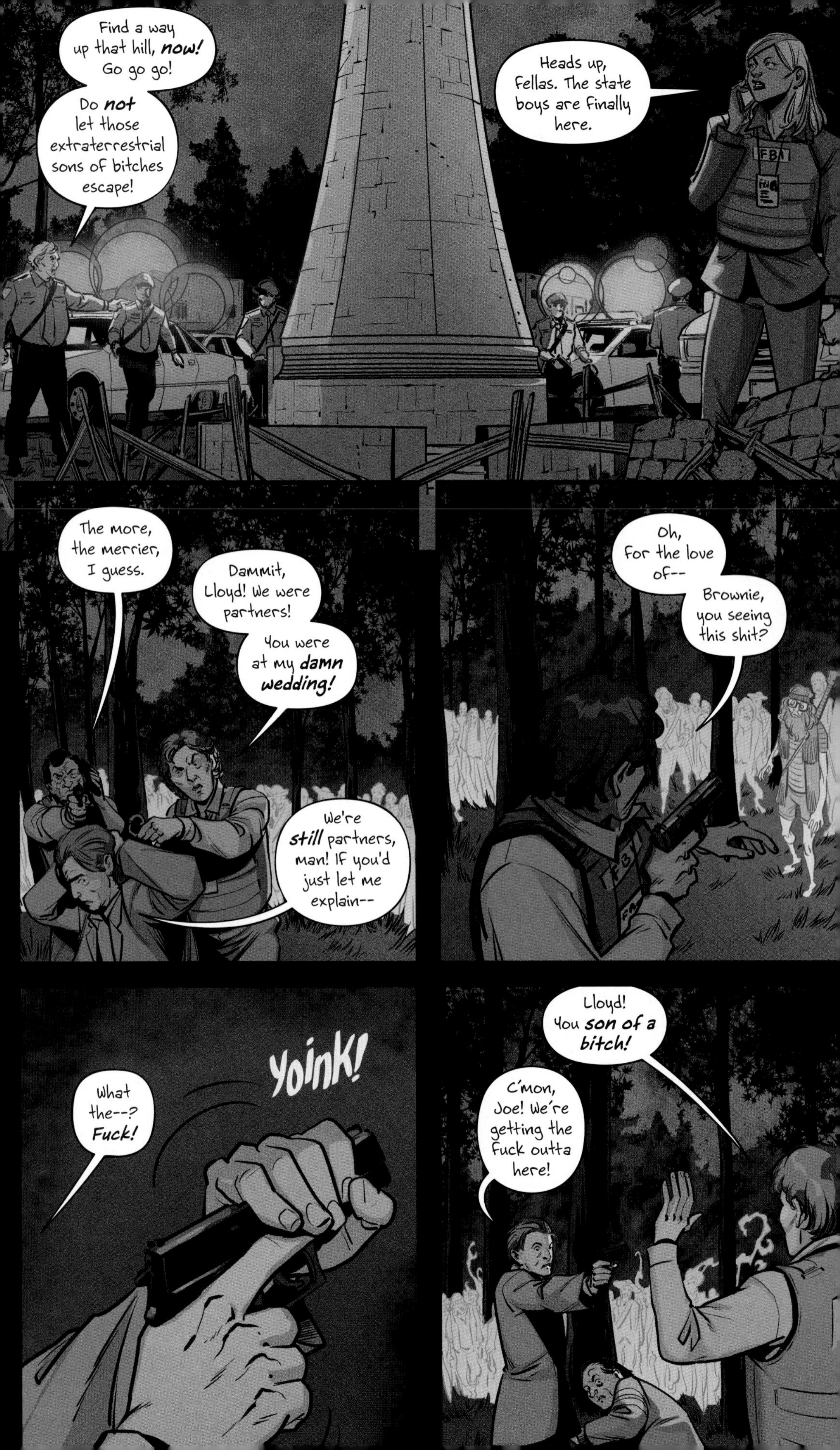
Find a way up that hill, **now!** Go go go!
Do **not** let those extraterrestrial sons of bitches escape!
Heads up, fellas. The state boys are finally here.
The more, the merrier, I guess.
Dammit, Lloyd! We were partners!
You were at my **damn wedding!**
We're **still** partners, man! If you'd just let me explain--
Oh, for the love of--
Brownie, you seeing this shit?
What the--? **Fuck!**
YOINK!
Lloyd! You **son of a bitch!**
C'mon, Joe! We're getting the fuck outta here!

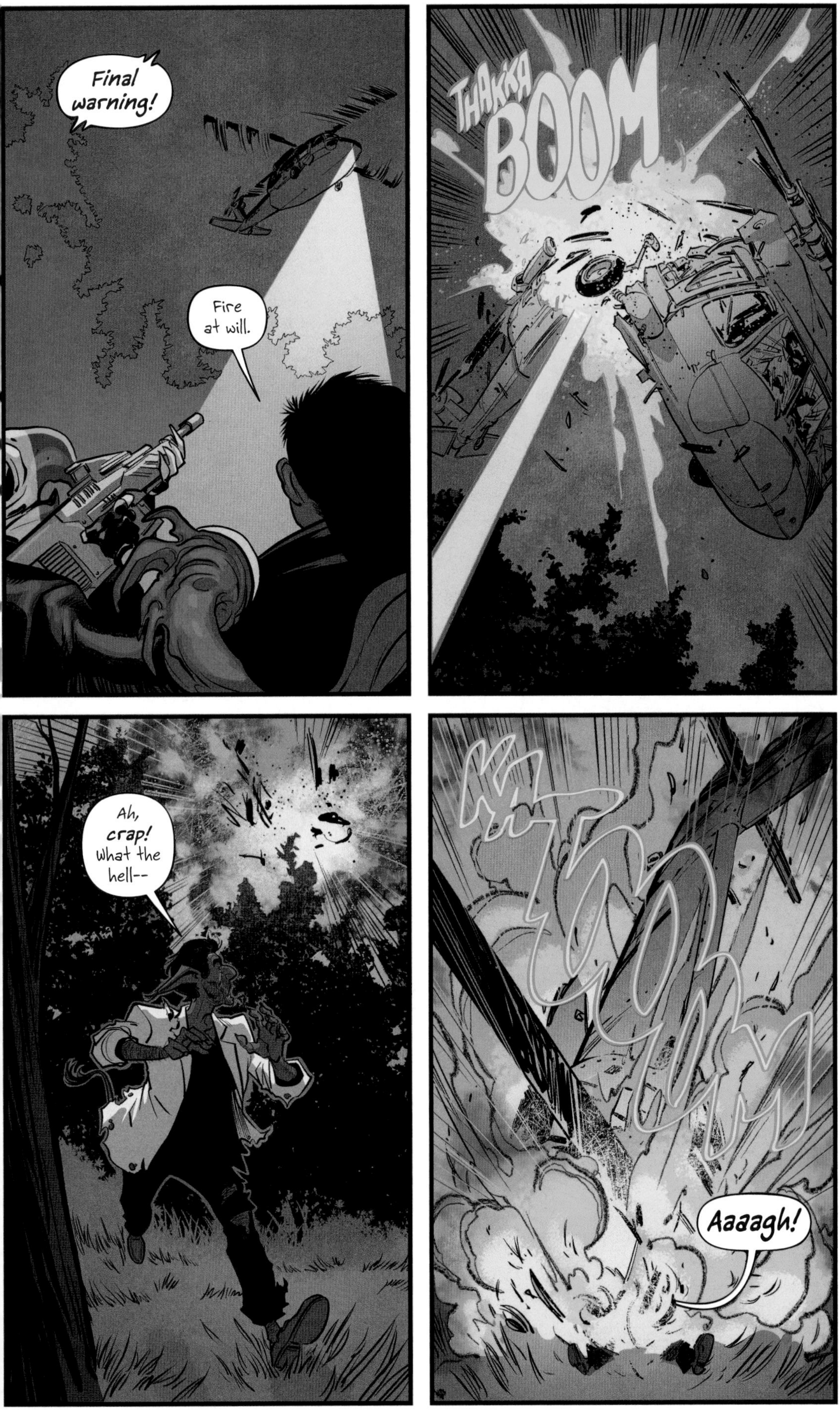
Final warning!
Fire at will.
THAKKA BOOM
Ah, crap! What the hell--
Aaaagh!

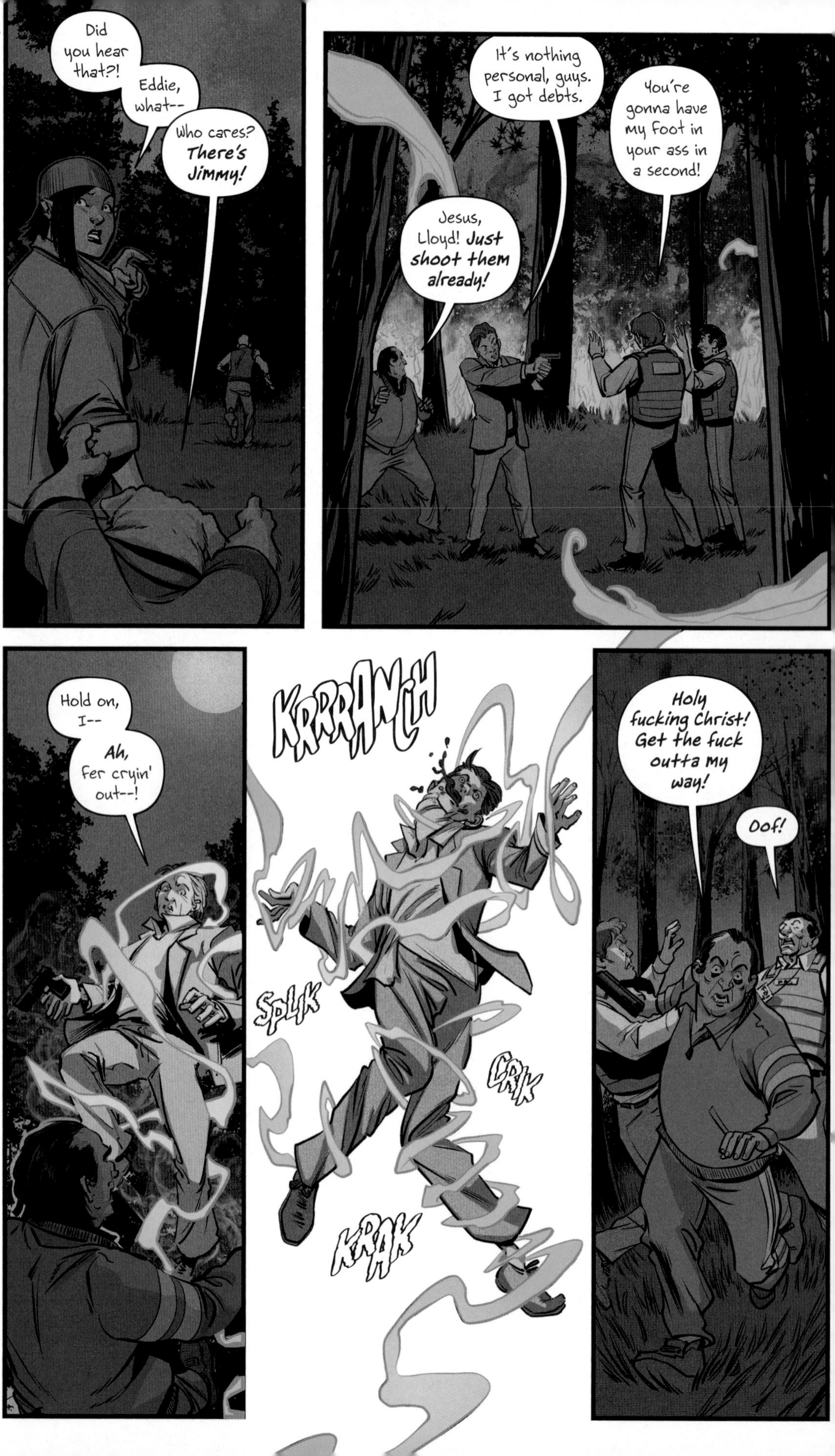
Did you hear that?!
Eddie, what--
Who cares? There's Jimmy!
It's nothing personal, guys. I got debts.
You're gonna have my foot in your ass in a second!
Jesus, Lloyd! Just shoot them already!
Hold on, I--
Ah, fer cryin' out--!
KRRRANCH
SPLIK
CRIK
KRAK
Holy fucking Christ! Get the fuck outta my way!
Oof!

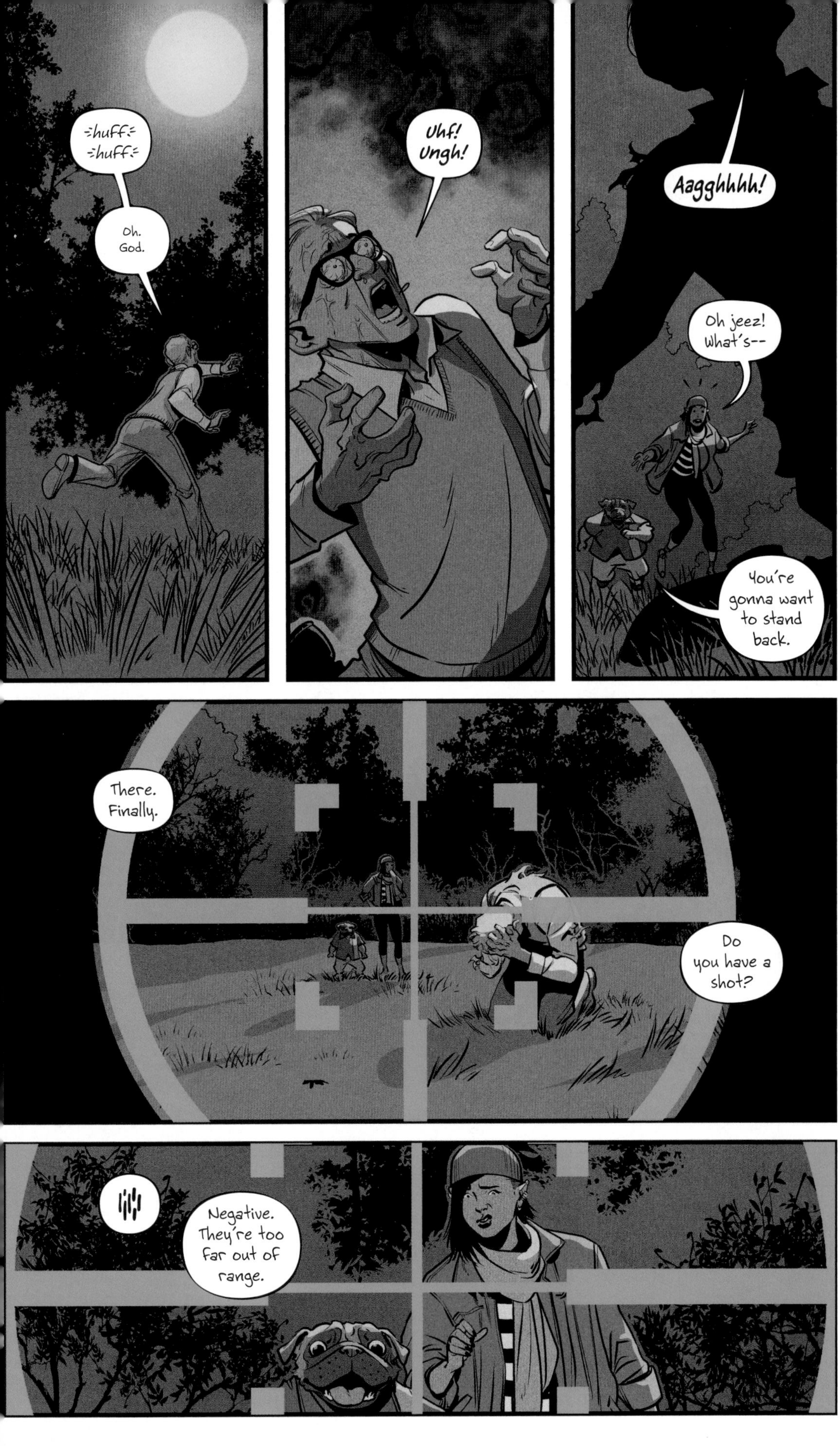

=huff=
=huff=
Oh. God.
Uhf! Ungh!
Aagghhhh!
Oh jeez! What's--
You're gonna want to stand back.
There. Finally.
Do you have a shot?
Negative. They're too far out of range.

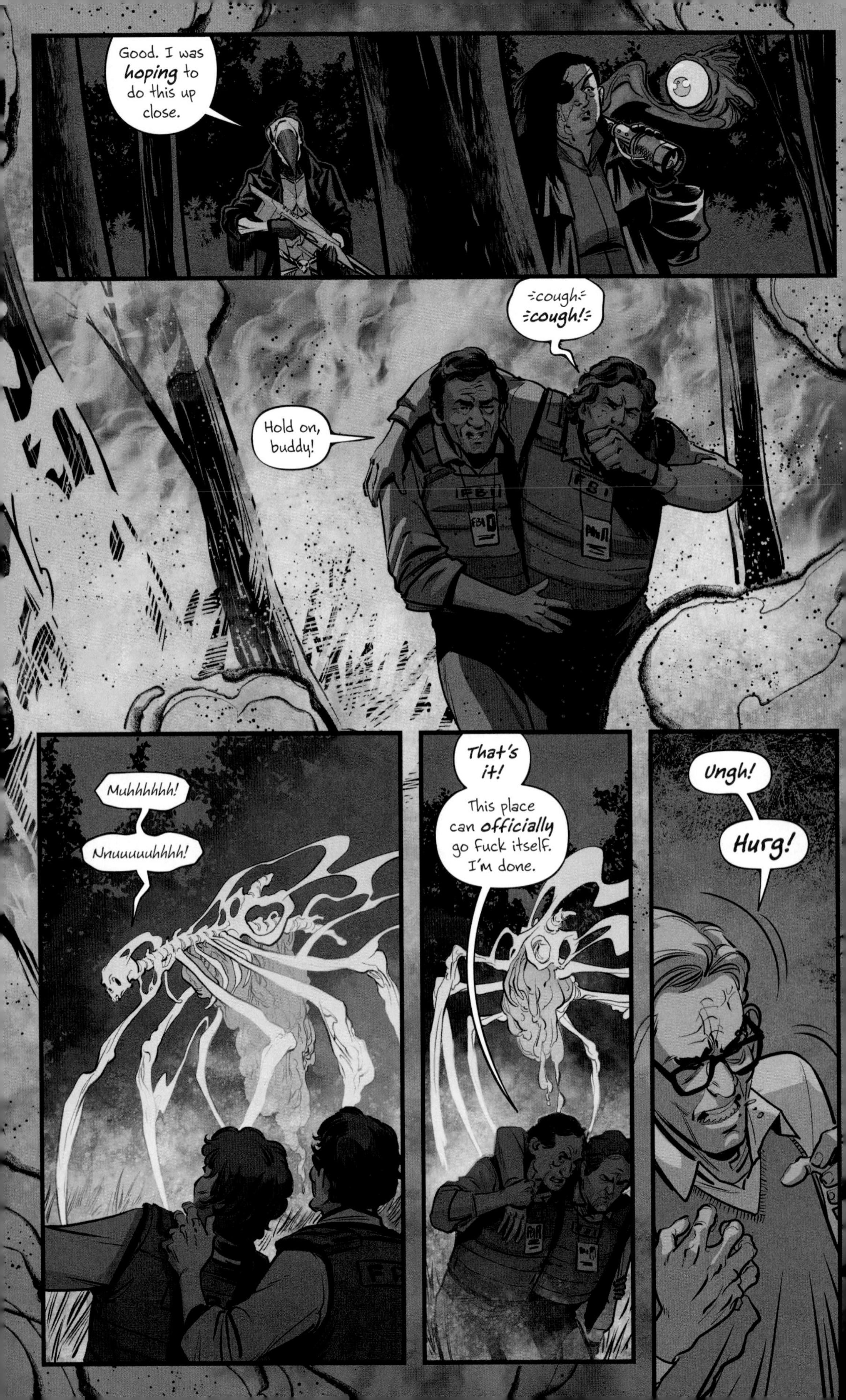
Good. I was hoping to do this up close.
cough cough!
Hold on, buddy!
Muhhhhhh!
Nnuuuuuhhhh!
That's it!
This place can officially go fuck itself. I'm done.
Ungh!
Hurg!

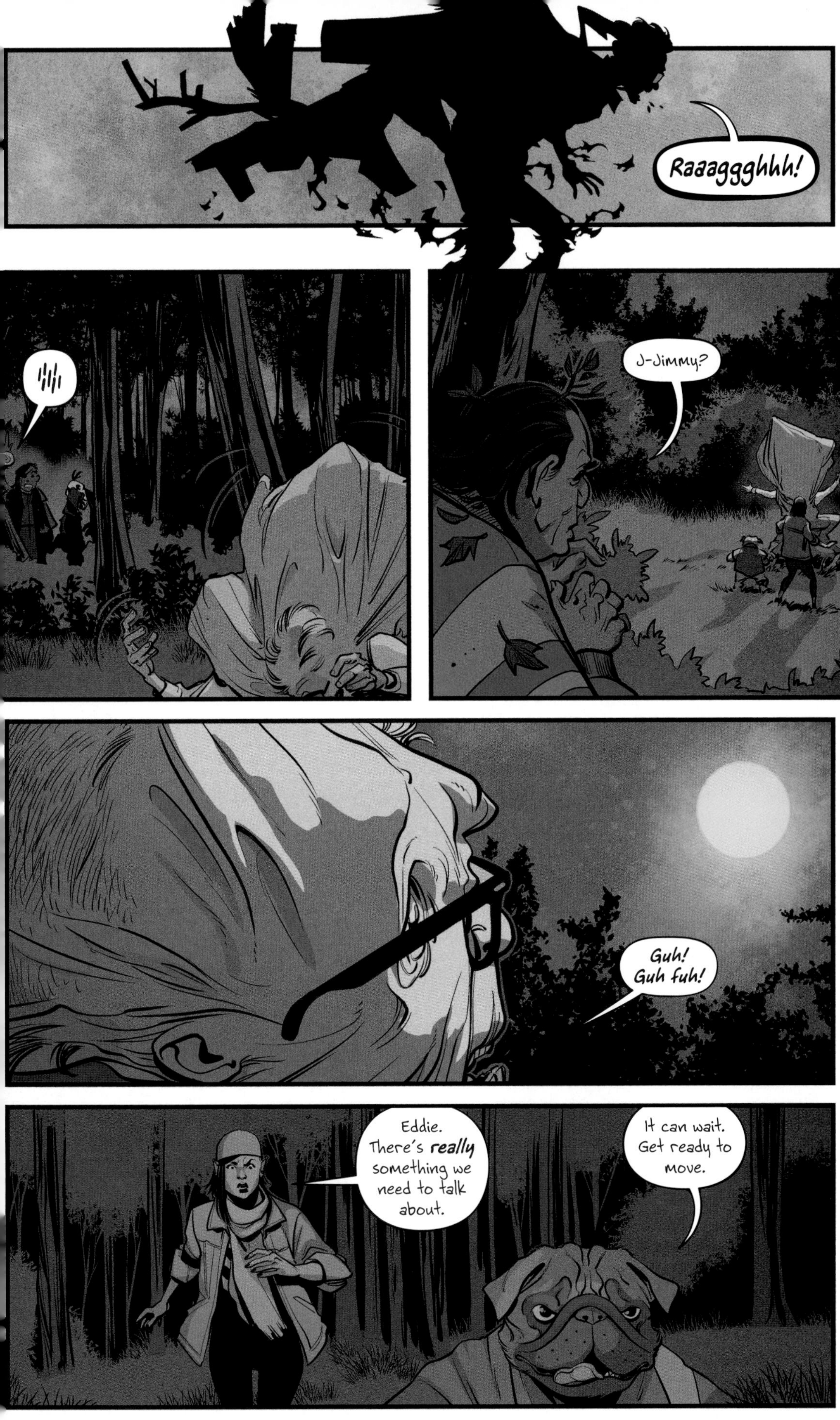
Raaaggghhh!
!!!!
J-Jimmy?
Guh!
Guh fuh!
Eddie. There's **really** something we need to talk about.
It can wait. Get ready to move.

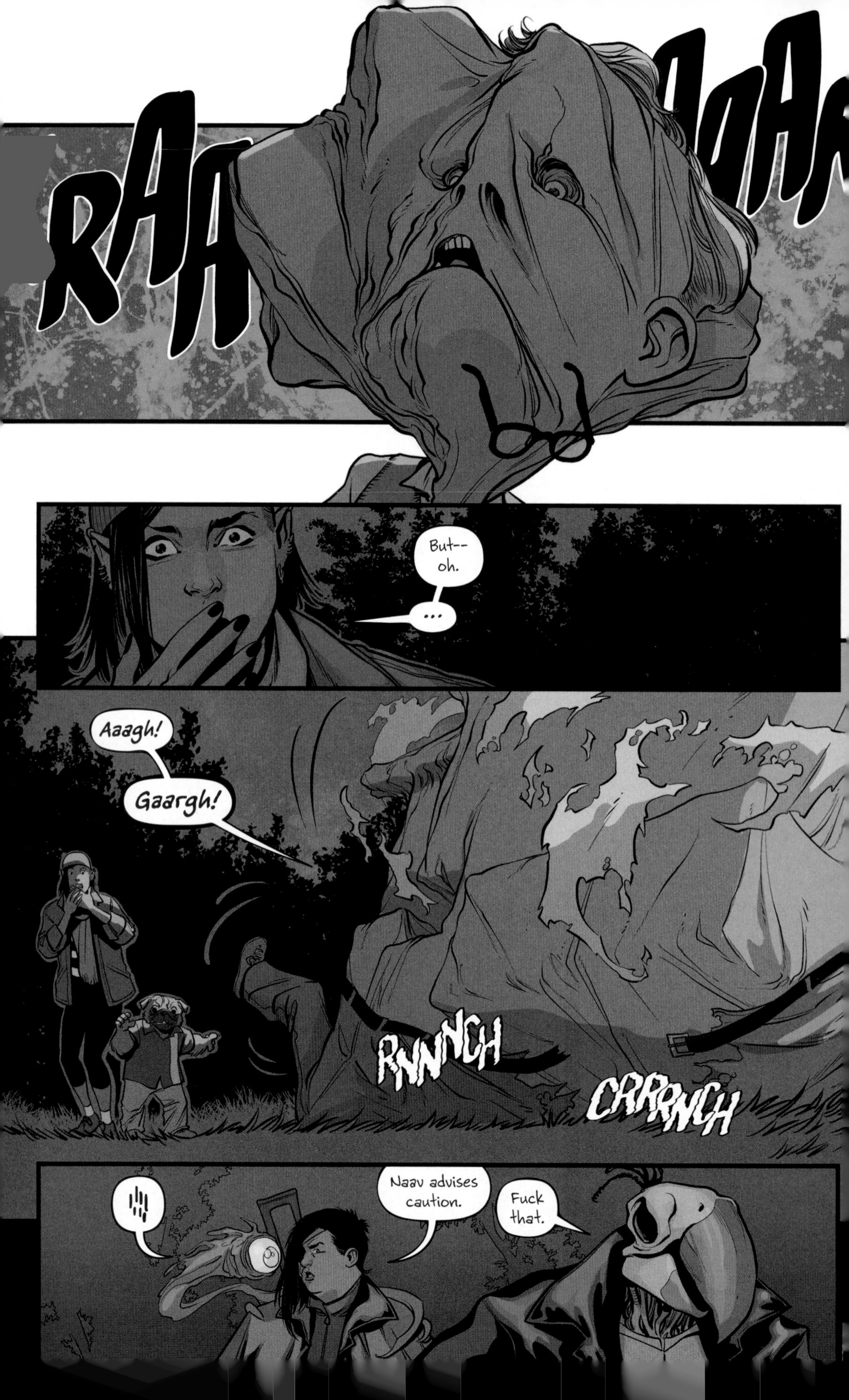
RAAAAAAAAA
But--
oh.
...
Aaagh!
Gaargh!
RNNNCH
CRRRNCH
!!!
Naav advises
caution.
Fuck
that.

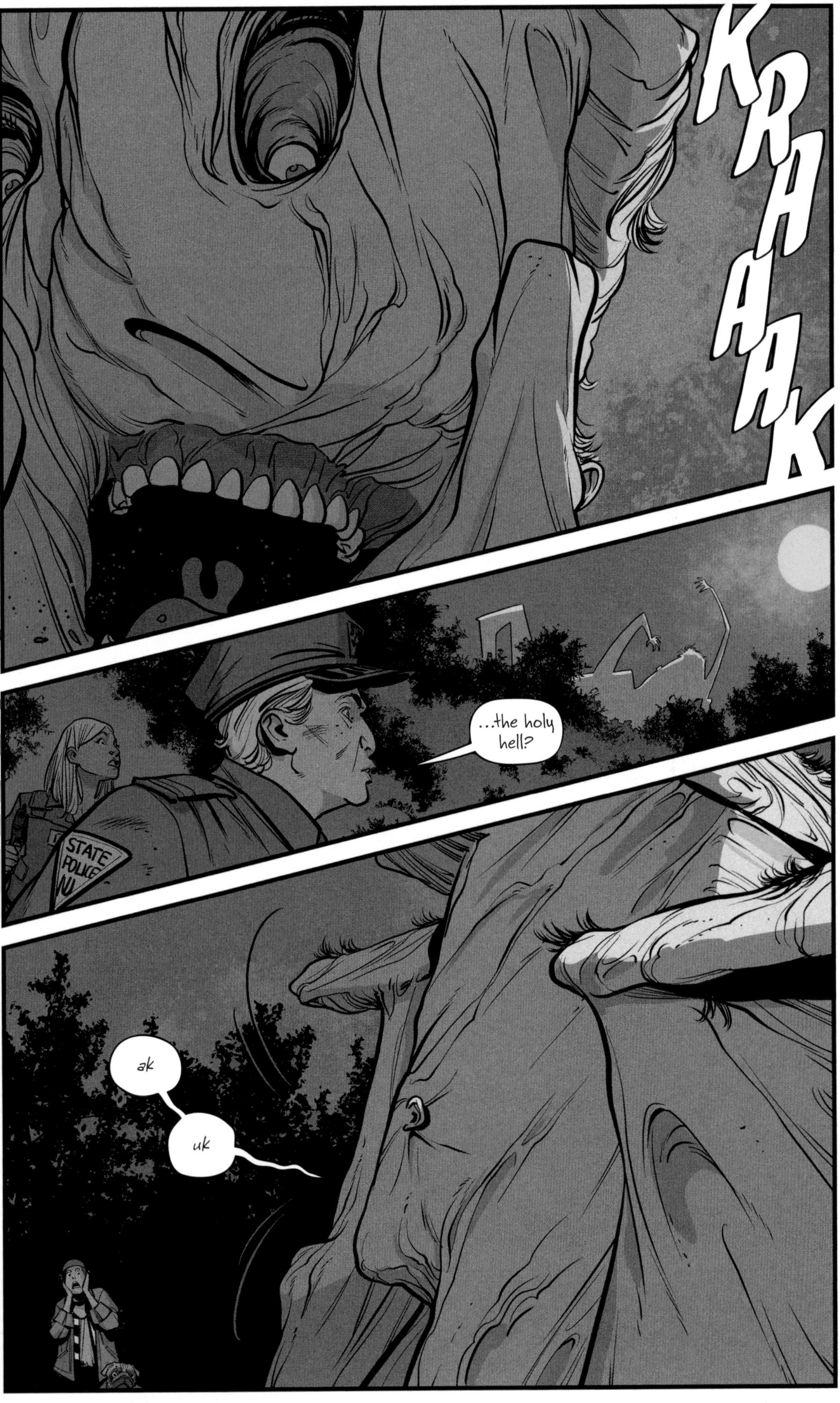
KRAAAAK
...the holy hell?
STATE POLICE NJ
ak
uk

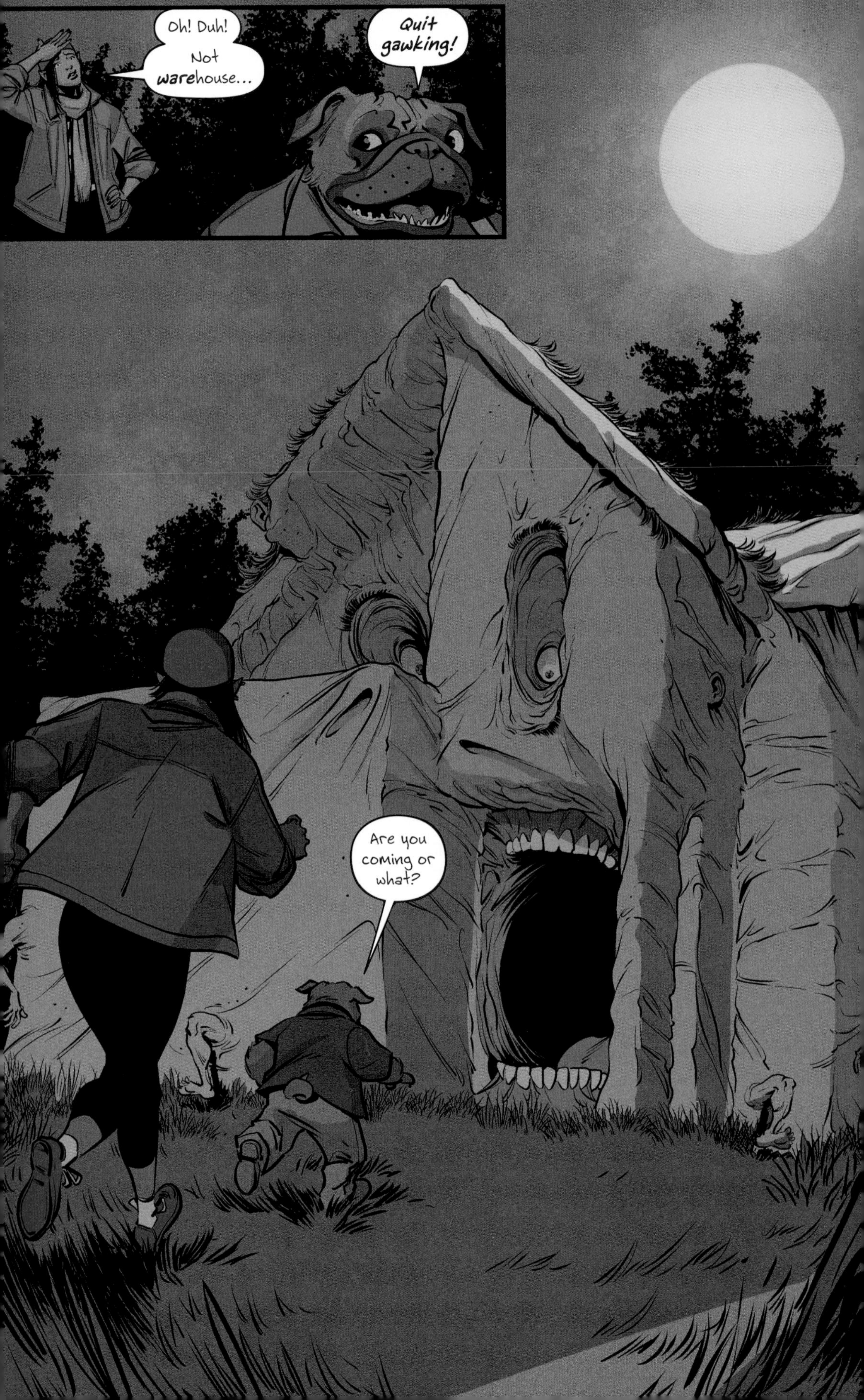
Oh! Duh!
Not warehouse...
Quit gawking!
Are you coming or what?

There!
Shit!
PRRRZXT
Uk! Uk!
Fuck! Move it!
Wait?
Agreed. We will wait here for them to return.
Not when we are so close.
Takk! Stop!

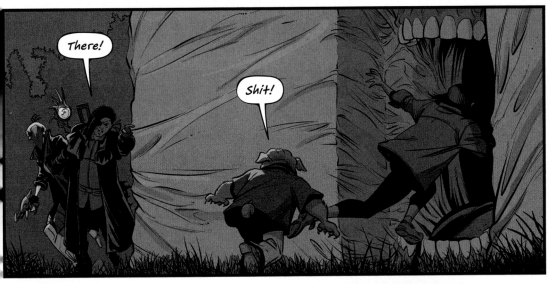

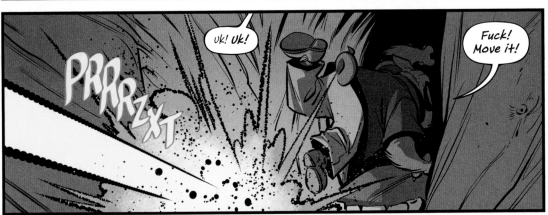

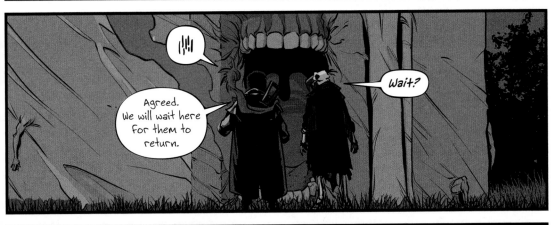

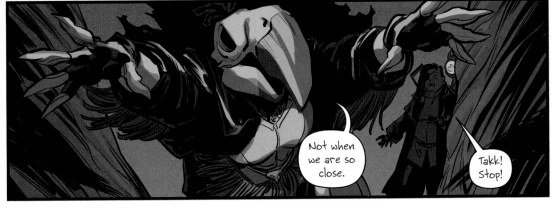

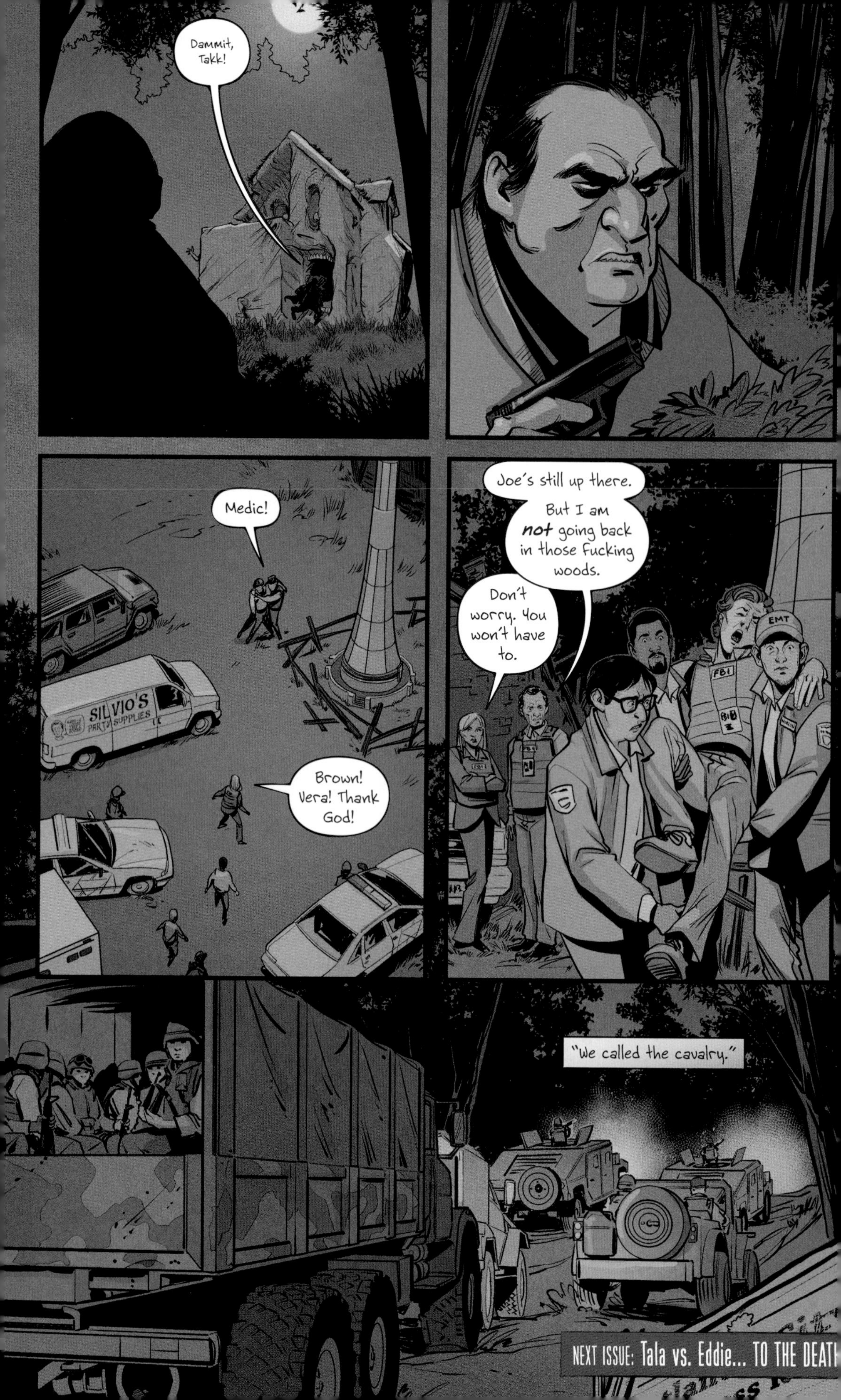

Dammit, Takk!
Medic!
SILVIO'S PARTY SUPPLIES
Brown! Vera! Thank God!
Joe's still up there.
But I am **not** going back in those fucking woods.
Don't worry. You won't have to.
FBI
EMT
"We called the cavalry."
NEXT ISSUE: Tala vs. Eddie... TO THE DEATH

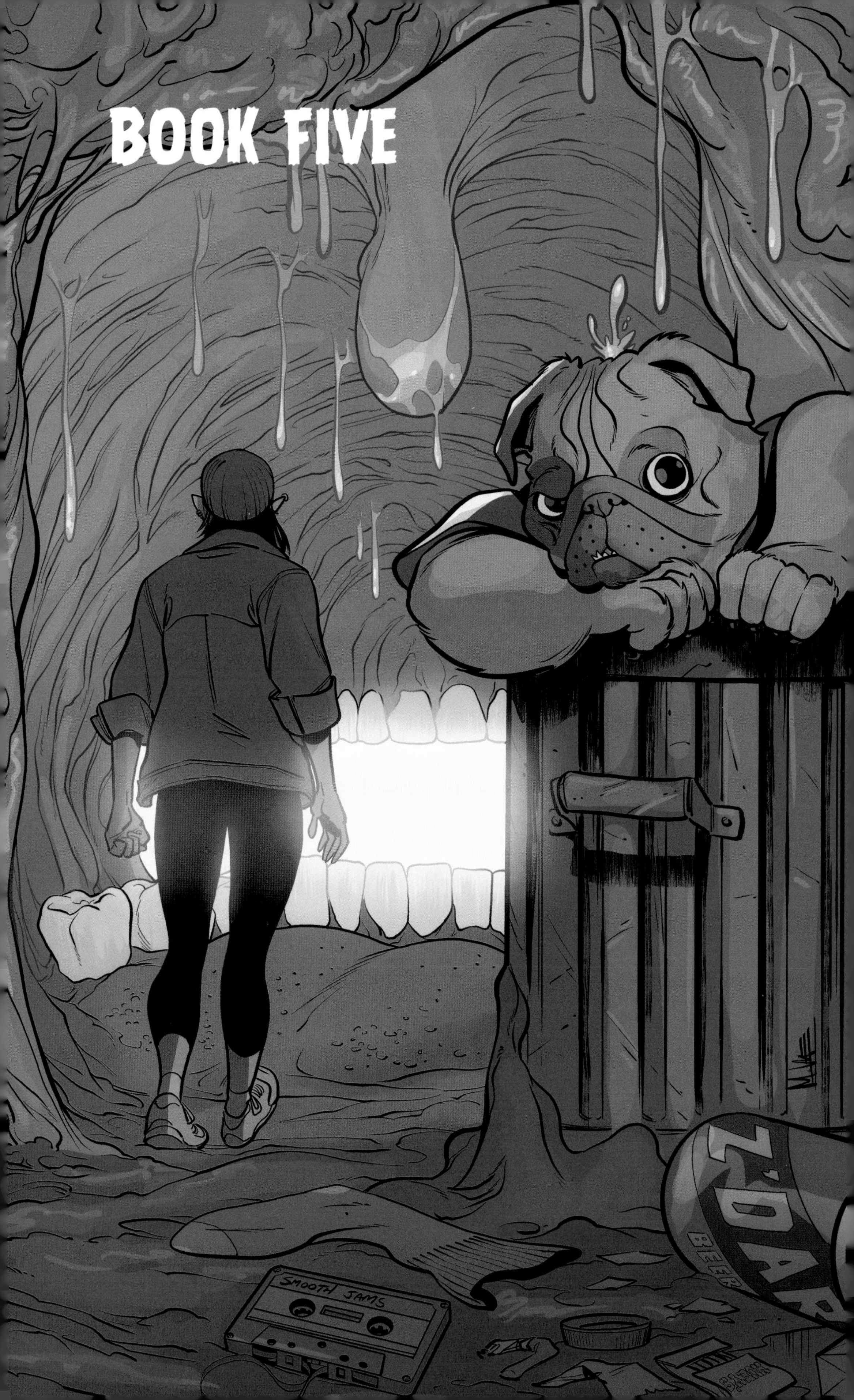
BOOK FIVE
SMOOTH JAMS
BEER

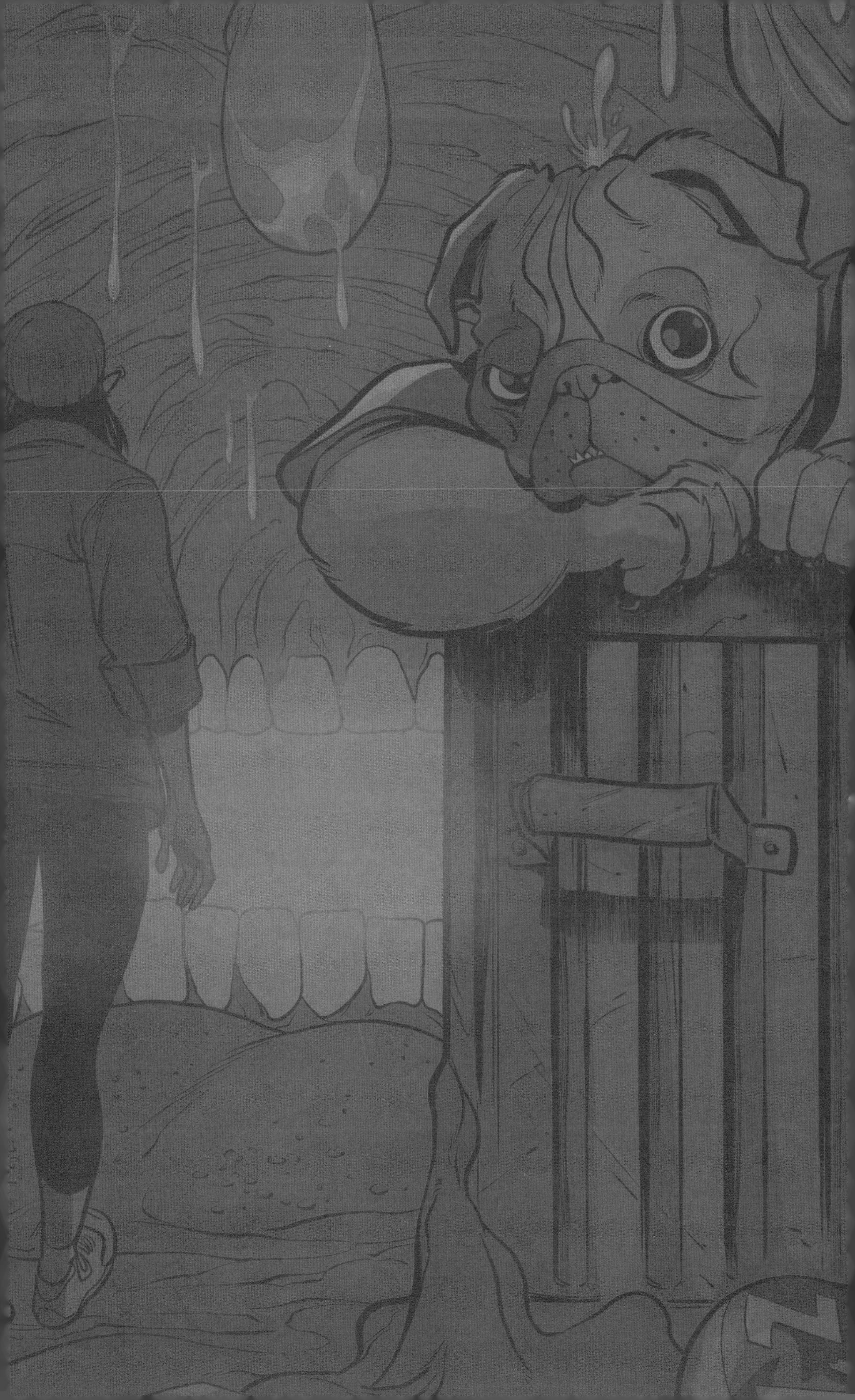

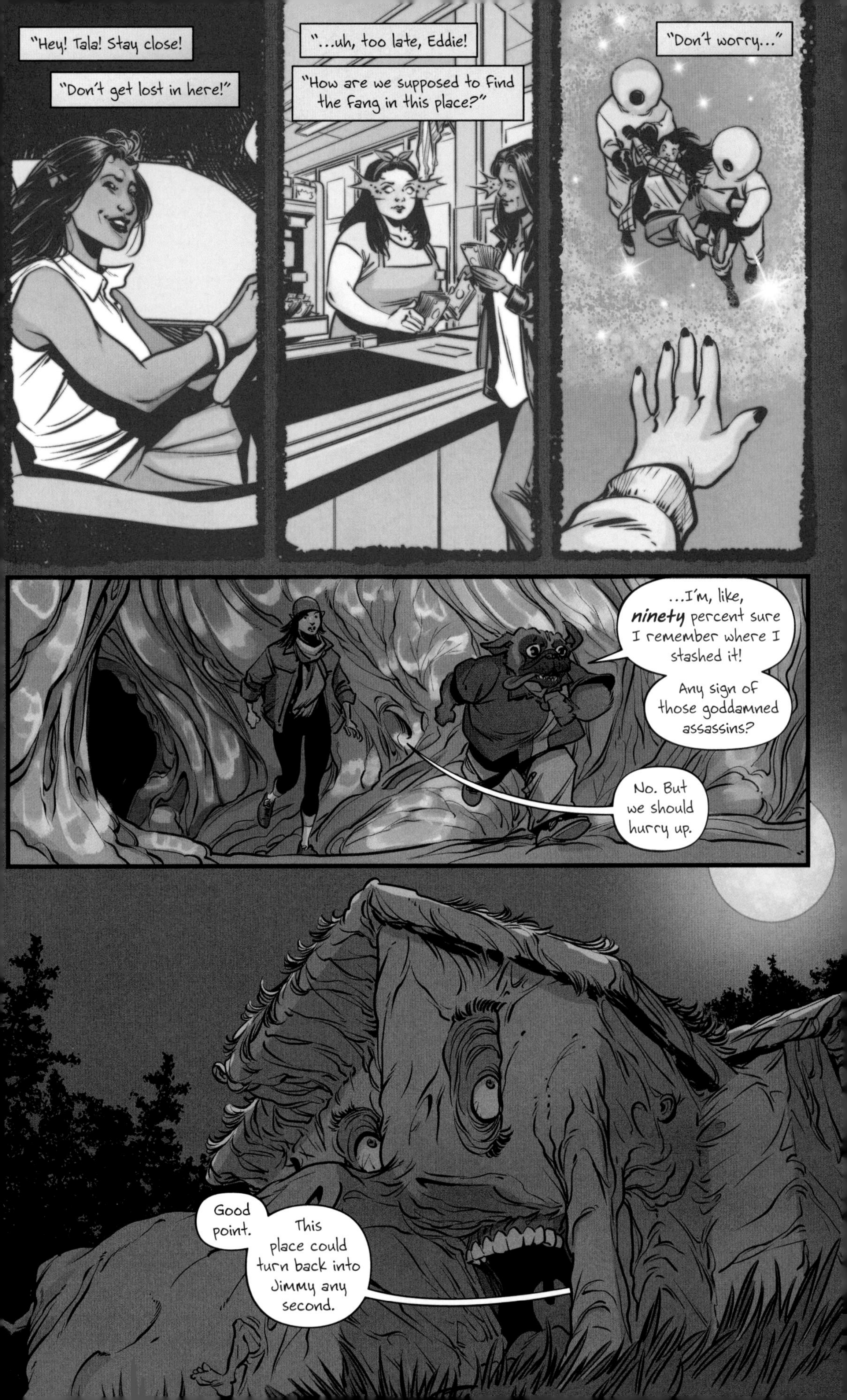
"Hey! Tala! Stay close!
"Don't get lost in here!"
"...uh, too late, Eddie!
"How are we supposed to find the fang in this place?"
"Don't worry..."
...I'm, like, **ninety** percent sure I remember where I stashed it!
Any sign of those goddamned assassins?
No. But we should hurry up.
Good point.
This place could turn back into Jimmy any second.

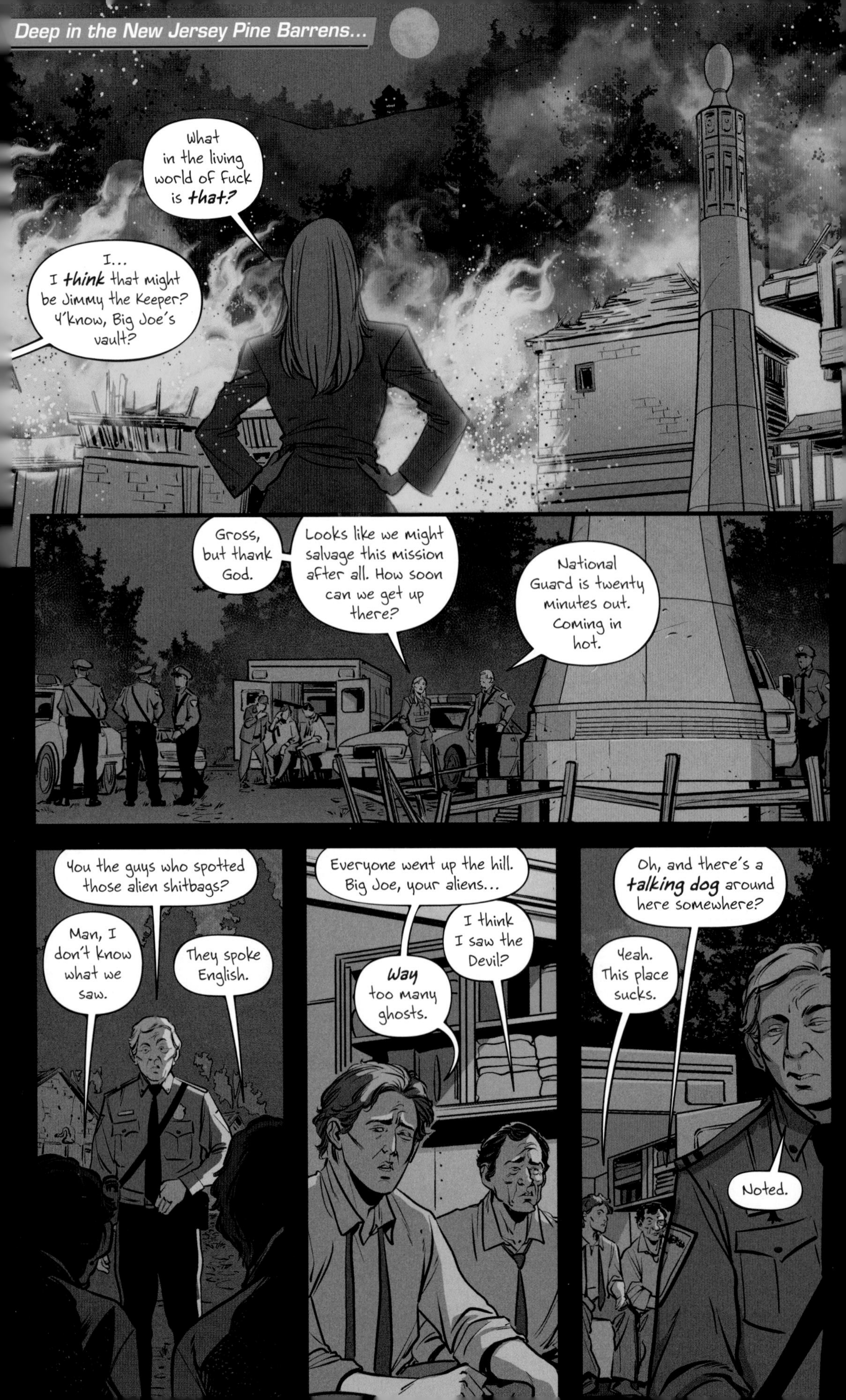
Deep in the New Jersey Pine Barrens...
What in the living world of fuck is *that?*
I... I *think* that might be Jimmy the Keeper? Y'know, Big Joe's vault?
Gross, but thank God.
Looks like we might salvage this mission after all. How soon can we get up there?
National Guard is twenty minutes out. Coming in hot.
You the guys who spotted those alien shitbags?
Man, I don't know what we saw.
They spoke English.
Everyone went up the hill. Big Joe, your aliens...
Way too many ghosts.
I think I saw the Devil?
Oh, and there's a *talking dog* around here somewhere?
Yeah. This place sucks.
Noted.

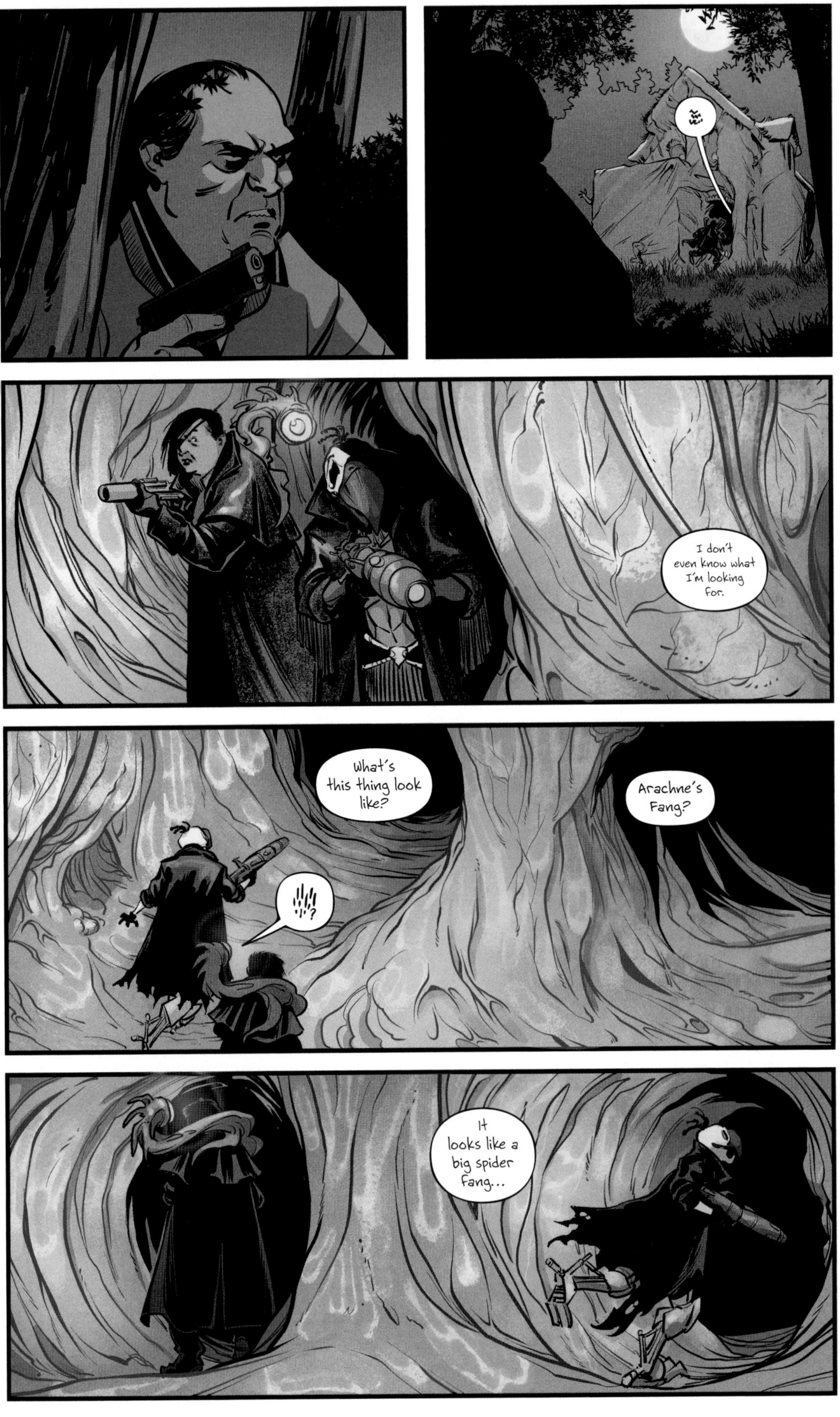
I don't even know what I'm looking for.
What's this thing look like?
Arachne's Fang?
It looks like a big spider fang...

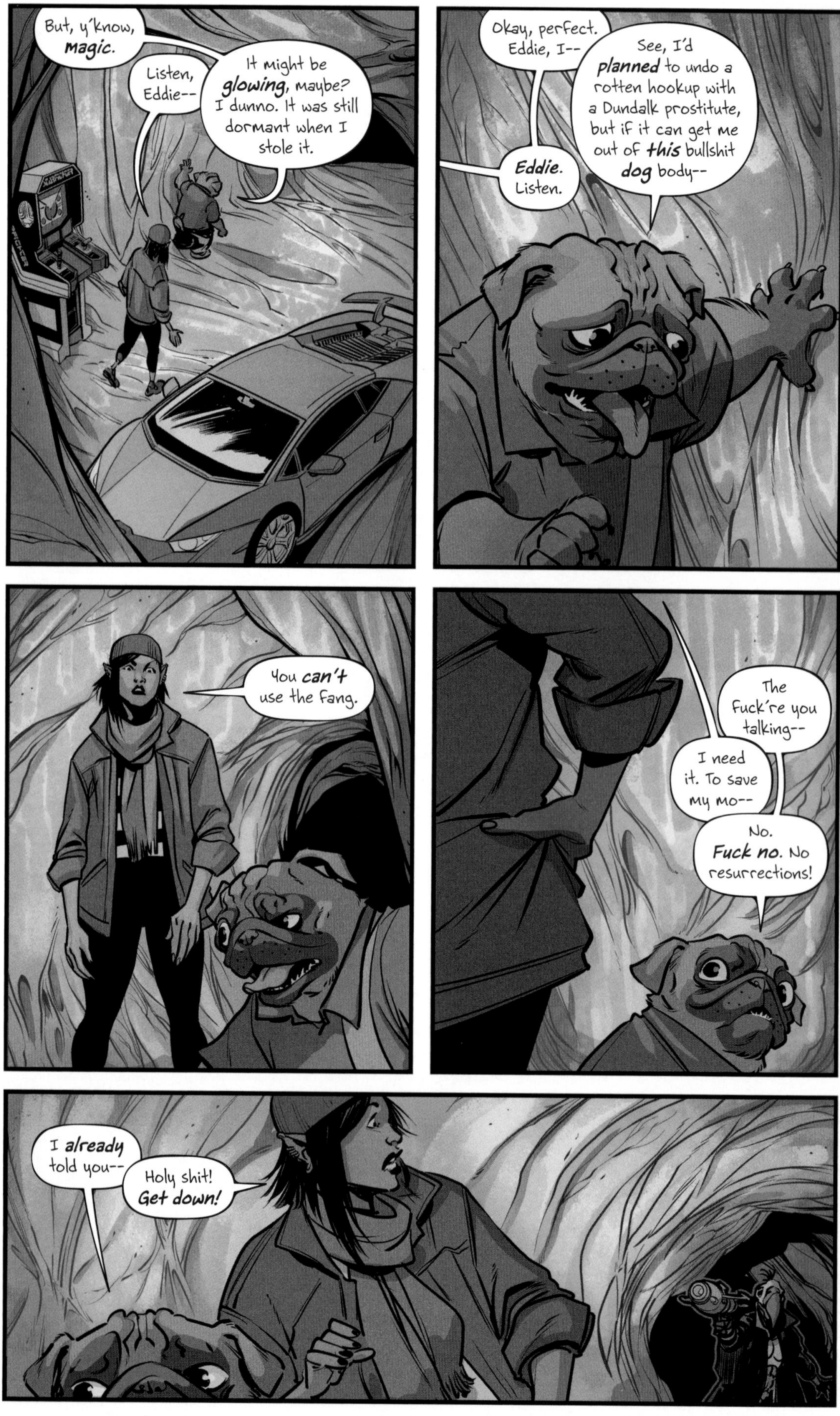

But, y'know, **magic**.
Listen, Eddie--
It might be **glowing**, maybe? I dunno. It was still dormant when I stole it.
Okay, perfect. Eddie, I--
See, I'd **planned** to undo a rotten hookup with a Dundalk prostitute, but if it can get me out of **this** bullshit **dog** body--
Eddie. Listen.
You **can't** use the fang.
The fuck're you talking--
I need it. To save my mo--
No. **Fuck no.** No resurrections!
I **already** told you--
Holy shit! **Get down!**

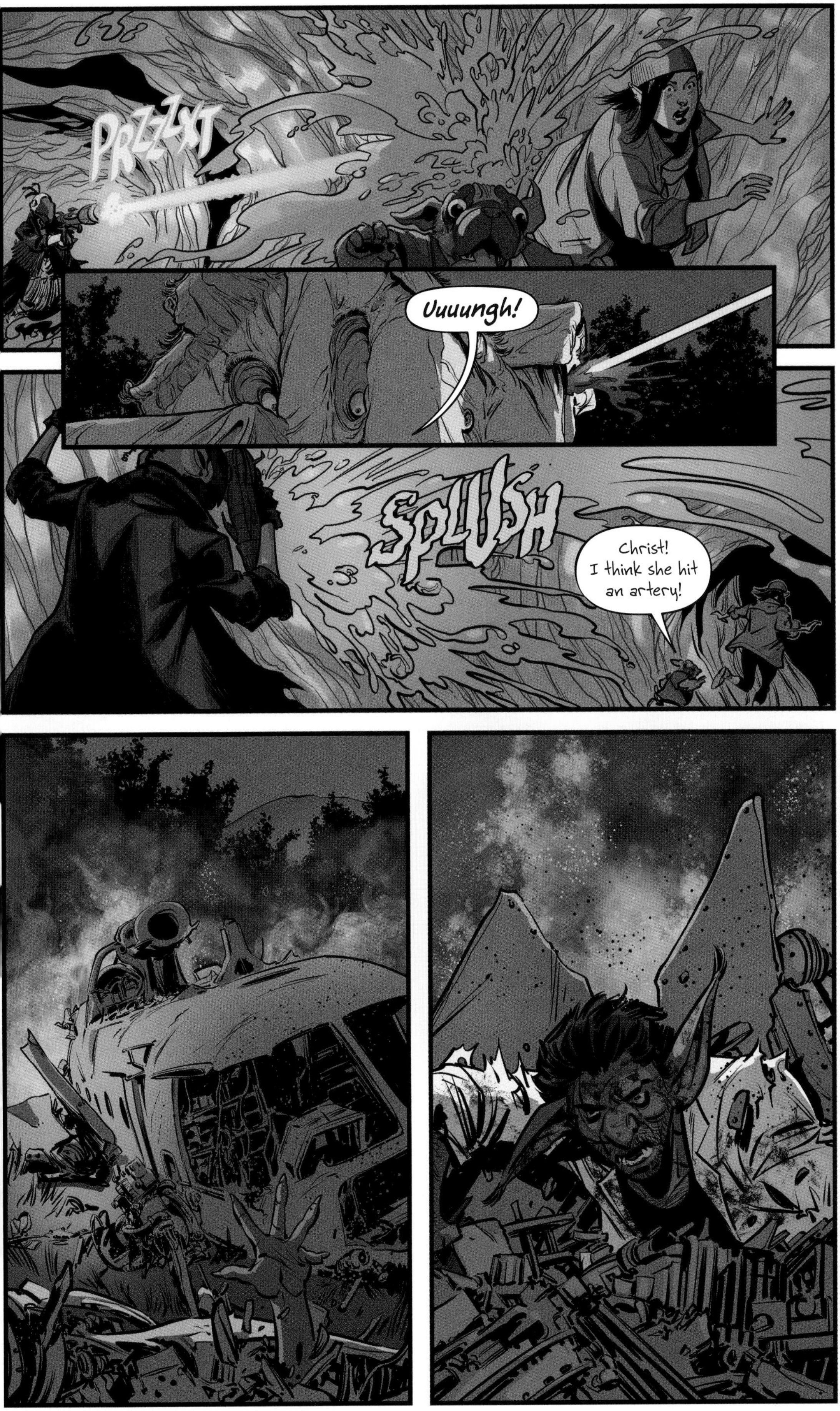
PRZZZXT
Uuuungh!
SPLUSH
Christ! I think she hit an artery!

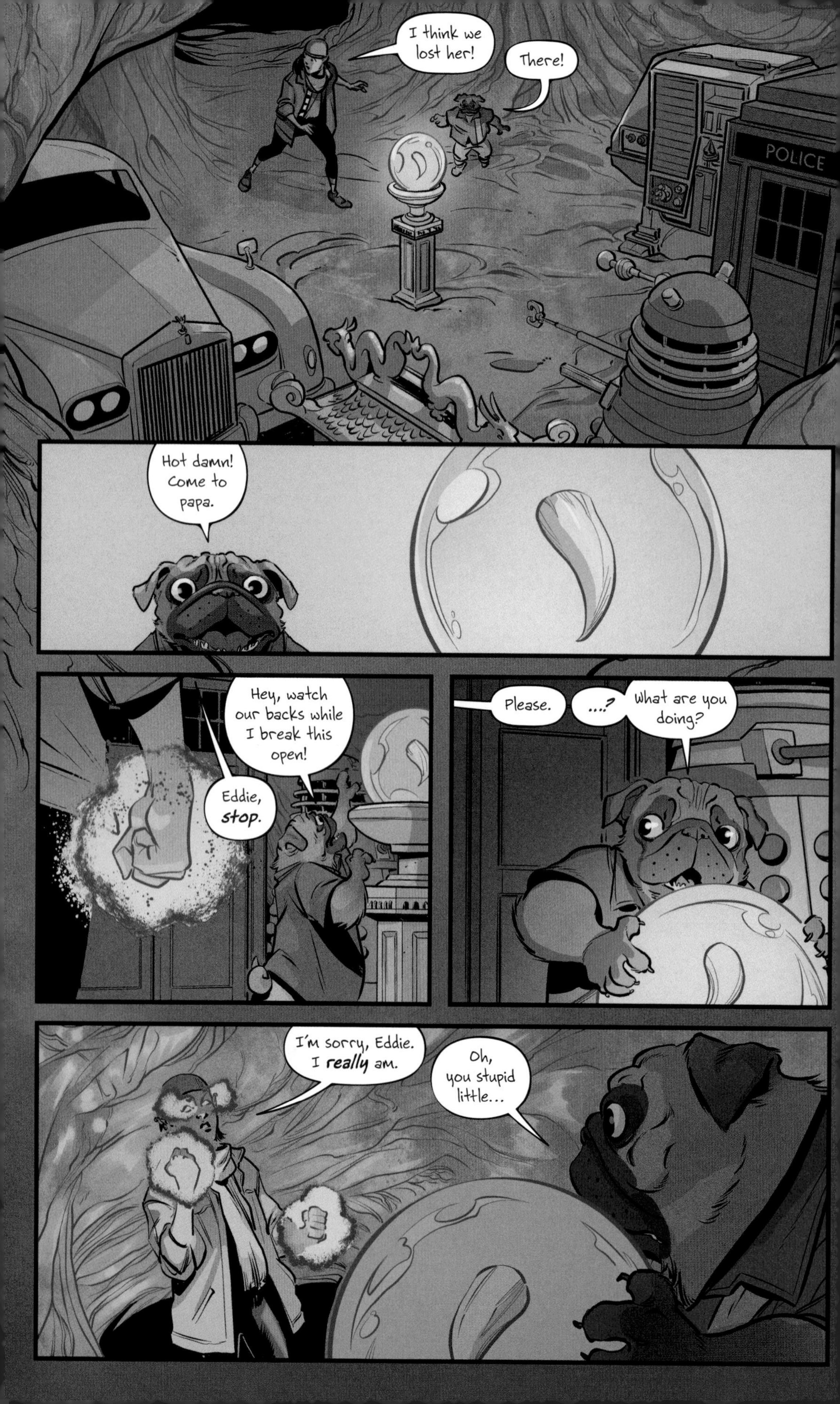

I think we lost her!
There!
POLICE
Hot damn! Come to papa.
Hey, watch our backs while I break this open!
Eddie, **stop.**
Please.
...?
What are you doing?
I'm sorry, Eddie. I **really** am.
Oh, you stupid little...

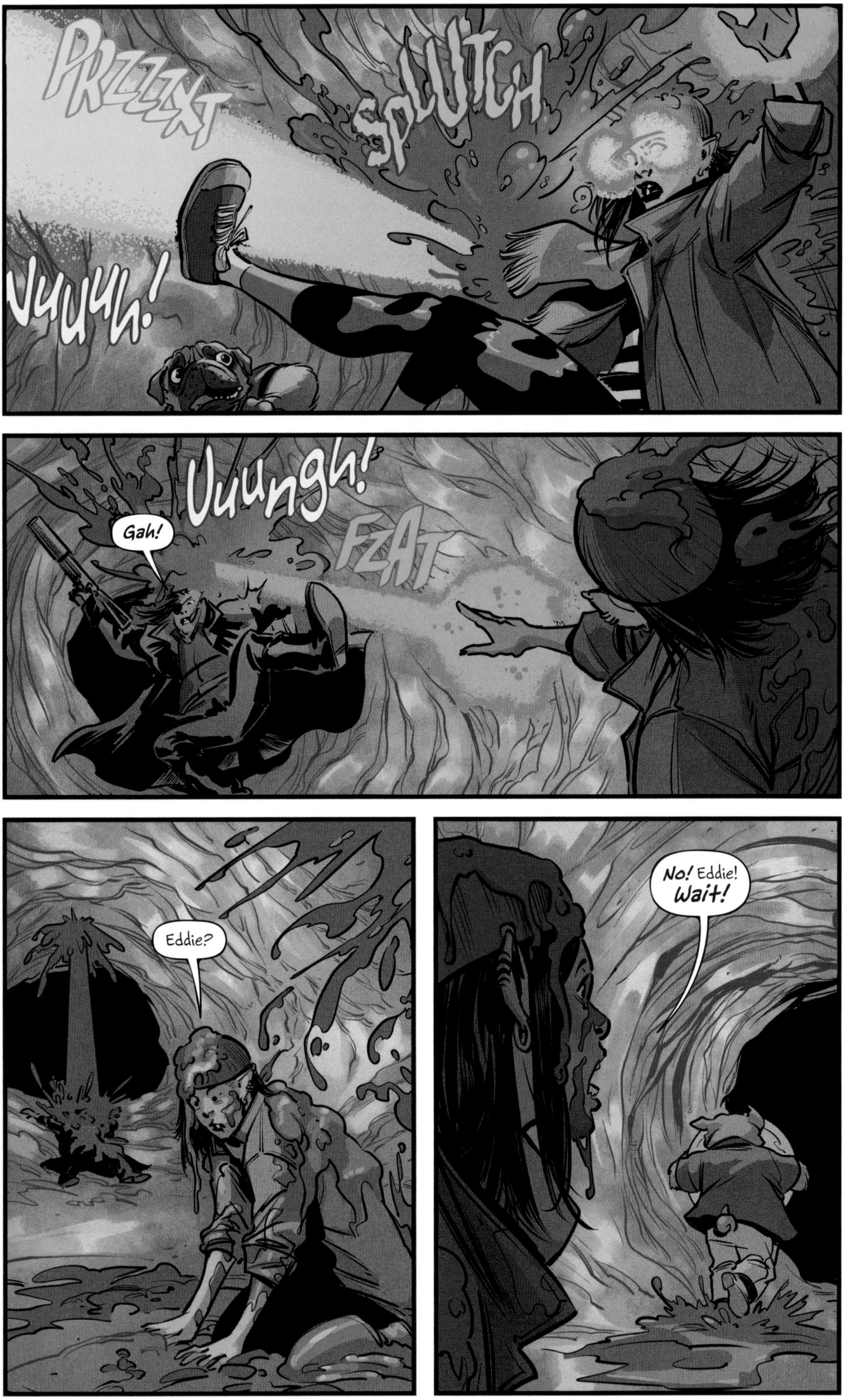
PRZZZXT
SPLUTCH
Uuuuh!
Uuungh!
Gah!
FZAT
Eddie?
No! Eddie! Wait!

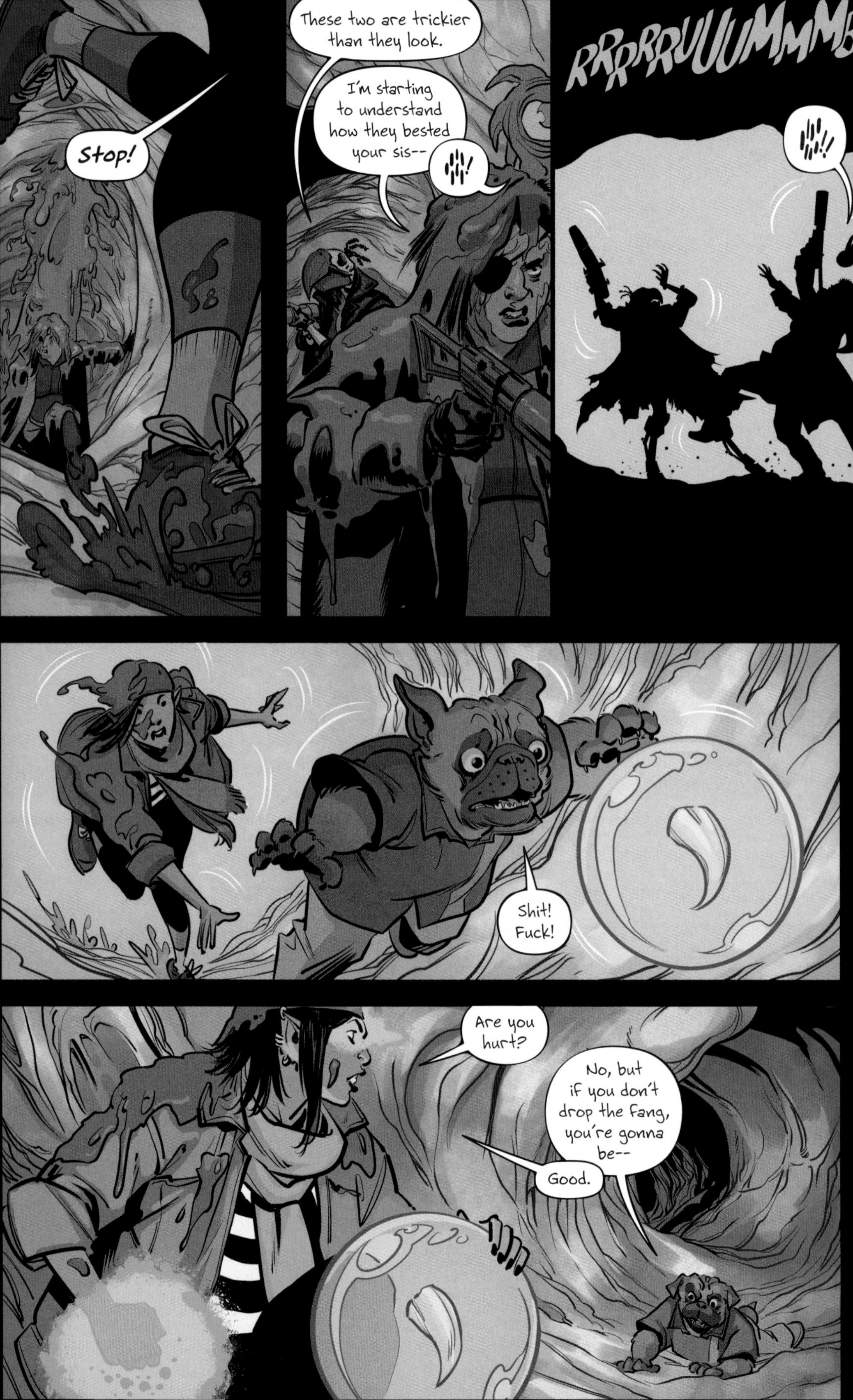
Stop!
These two are trickier than they look.
I'm starting to understand how they bested your sis--
!!!
RRRRRRUUUMMMB
!!!
Shit! Fuck!
Are you hurt?
No, but if you don't drop the fang, you're gonna be--
Good.

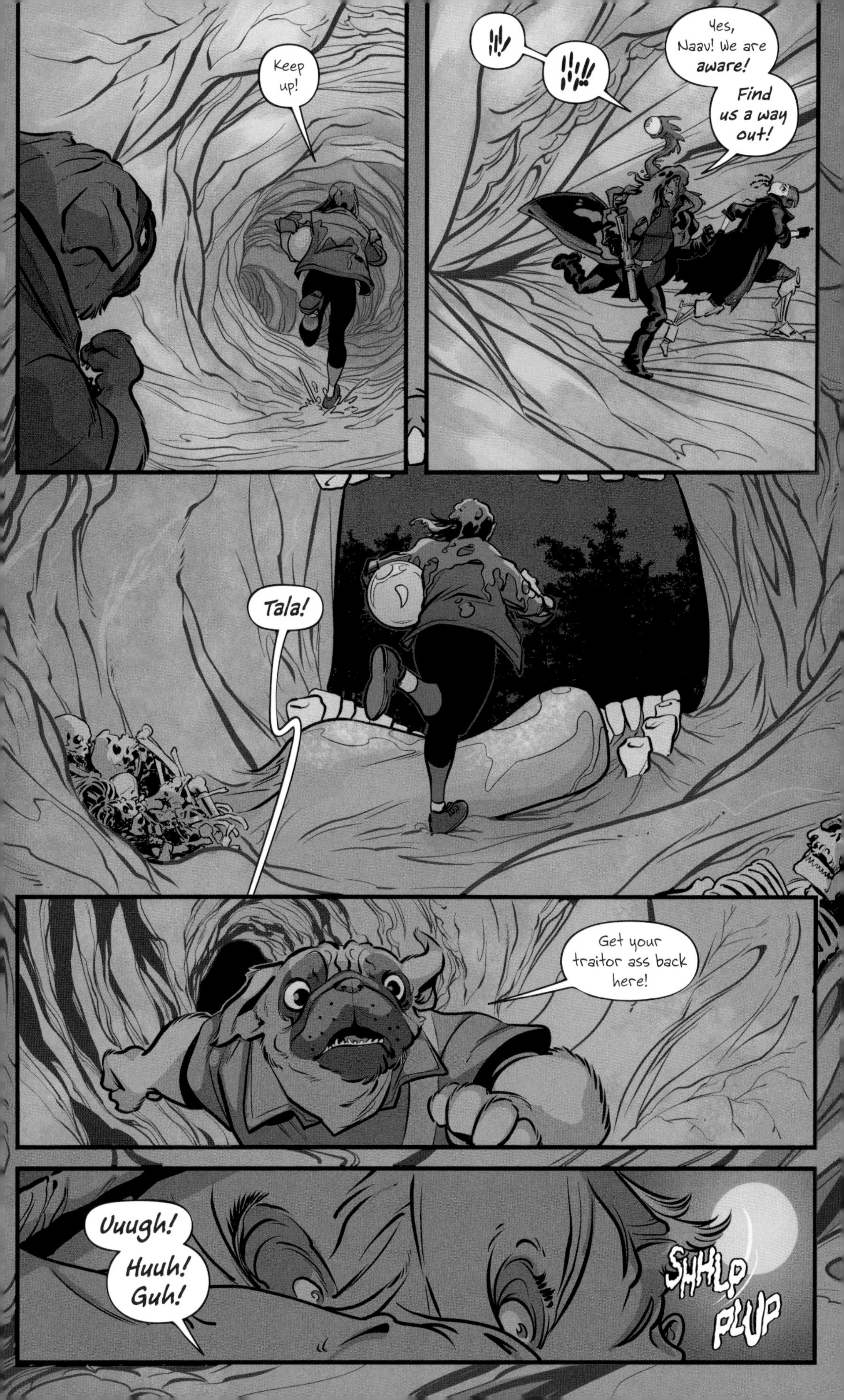
Keep up!
!!/
!!?!!
Yes, Naav! We are aware!
Find us a way out!
Tala!
Get your traitor ass back here!
Uuugh!
Huuh!
Guh!
SHHLP
PLUP

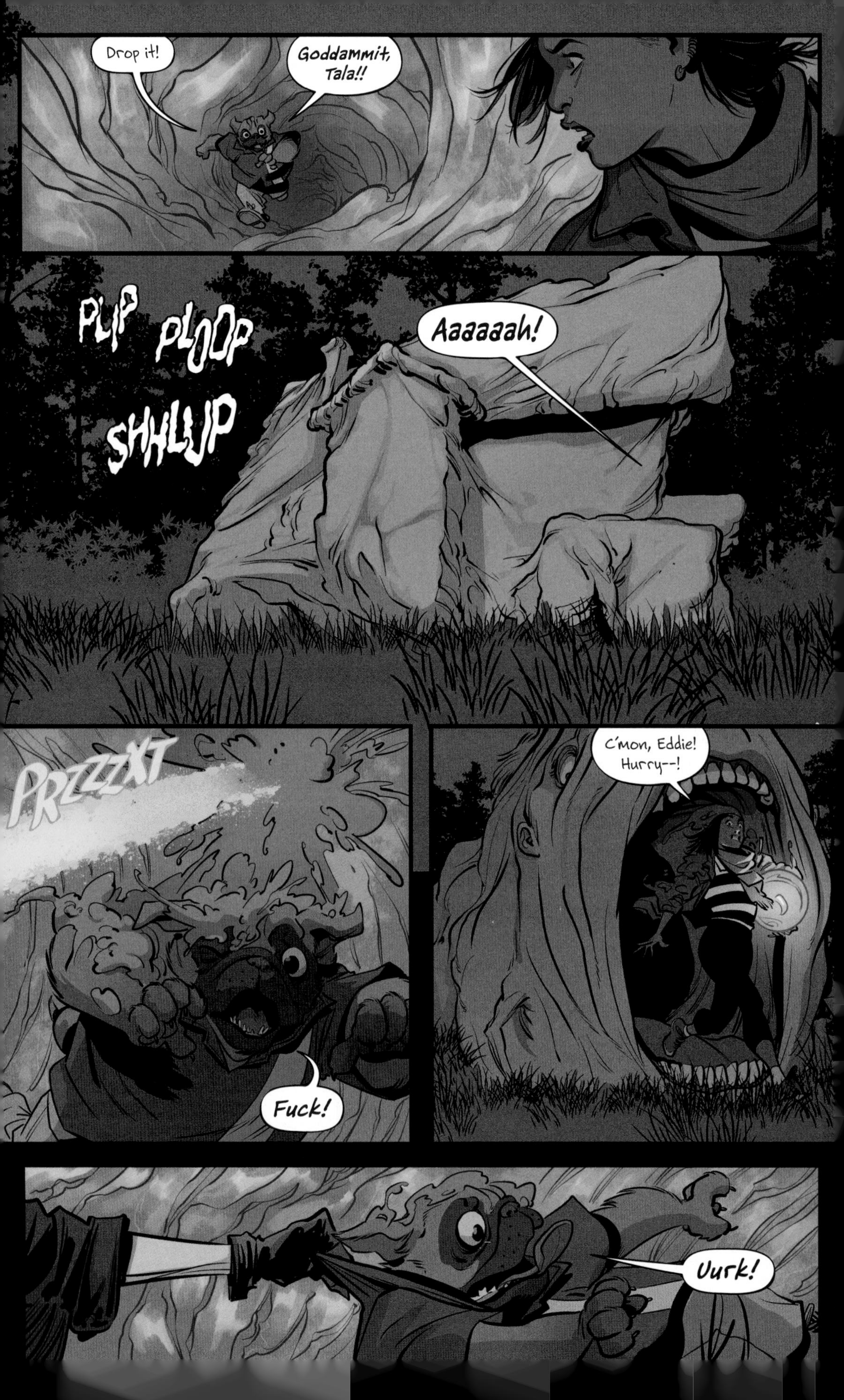
Drop it!
Goddammit, Tala!!
PLIP
PLOOP
SHHLUP
Aaaaaah!
PRZZZXT
Fuck!
C'mon, Eddie! Hurry--!
Uurk!

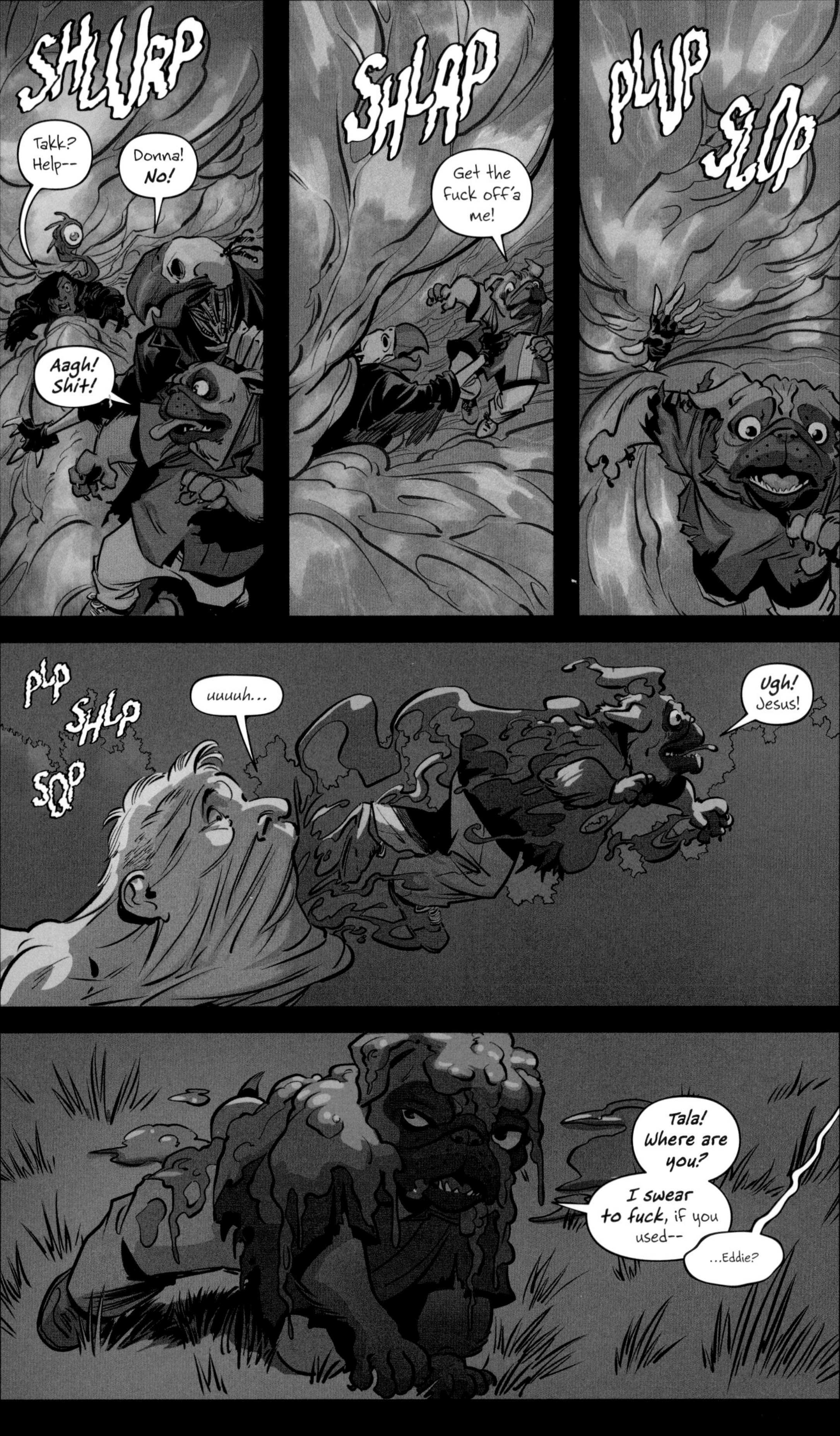
SHLURP
Takk? Help--
Donna! No!
Aagh! Shit!
SHLAP
Get the fuck off'a me!
PLUP
SLOP
PLP
SHLP
SQP
uuuuh...
Ugh! Jesus!
Tala! Where are you?
I swear to fuck, if you used--
...Eddie?

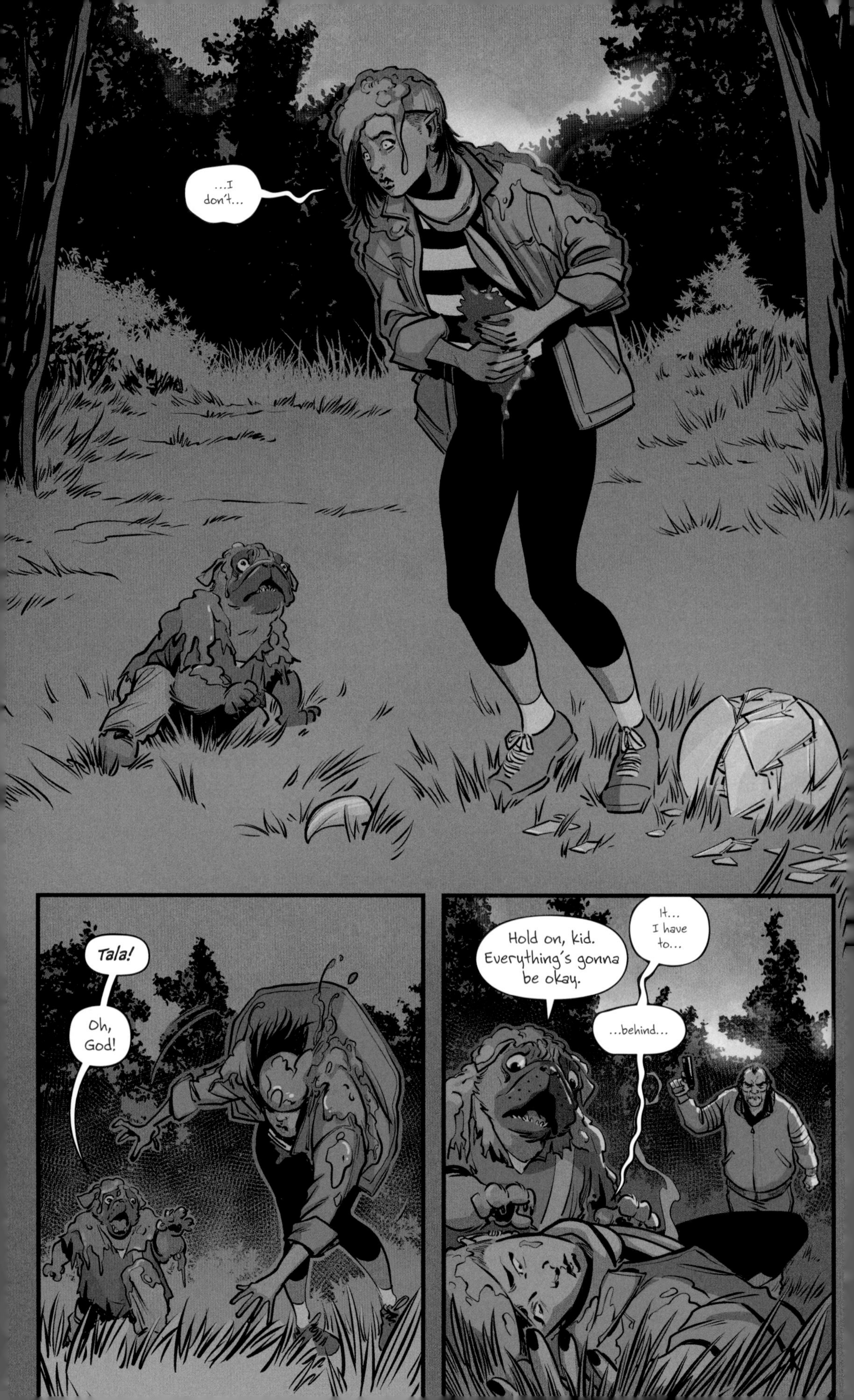

...I don't...
Tala!
Oh, God!
Hold on, kid. Everything's gonna be okay.
It... I have to...
...behind...

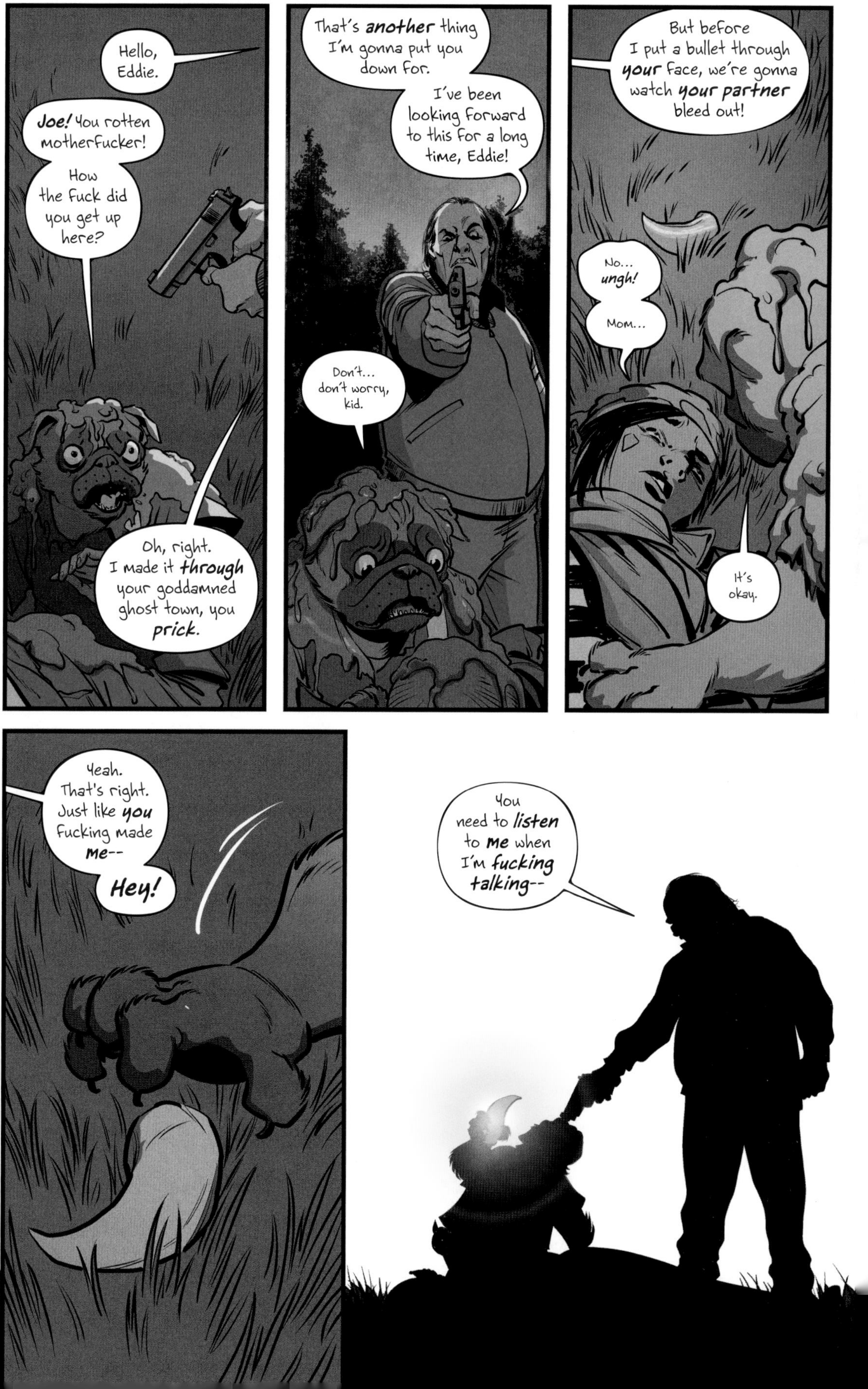
Hello, Eddie.
Joe! You rotten motherfucker!
How the fuck did you get up here?
Oh, right. I made it through your goddamned ghost town, you prick.
That's another thing I'm gonna put you down for.
I've been looking forward to this for a long time, Eddie!
Don't... don't worry, kid.
But before I put a bullet through your face, we're gonna watch your partner bleed out!
No... ungh!
Mom...
It's okay.
Yeah. That's right. Just like you fucking made me--
Hey!
You need to listen to me when I'm fucking talking--

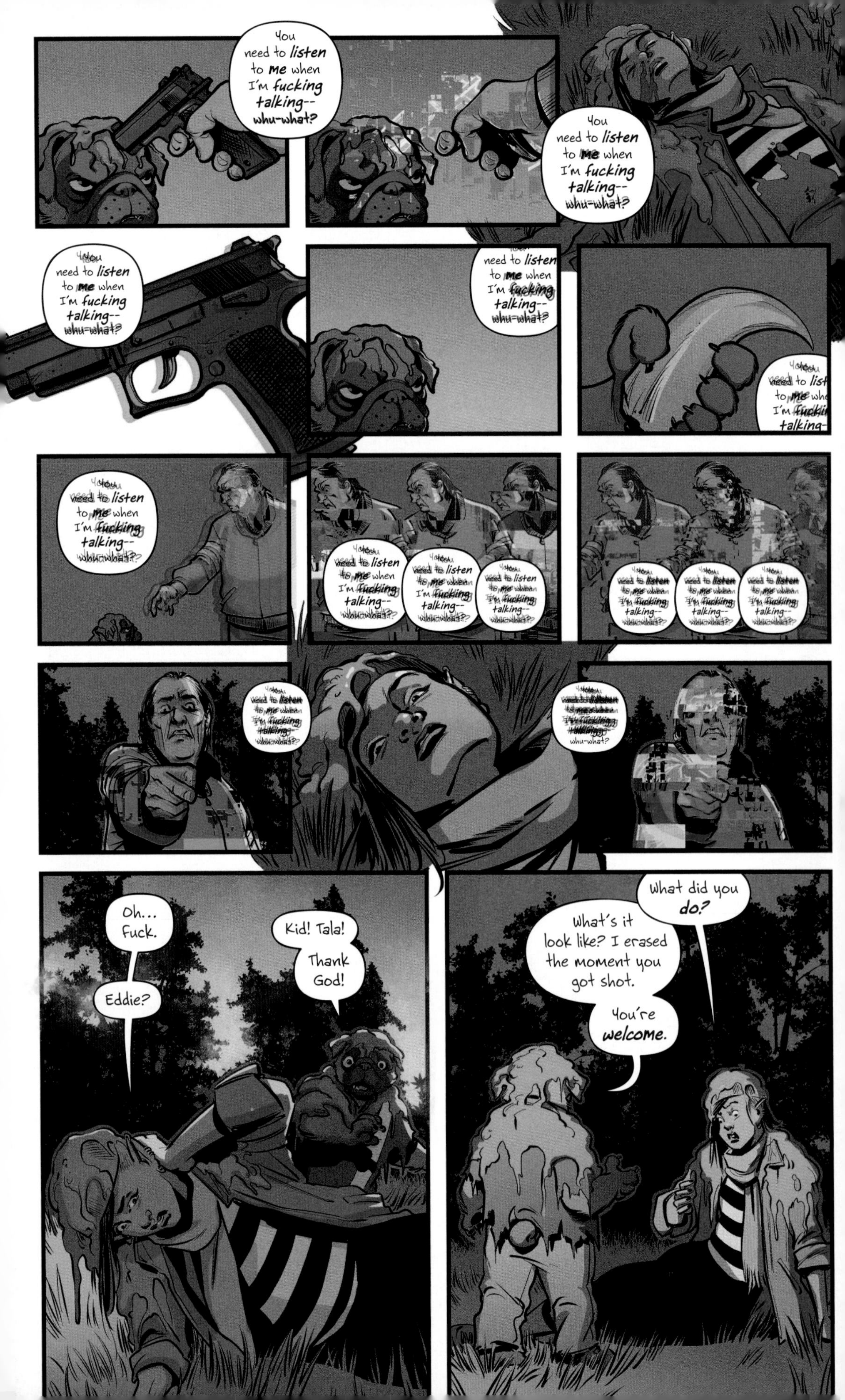
You need to listen to me when I'm fucking talking-- whu-what?
You need to listen to me when I'm fucking talking-- whu-what?
You need to listen to me when I'm fucking talking-- whu-what?
You need to listen to me when I'm fucking talking-- whu-what?
You need to listen to me when I'm fucking talking-- whu-what?
You need to listen to me when I'm fucking talking-- whu-what?
Oh... Fuck.
Eddie?
Kid! Tala!
Thank God!
What did you do?
What's it look like? I erased the moment you got shot.
You're welcome.

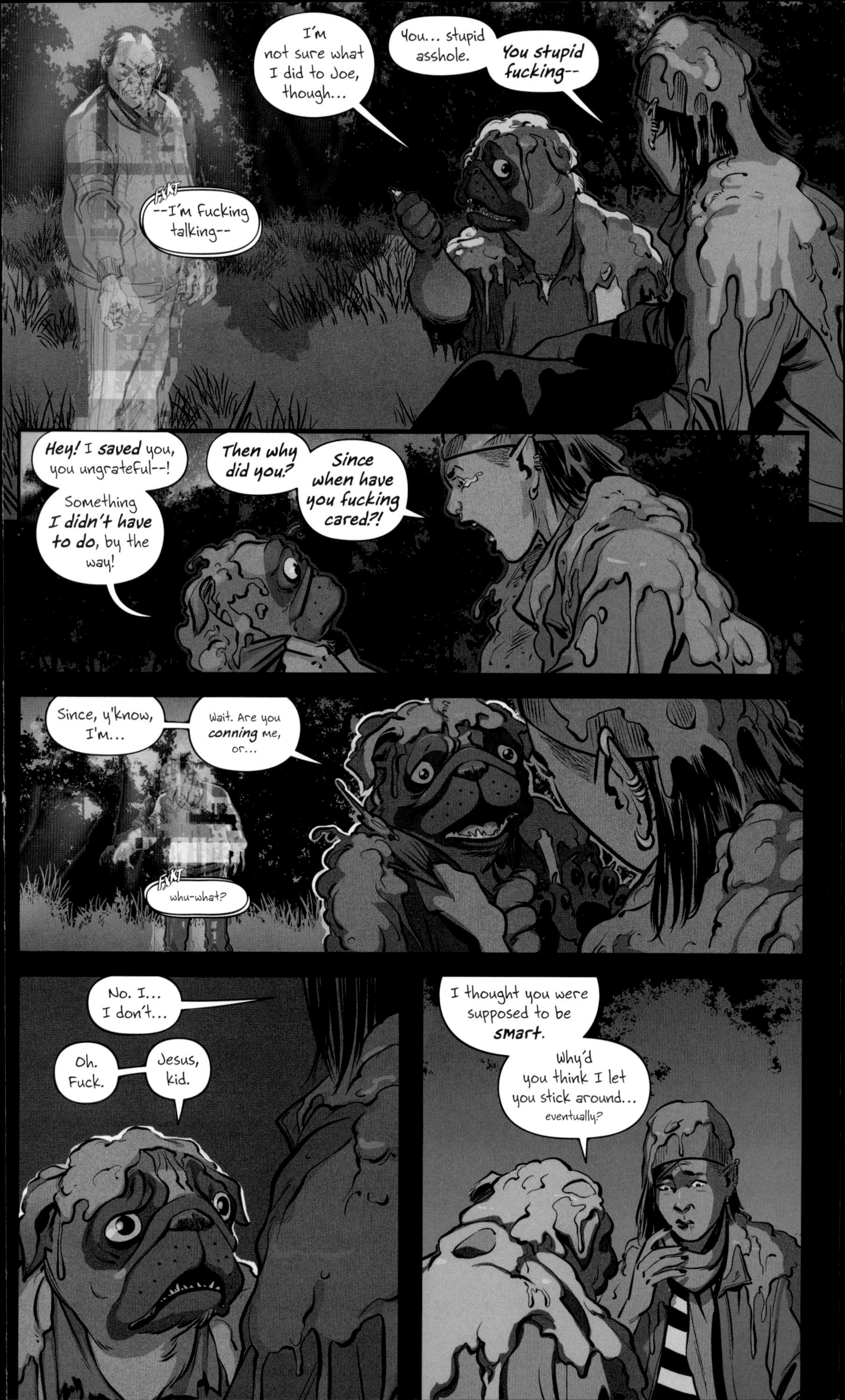
I'm not sure what I did to Joe, though...
You... stupid asshole.
You stupid fucking--
FXKT
--I'm fucking talking--
Hey! I saved you, you ungrateful--!
Something I didn't have to do, by the way!
Then why did you?
Since when have you fucking cared?!
Since, y'know, I'm...
Wait. Are you conning me, or...
FXKT
whu-what?
No. I... I don't...
Oh. Fuck.
Jesus, kid.
I thought you were supposed to be smart.
Why'd you think I let you stick around... eventually?

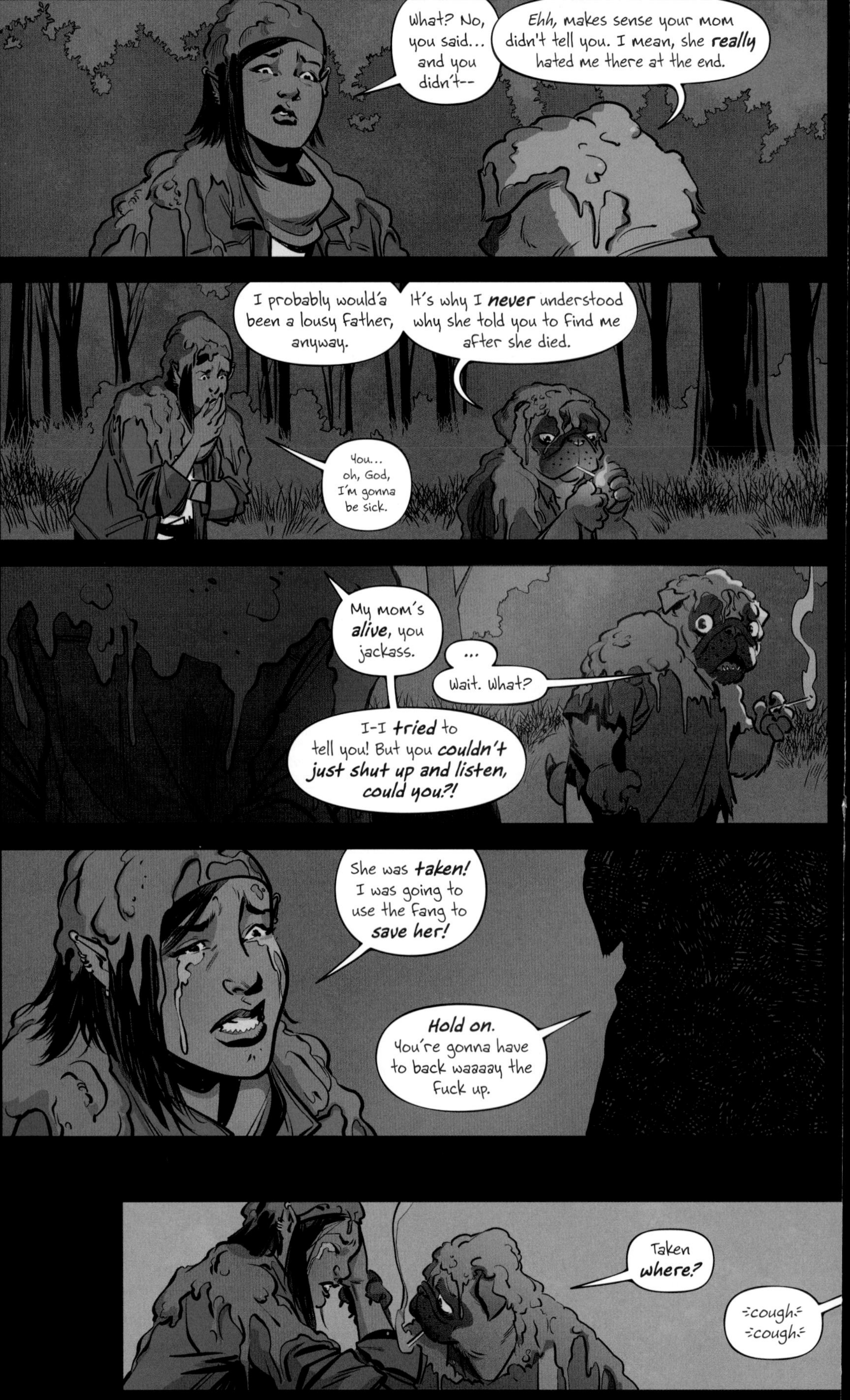
What? No, you said... and you didn't--
Ehh, makes sense your mom didn't tell you. I mean, she **really** hated me there at the end.
I probably would'a been a lousy father, anyway.
It's why I **never** understood why she told you to find me after she died.
You... oh, God, I'm gonna be sick.
My mom's **alive**, you jackass.
...
Wait. What?
I-I **tried** to tell you! But you **couldn't just shut up and listen, could you?!**
She was **taken!** I was going to use the Fang to **save her!**
Hold on. You're gonna have to back waaaay the fuck up.
Taken **where?**
=cough= =cough=

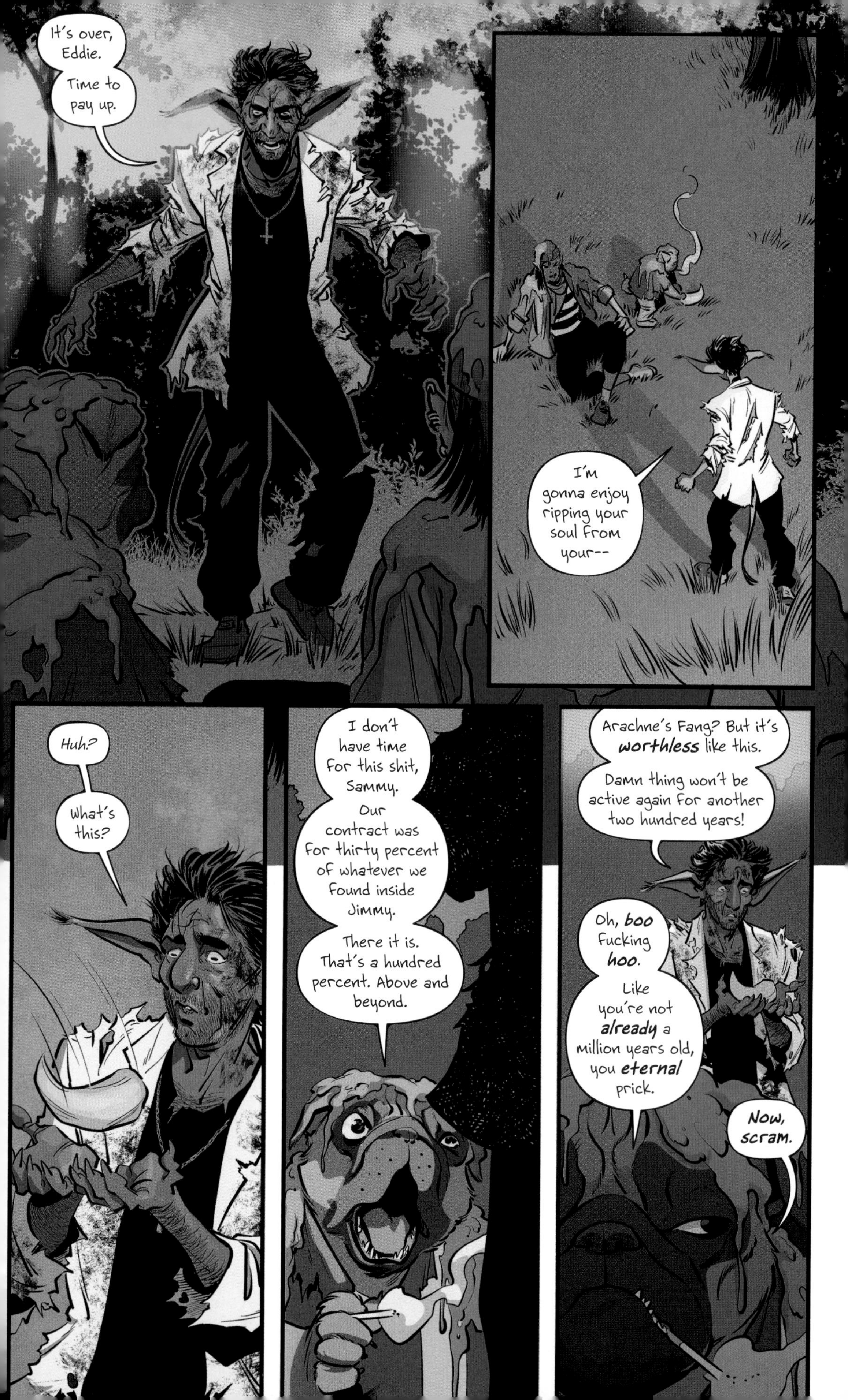

It's over, Eddie.
Time to pay up.
I'm gonna enjoy ripping your soul from your--
Huh?
What's this?
I don't have time for this shit, Sammy.
Our contract was for thirty percent of whatever we found inside Jimmy.
There it is. That's a hundred percent. Above and beyond.
Arachne's Fang? But it's **worthless** like this.
Damn thing won't be active again for another two hundred years!
Oh, **boo** fucking **hoo.**
Like you're not **already** a million years old, you **eternal** prick.
Now, scram.

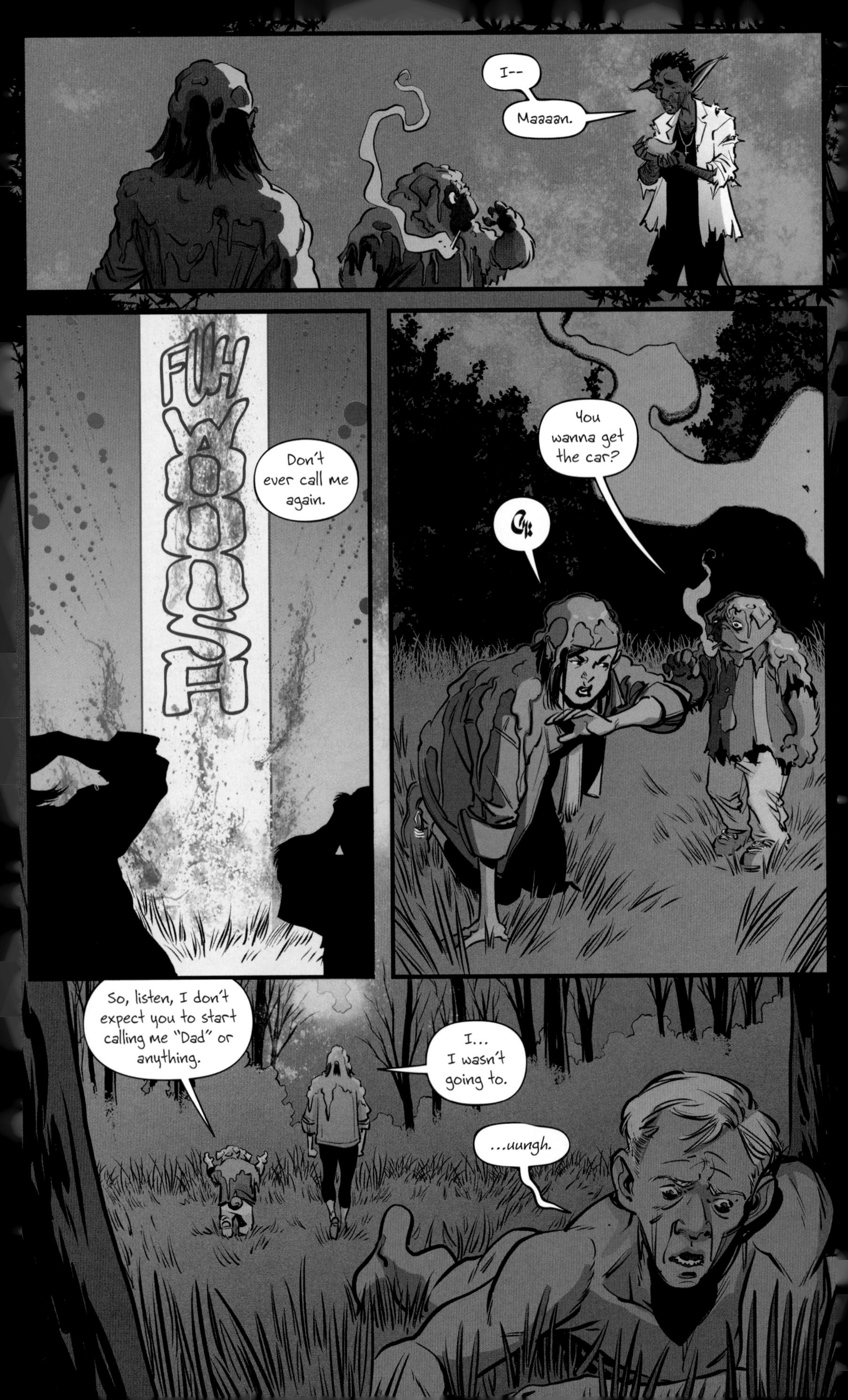
I--
Maaaan.
FUH WOOOSH
Don't ever call me again.
You wanna get the car?
So, listen, I don't expect you to start calling me "Dad" or anything.
I... I wasn't going to.
...uungh.

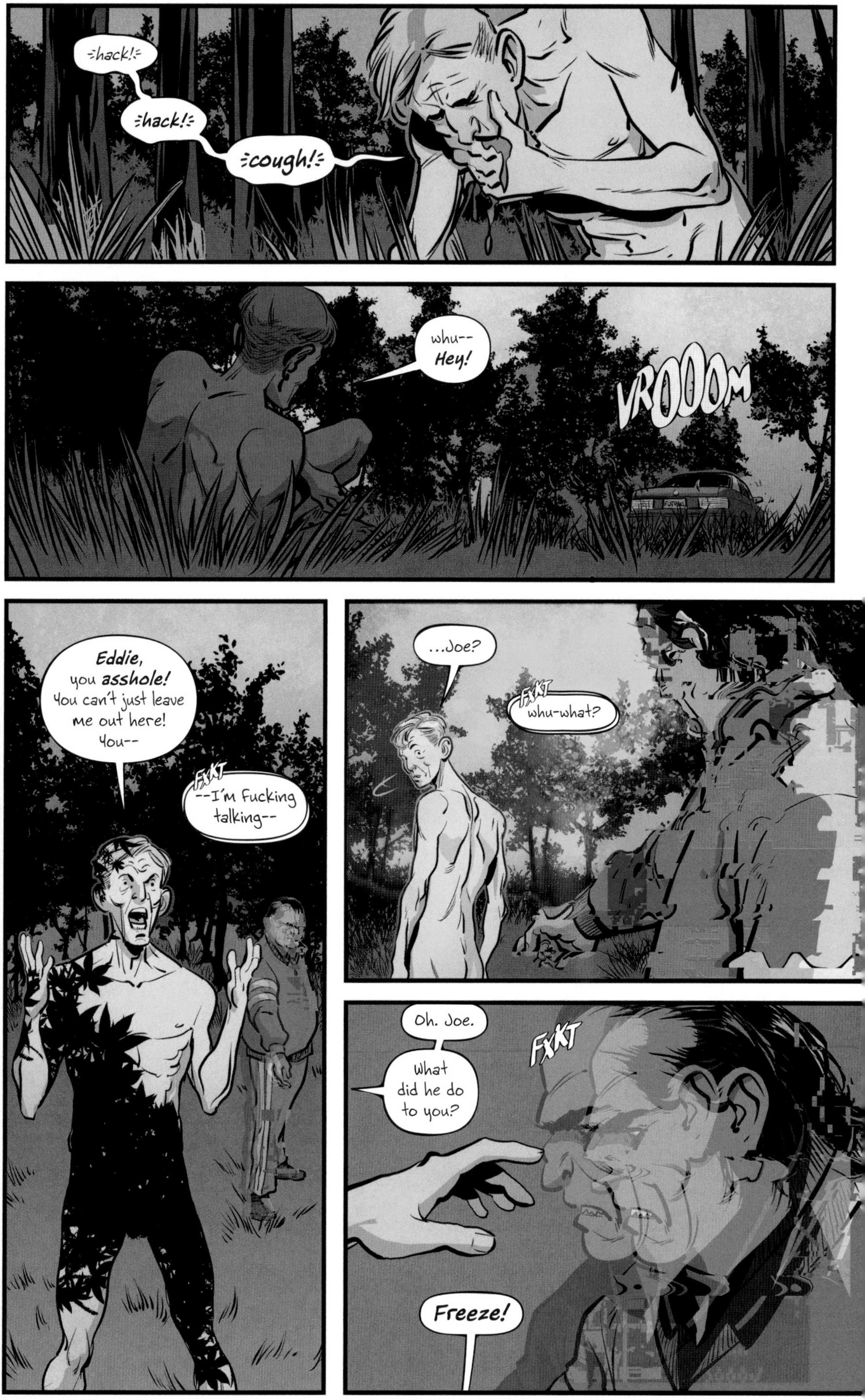

hack!
hack!
cough!
whu-- Hey!
VROOOM
Eddie, you asshole! You can't just leave me out here! You--
FXKT
--I'm fucking talking--
...Joe?
FXKT
whu-what?
Oh. Joe.
What did he do to you?
FXKT
Freeze!

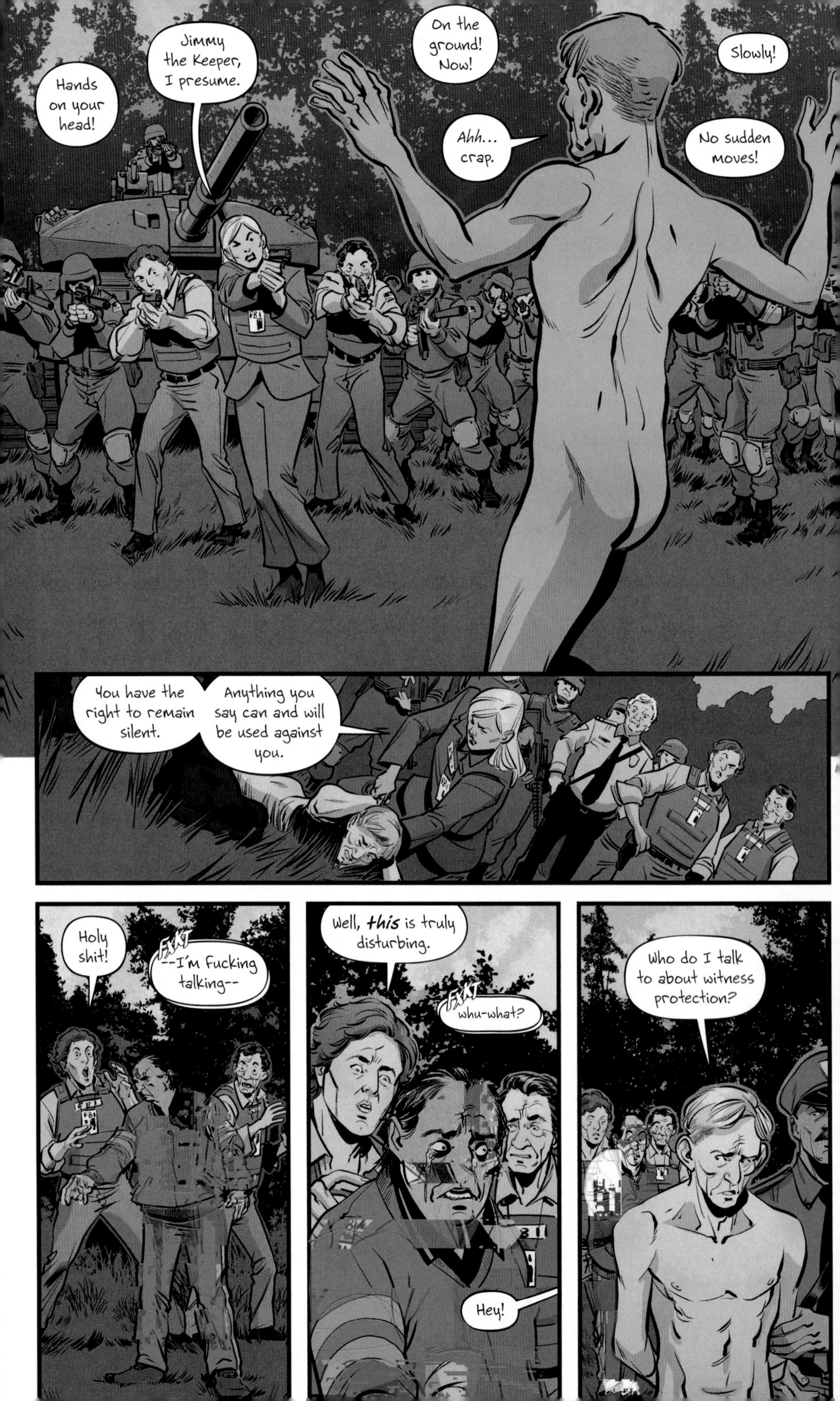
Hands on your head!
Jimmy the Keeper, I presume.
On the ground! Now!
Ahh... crap.
Slowly!
No sudden moves!
You have the right to remain silent.
Anything you say can and will be used against you.
Holy shit!
FXXT
--I'm fucking talking--
Well, this is truly disturbing.
FXXT
whu-what?
Hey!
Who do I talk to about witness protection?

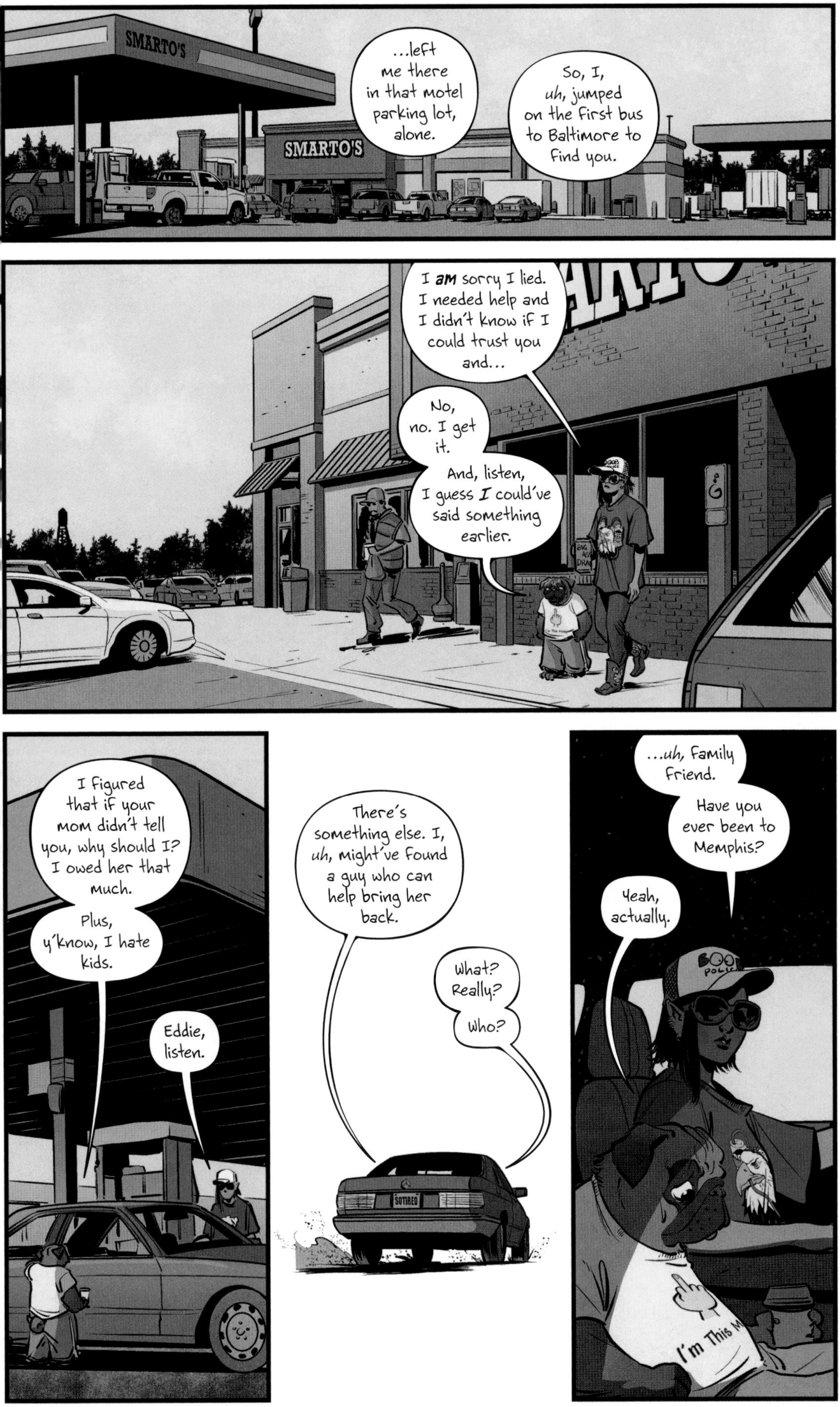
SMARTO'S
SMARTO'S
...left me there in that motel parking lot, alone.
So, I, *uh*, jumped on the first bus to Baltimore to find you.
I **am** sorry I lied. I needed help and I didn't know if I could trust you and...
No, no. I get it.
And, listen, I guess *I* could've said something earlier.
I figured that if your mom didn't tell you, why should I? I owed her that much.
Plus, y'know, I hate kids.
Eddie, listen.
There's something else. I, *uh*, might've found a guy who can help bring her back.
SOTIRED
What? Really?
Who?
...*uh*, family friend.
Have you ever been to Memphis?
Yeah, actually.

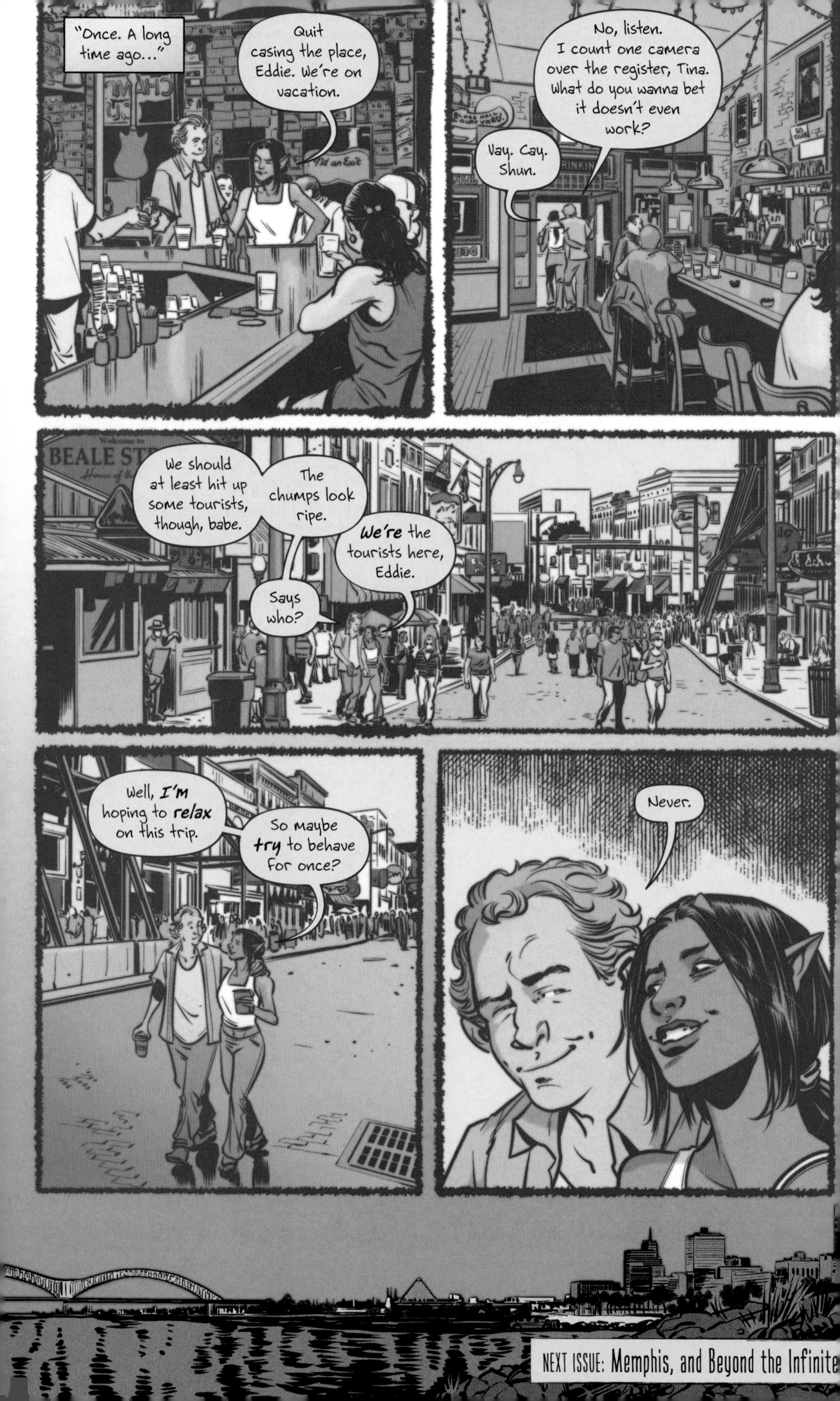
"Once. A long time ago..."
Quit casing the place, Eddie. We're on vacation.
No, listen. I count one camera over the register, Tina. What do you wanna bet it doesn't even work?
Vay. Cay. Shun.
BEALE ST
We should at least hit up some tourists, though, babe.
The chumps look ripe.
We're the tourists here, Eddie.
Says who?
Well, I'm hoping to relax on this trip.
So maybe try to behave for once?
Never.
NEXT ISSUE: Memphis, and Beyond the Infinite

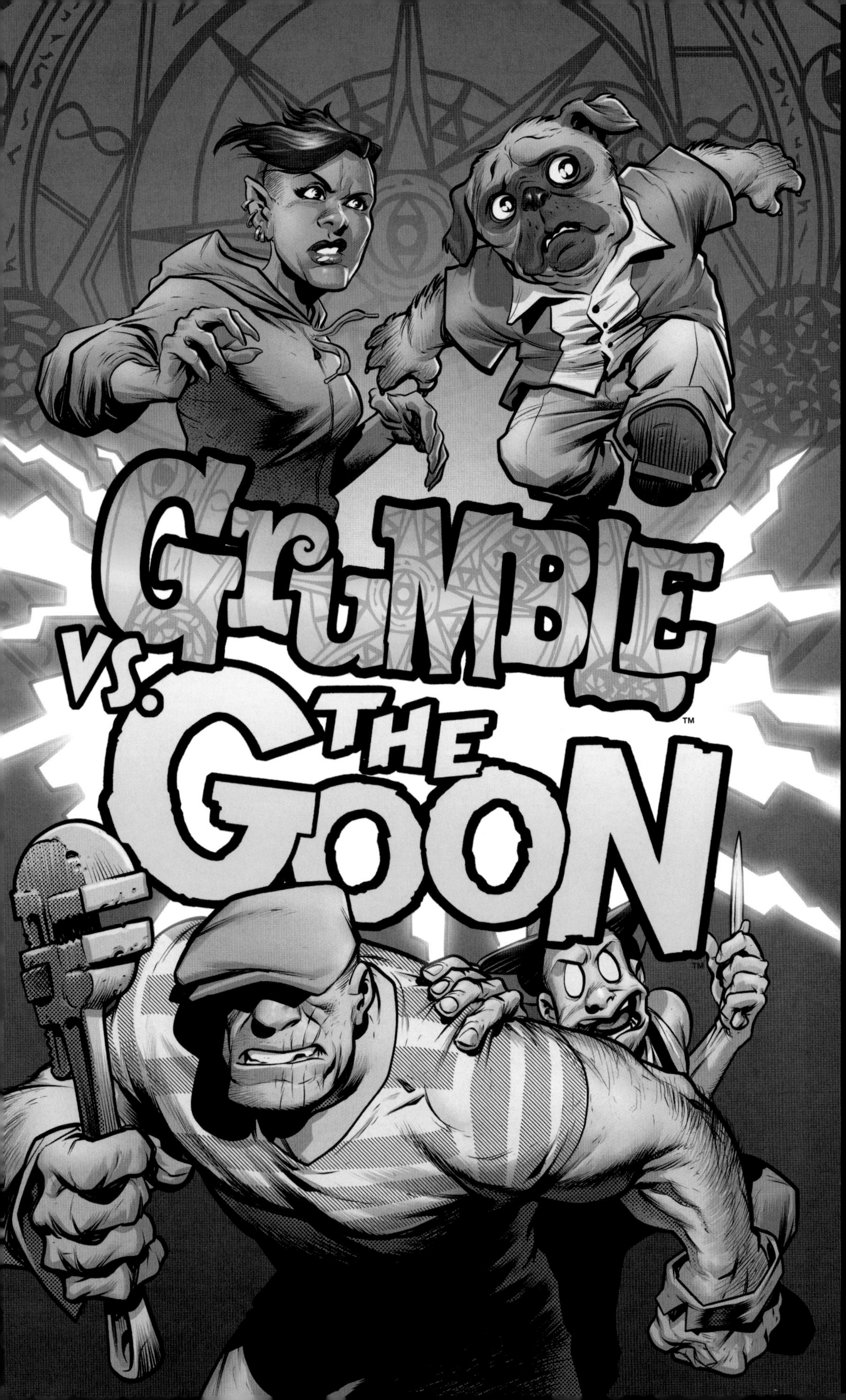
GRUMBLE
VS.
THE GOON™

GRUMBLE vs. THE GOON

WRITTEN BY:
RAFER ROBERTS AND ERIC POWELL

ART BY:
MIKE NORTON AND ERIC POWELL

COLORS BY:
MARISSA LOUISE

LETTERED BY:
CRANK!

EDITED BY:
TRACY MARSH

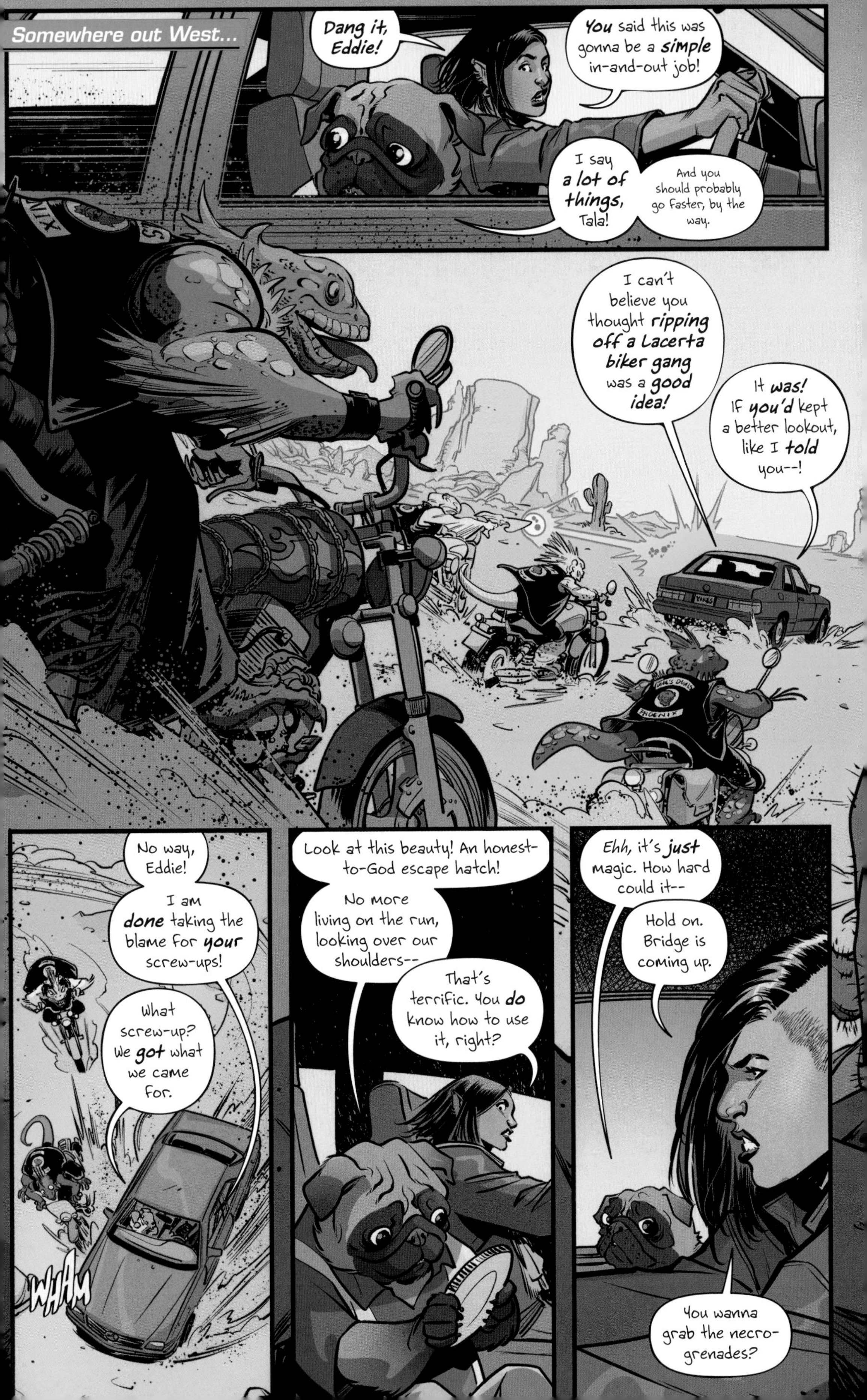
Somewhere out West...
Dang it, Eddie!
You said this was gonna be a simple in-and-out job!
I say a lot of things, Tala!
And you should probably go faster, by the way.
I can't believe you thought ripping off a Lacerta biker gang was a good idea!
It was! If you'd kept a better lookout, like I told you--!
No way, Eddie!
I am done taking the blame for your screw-ups!
What screw-up? We got what we came for.
WHAM
Look at this beauty! An honest-to-God escape hatch!
No more living on the run, looking over our shoulders--
That's terrific. You do know how to use it, right?
Ehh, it's just magic. How hard could it--
Hold on. Bridge is coming up.
You wanna grab the necro-grenades?

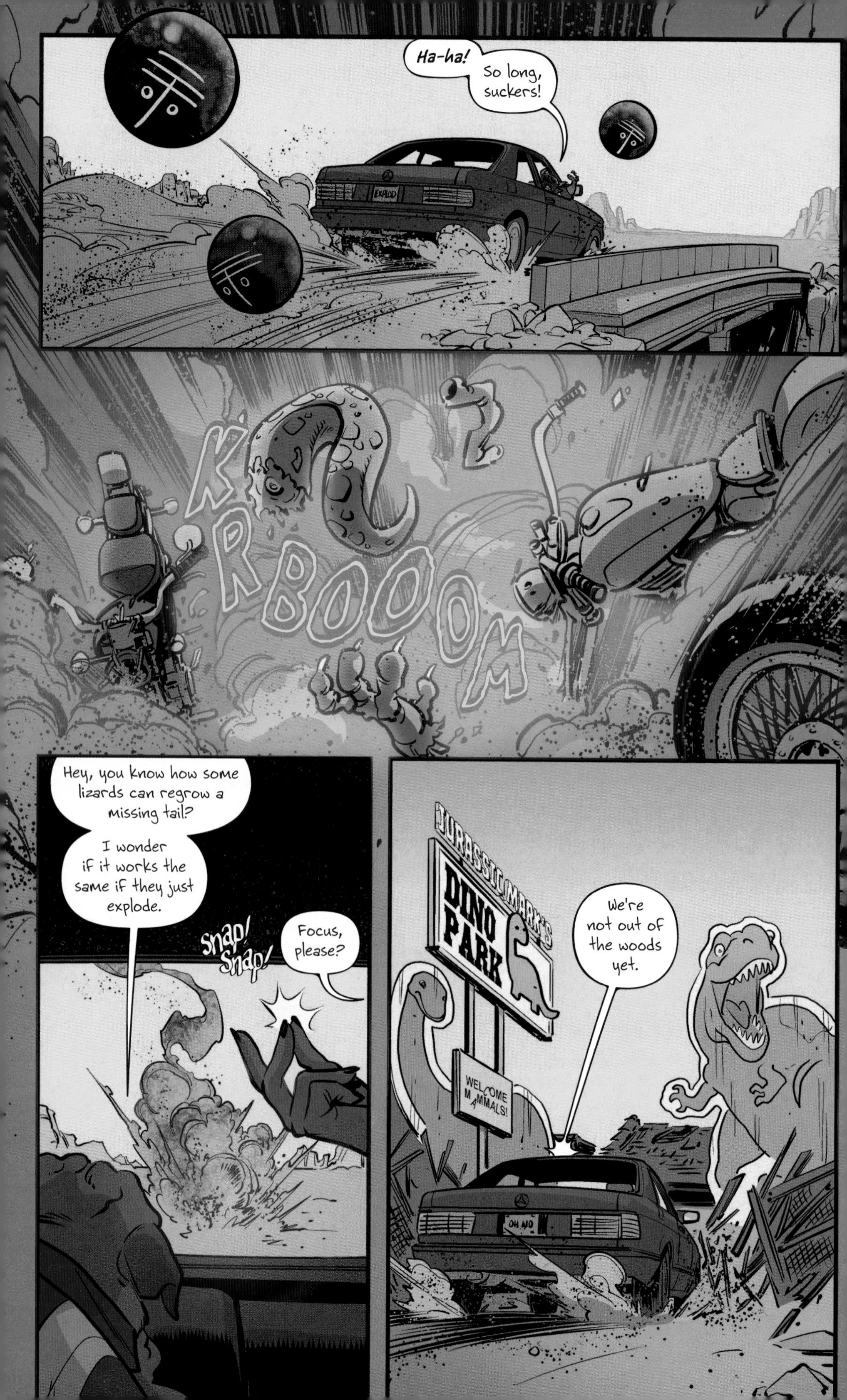
Ha-ha!
So long, suckers!
EXPLOD
KRBOOOM
Hey, you know how some lizards can regrow a missing tail?
I wonder if it works the same if they just explode.
Snap! Snap!
Focus, please?
JURASSIC MARK'S DINO PARK
WELCOME MAMMALS!
We're not out of the woods yet.
OH NO

OK, *there!* That's the place Dicky Ramora told me about!

GIFT SHOP

NO TROLS

Ugh! This dump smells *awful.*

Hurry up and open the portal.

Yeah, funny thing...

Are you *kidding me?* You said--!

BEHOLD. DINOCHICKEN!

buck bock?

GO EXTINCT!

Hey! What the--

YONK

buck bock!

Whoa.

BRRVRRRRMMM

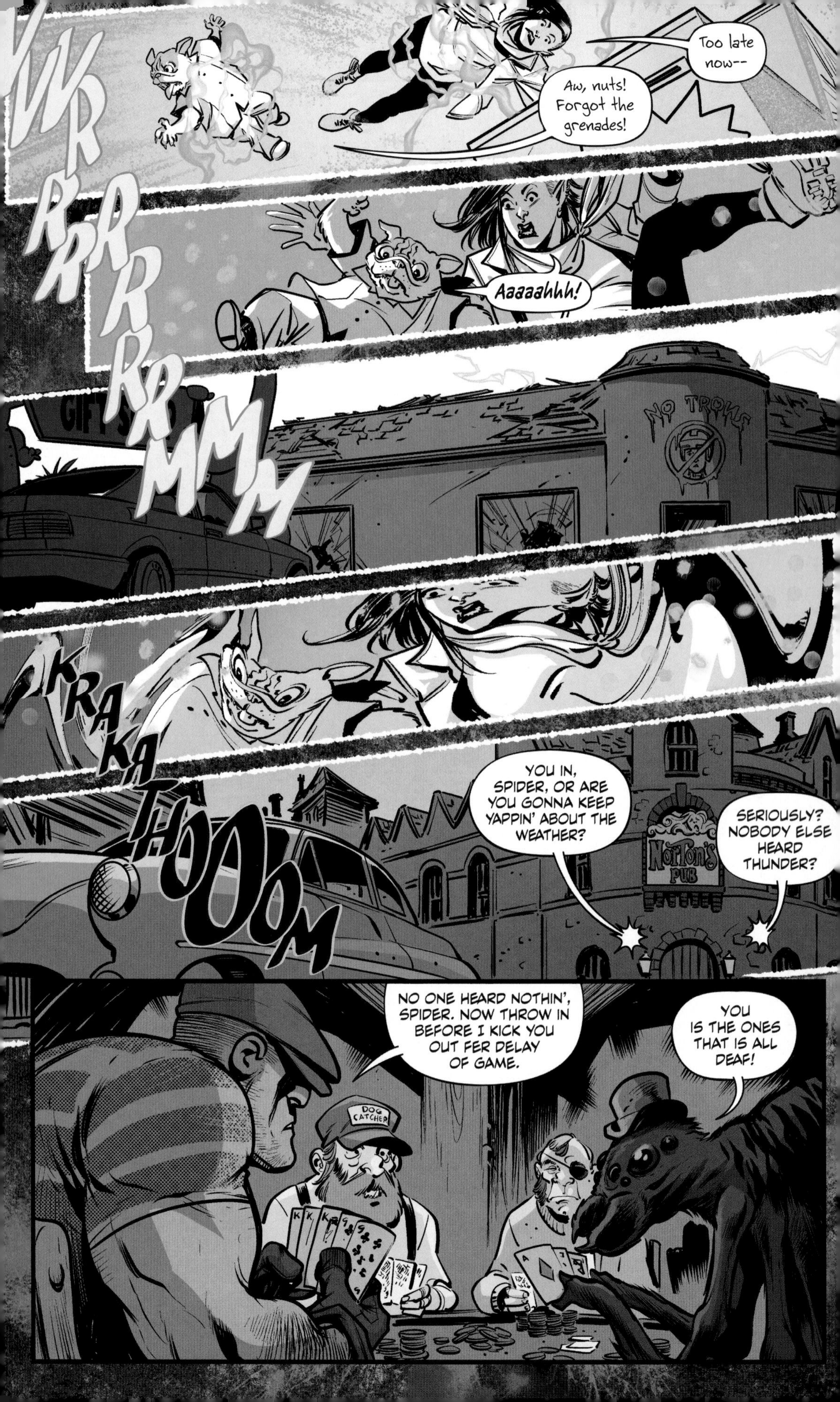
VVVRRRRRRRRMMMM
Aw, nuts! Forgot the grenades!
Too late now--
Aaaaahhh!
GIFT S
NO TROLLS
KRAKATHOOOOM
YOU IN, SPIDER, OR ARE YOU GONNA KEEP YAPPIN' ABOUT THE WEATHER?
NORTON'S PUB
SERIOUSLY? NOBODY ELSE HEARD THUNDER?
NO ONE HEARD NOTHIN', SPIDER. NOW THROW IN BEFORE I KICK YOU OUT FER DELAY OF GAME.
YOU IS THE ONES THAT IS ALL DEAF!
DOG CATCHER

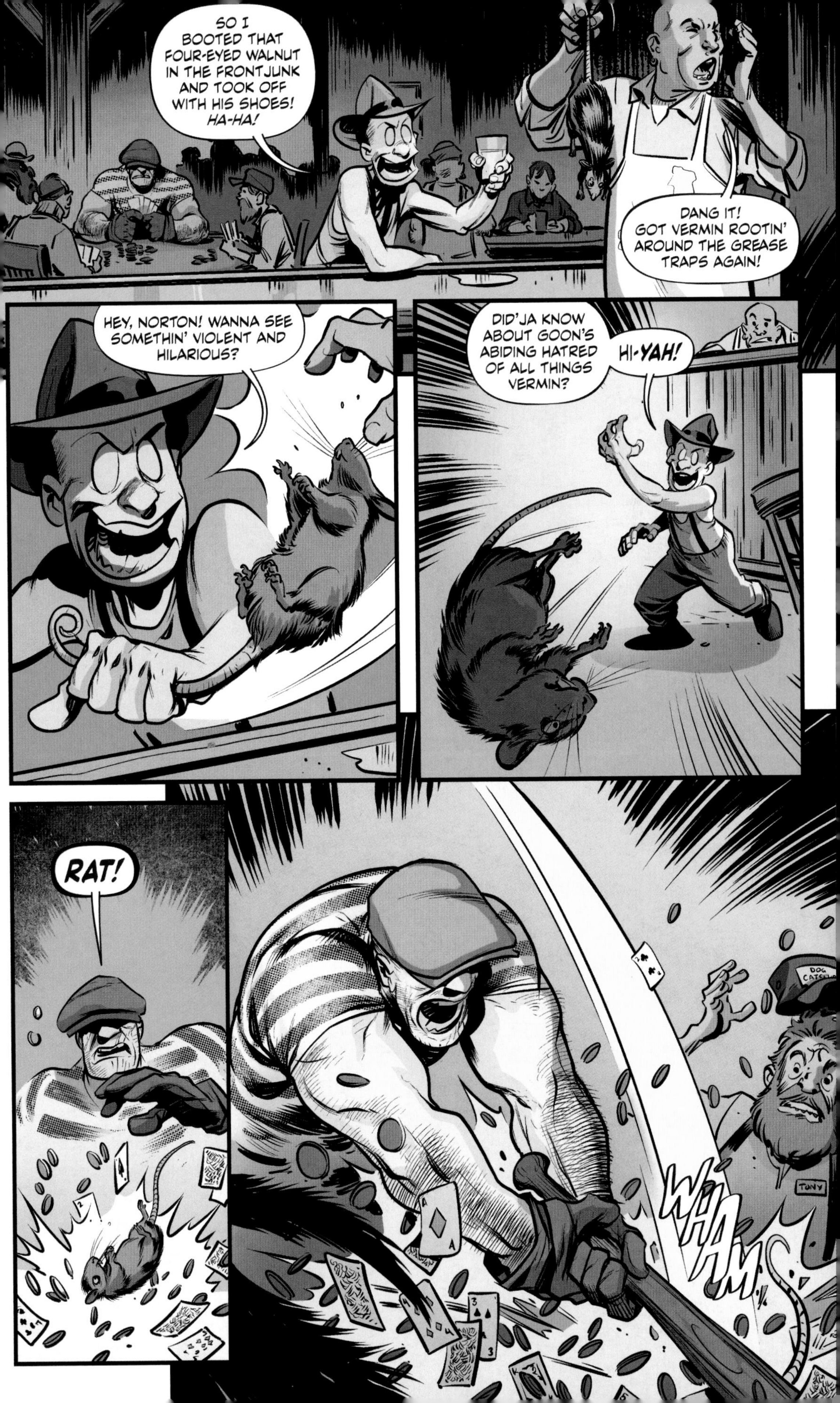
SO I BOOTED THAT FOUR-EYED WALNUT IN THE FRONTJUNK AND TOOK OFF WITH HIS SHOES! HA-HA!
DANG IT! GOT VERMIN ROOTIN' AROUND THE GREASE TRAPS AGAIN!
HEY, NORTON! WANNA SEE SOMETHIN' VIOLENT AND HILARIOUS?
DID'JA KNOW ABOUT GOON'S ABIDING HATRED OF ALL THINGS VERMIN?
HI-YAH!
RAT!
DOG
WHAM
TONY

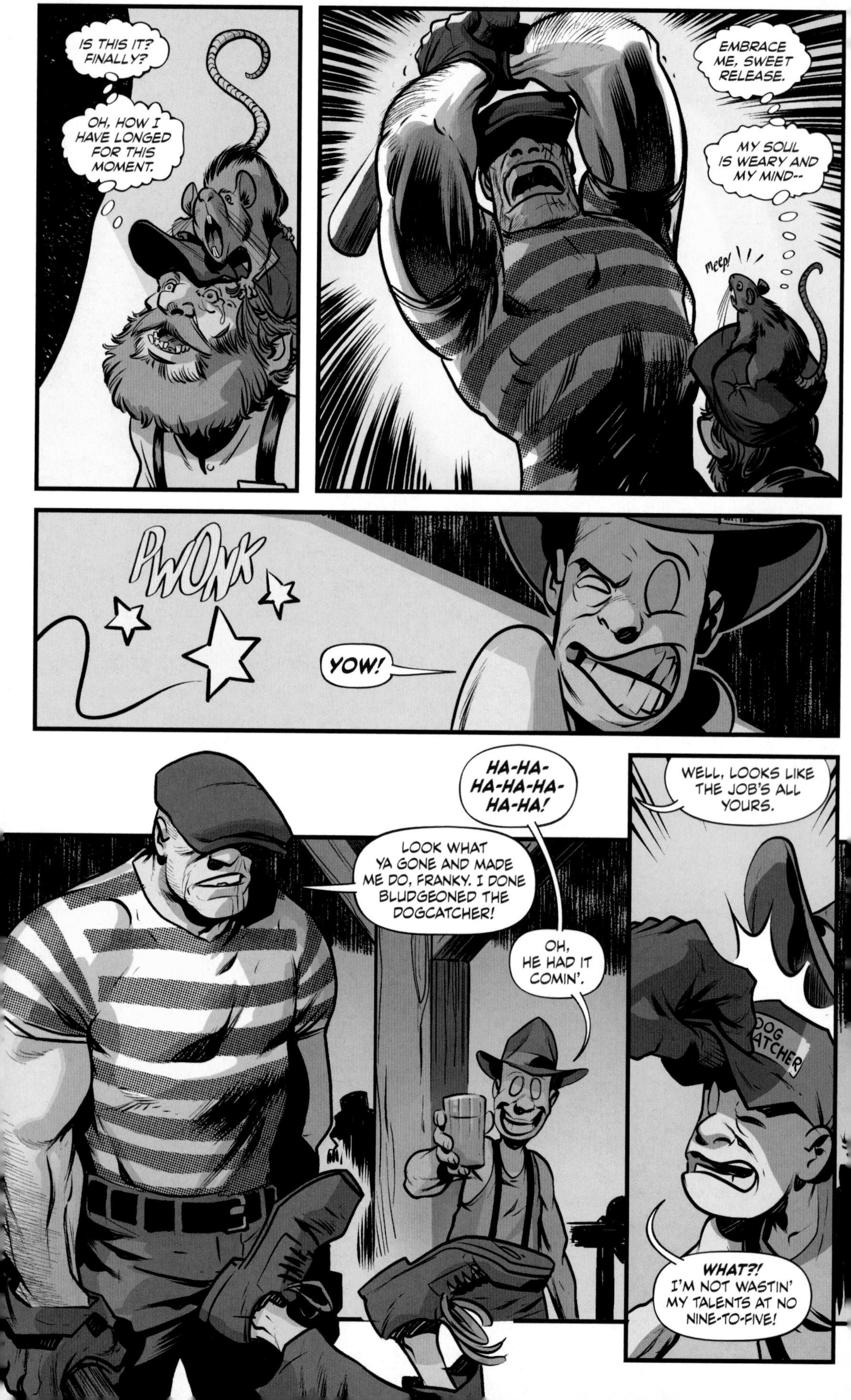
IS THIS IT? FINALLY?
OH, HOW I HAVE LONGED FOR THIS MOMENT.
EMBRACE ME, SWEET RELEASE.
MY SOUL IS WEARY AND MY MIND--
meep!
PWONK
YOW!
LOOK WHAT YA GONE AND MADE ME DO, FRANKY. I DONE BLUDGEONED THE DOGCATCHER!
HA-HA-HA-HA-HA-HA-HA!
OH, HE HAD IT COMIN'.
WELL, LOOKS LIKE THE JOB'S ALL YOURS.
DOG CATCHER
WHAT?! I'M NOT WASTIN' MY TALENTS AT NO NINE-TO-FIVE!

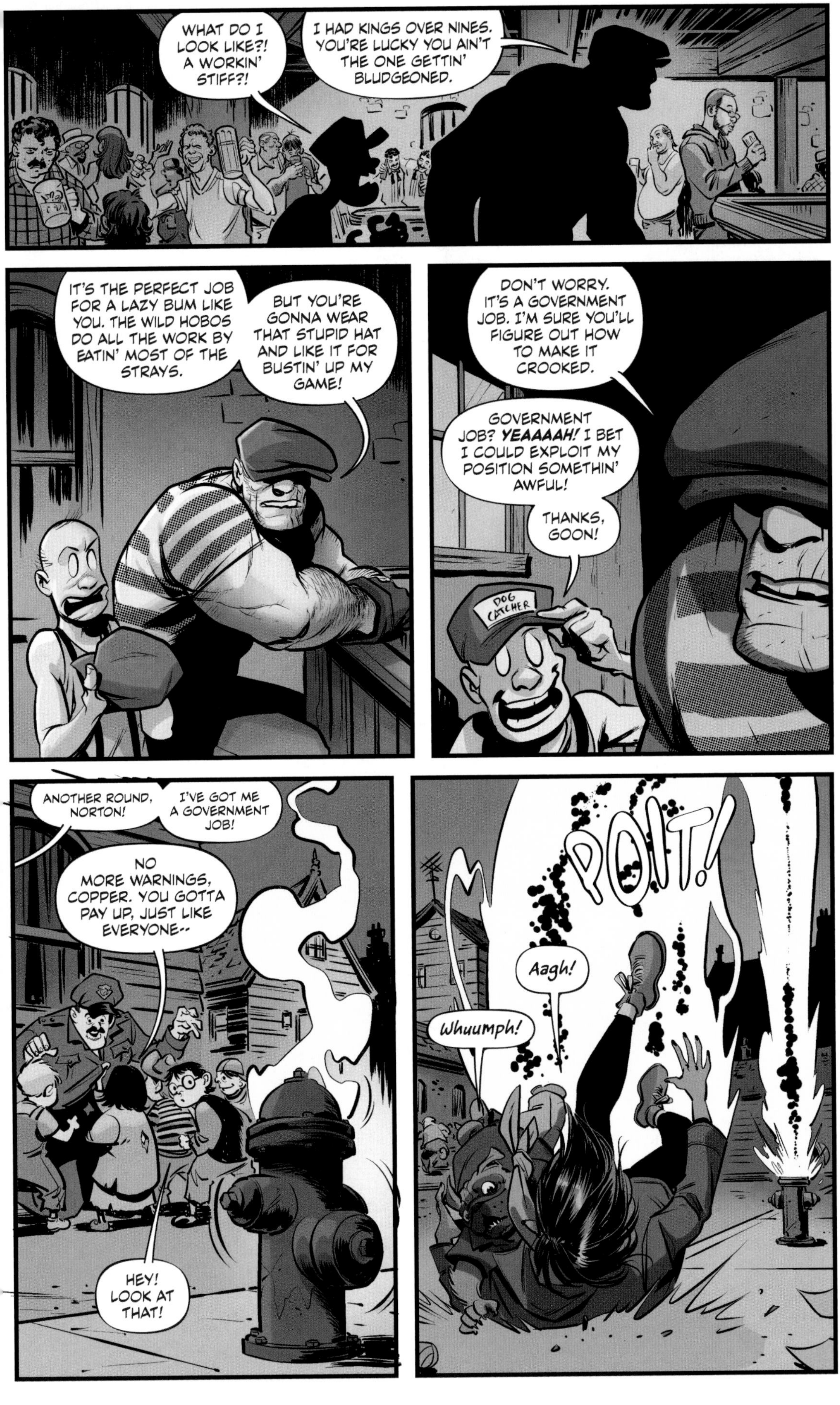
WHAT DO I LOOK LIKE?! A WORKIN' STIFF?!
I HAD KINGS OVER NINES. YOU'RE LUCKY YOU AIN'T THE ONE GETTIN' BLUDGEONED.
IT'S THE PERFECT JOB FOR A LAZY BUM LIKE YOU. THE WILD HOBOS DO ALL THE WORK BY EATIN' MOST OF THE STRAYS.
BUT YOU'RE GONNA WEAR THAT STUPID HAT AND LIKE IT FOR BUSTIN' UP MY GAME!
DON'T WORRY. IT'S A GOVERNMENT JOB. I'M SURE YOU'LL FIGURE OUT HOW TO MAKE IT CROOKED.
GOVERNMENT JOB? YEAAAAH! I BET I COULD EXPLOIT MY POSITION SOMETHIN' AWFUL!
THANKS, GOON!
DOG CATCHER
ANOTHER ROUND, NORTON!
I'VE GOT ME A GOVERNMENT JOB!
NO MORE WARNINGS, COPPER. YOU GOTTA PAY UP, JUST LIKE EVERYONE--
HEY! LOOK AT THAT!
POIT!
Aagh!
Whuumph!

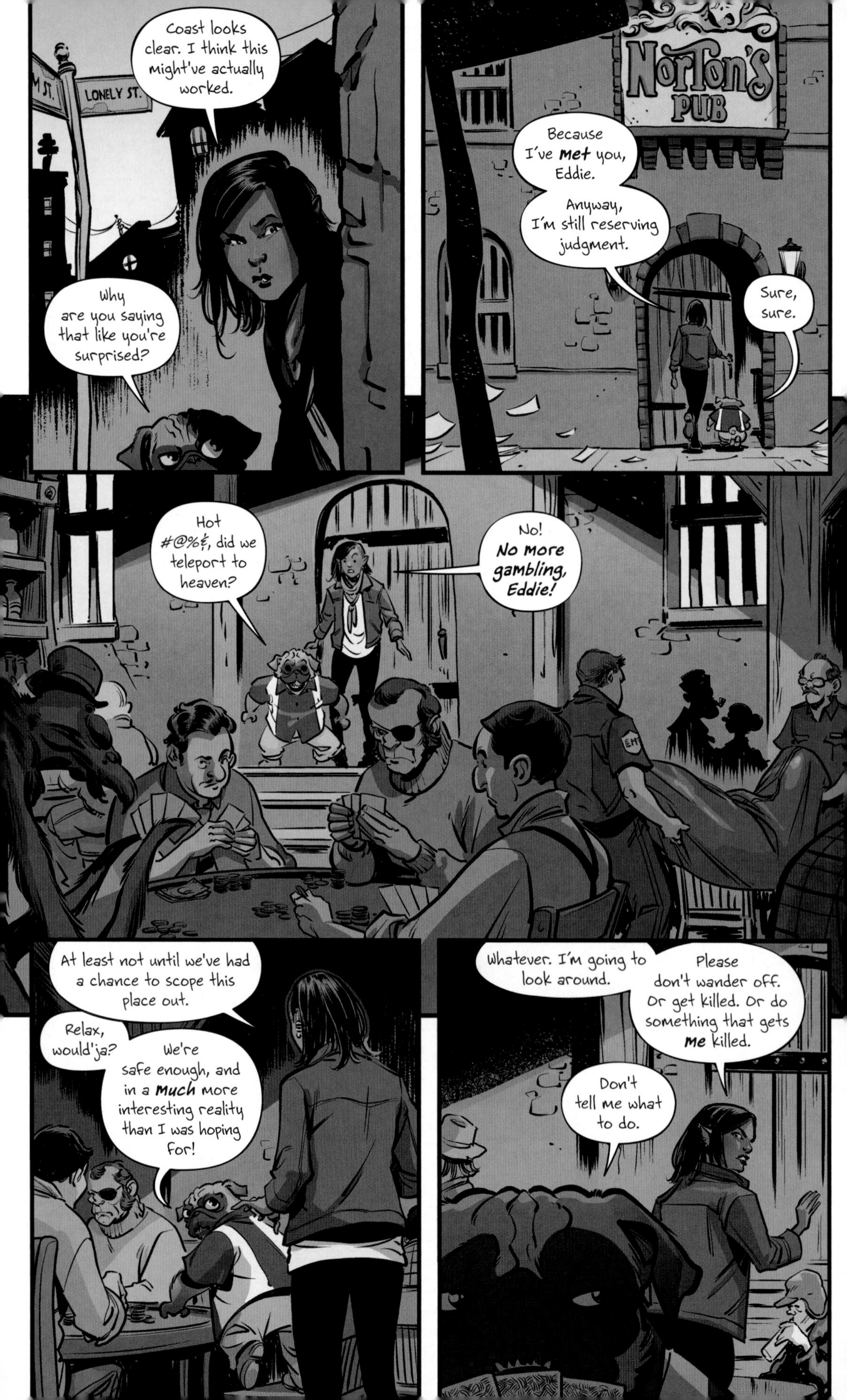
LONELY ST.
M ST.
Coast looks clear. I think this might've actually worked.
Why are you saying that like you're surprised?
Norton's PUB
Because I've **met** you, Eddie.
Anyway, I'm still reserving judgment.
Sure, sure.
Hot #@%&, did we teleport to heaven?
No! **No more gambling, Eddie!**
EMT
At least not until we've had a chance to scope this place out.
Relax, would'ja?
We're safe enough, and in a **much** more interesting reality than I was hoping for!
Whatever. I'm going to look around.
Please don't wander off. Or get killed. Or do something that gets **me** killed.
Don't tell me what to do.

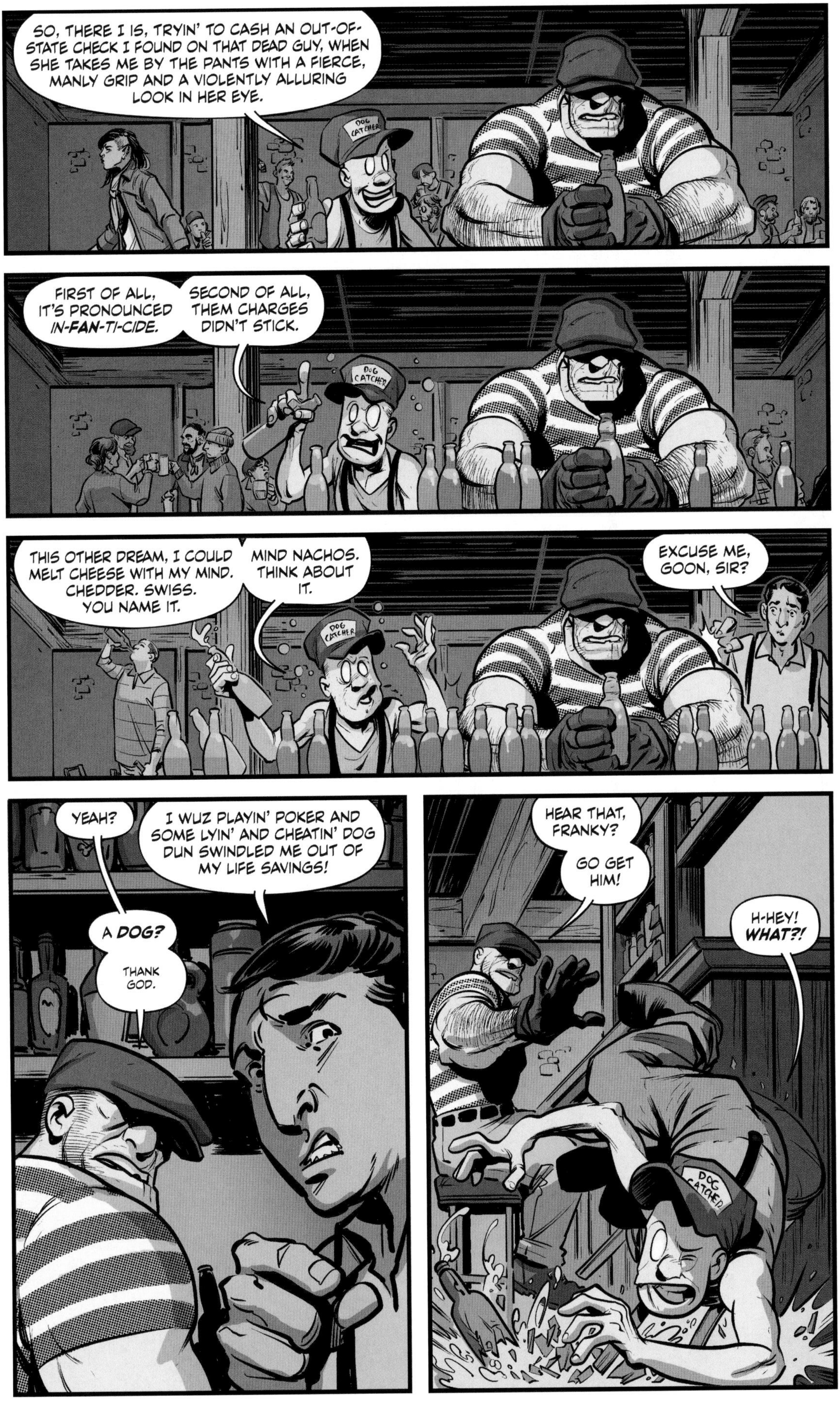
SO, THERE I IS, TRYIN' TO CASH AN OUT-OF-STATE CHECK I FOUND ON THAT DEAD GUY, WHEN SHE TAKES ME BY THE PANTS WITH A FIERCE, MANLY GRIP AND A VIOLENTLY ALLURING LOOK IN HER EYE.
DOG CATCHER
FIRST OF ALL, IT'S PRONOUNCED *IN-**FAN**-TI-CIDE.*
SECOND OF ALL, THEM CHARGES DIDN'T STICK.
DOG CATCHER
THIS OTHER DREAM, I COULD MELT CHEESE WITH MY MIND. CHEDDER. SWISS. YOU NAME IT.
MIND NACHOS. THINK ABOUT IT.
DOG CATCHER
EXCUSE ME, GOON, SIR?
YEAH?
I WUZ PLAYIN' POKER AND SOME LYIN' AND CHEATIN' DOG DUN SWINDLED ME OUT OF MY LIFE SAVINGS!
A **DOG?**
THANK GOD.
HEAR THAT, FRANKY?
GO GET HIM!
H-HEY! ***WHAT?!***
DOG CATCHER

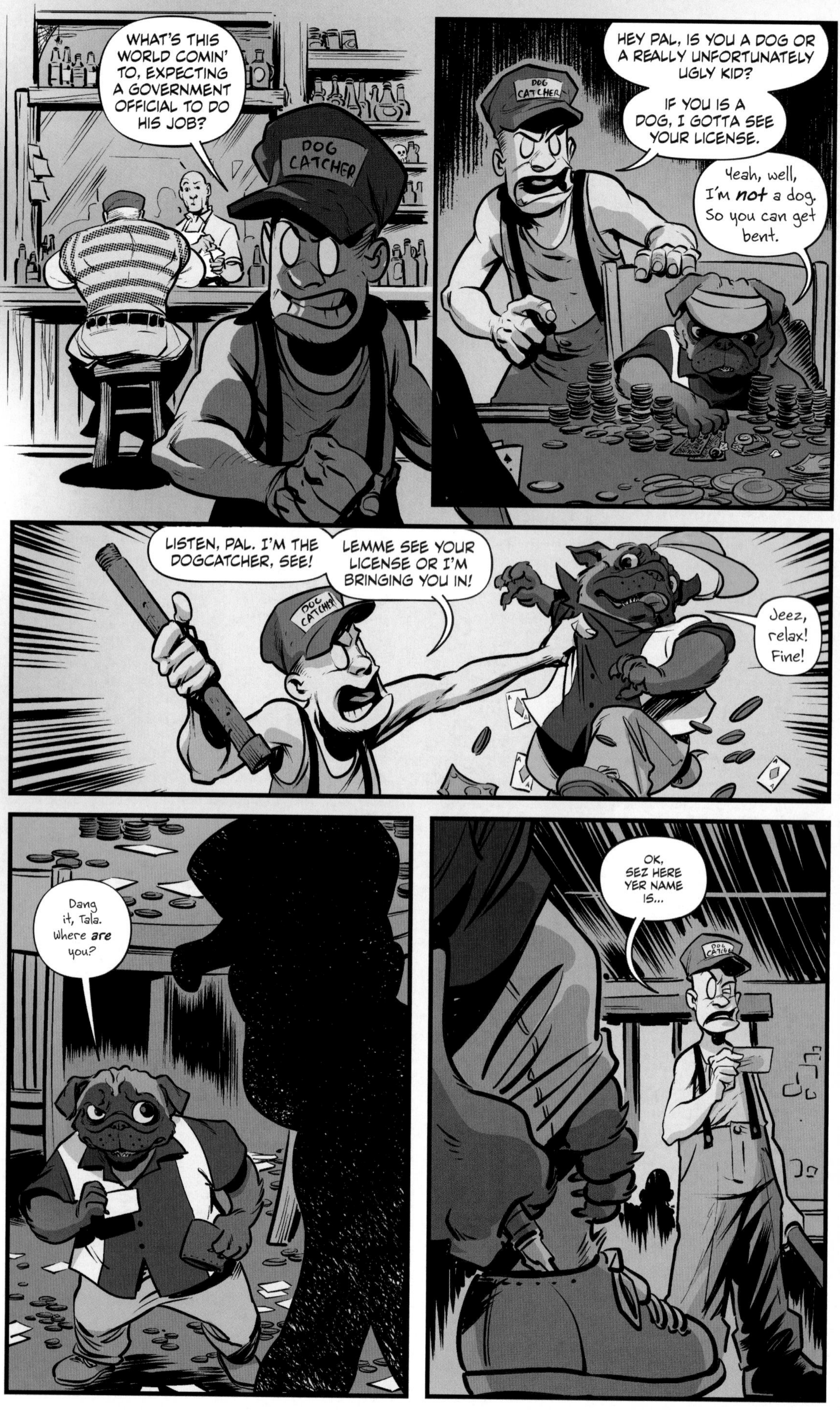

WHAT'S THIS WORLD COMIN' TO, EXPECTING A GOVERNMENT OFFICIAL TO DO HIS JOB?
DOG CATCHER
HEY PAL, IS YOU A DOG OR A REALLY UNFORTUNATELY UGLY KID?
IF YOU IS A DOG, I GOTTA SEE YOUR LICENSE.
Yeah, well, I'm **not** a dog. So you can get bent.
LISTEN, PAL. I'M THE DOGCATCHER, SEE!
LEMME SEE YOUR LICENSE OR I'M BRINGING YOU IN!
Jeez, relax! Fine!
Dang it, Tala. Where **are** you?
OK, SEZ HERE YER NAME IS...

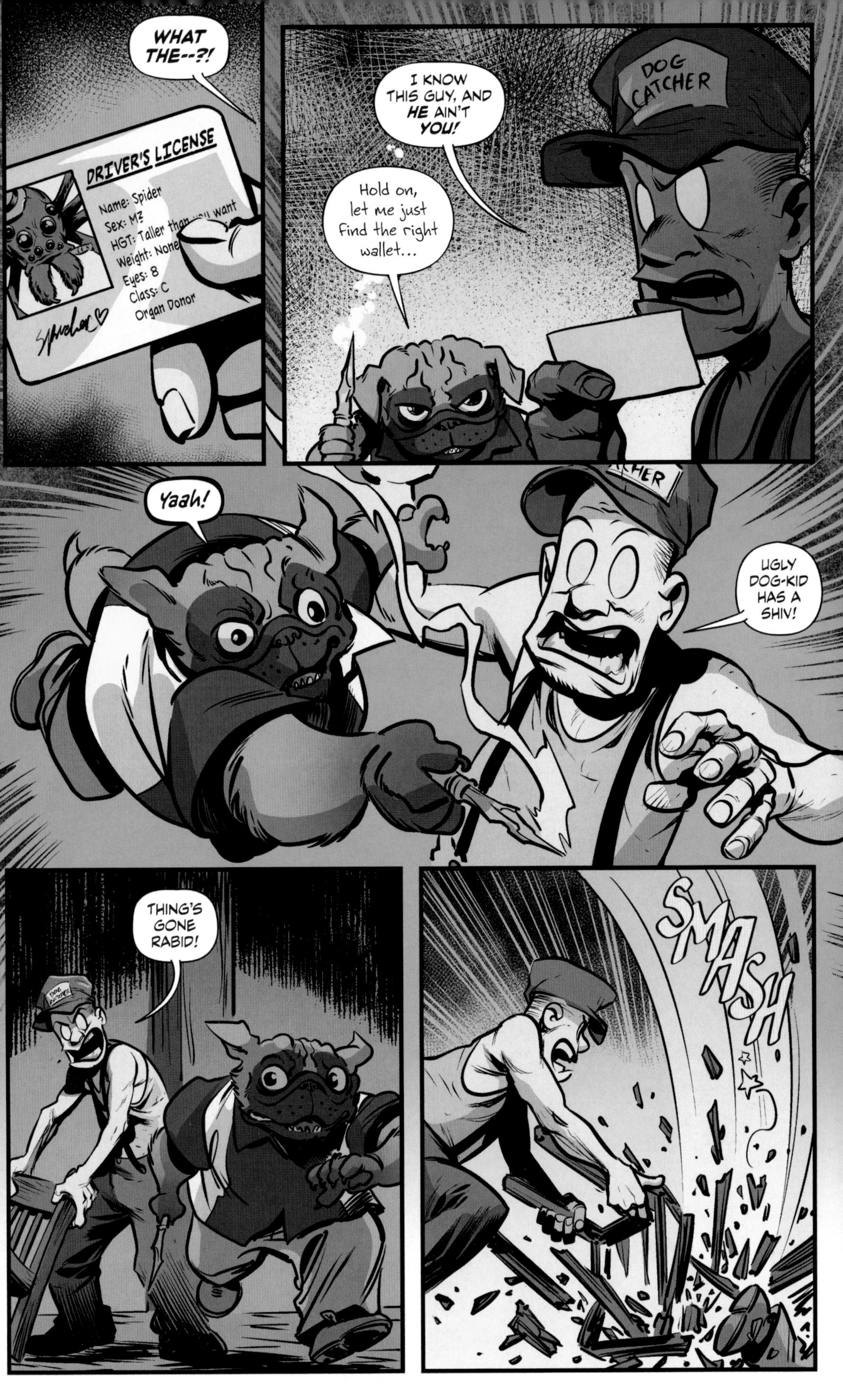
WHAT THE--?!
DRIVER'S LICENSE
Name: Spider
Sex: M?
HGT: Taller than you want
Weight: None
Eyes: 8
Class: C
Organ Donor
Hold on, let me just find the right wallet...
I KNOW THIS GUY, AND HE AIN'T YOU!
DOG CATCHER
Yaah!
UGLY DOG-KID HAS A SHIV!
THING'S GONE RABID!
SMASH

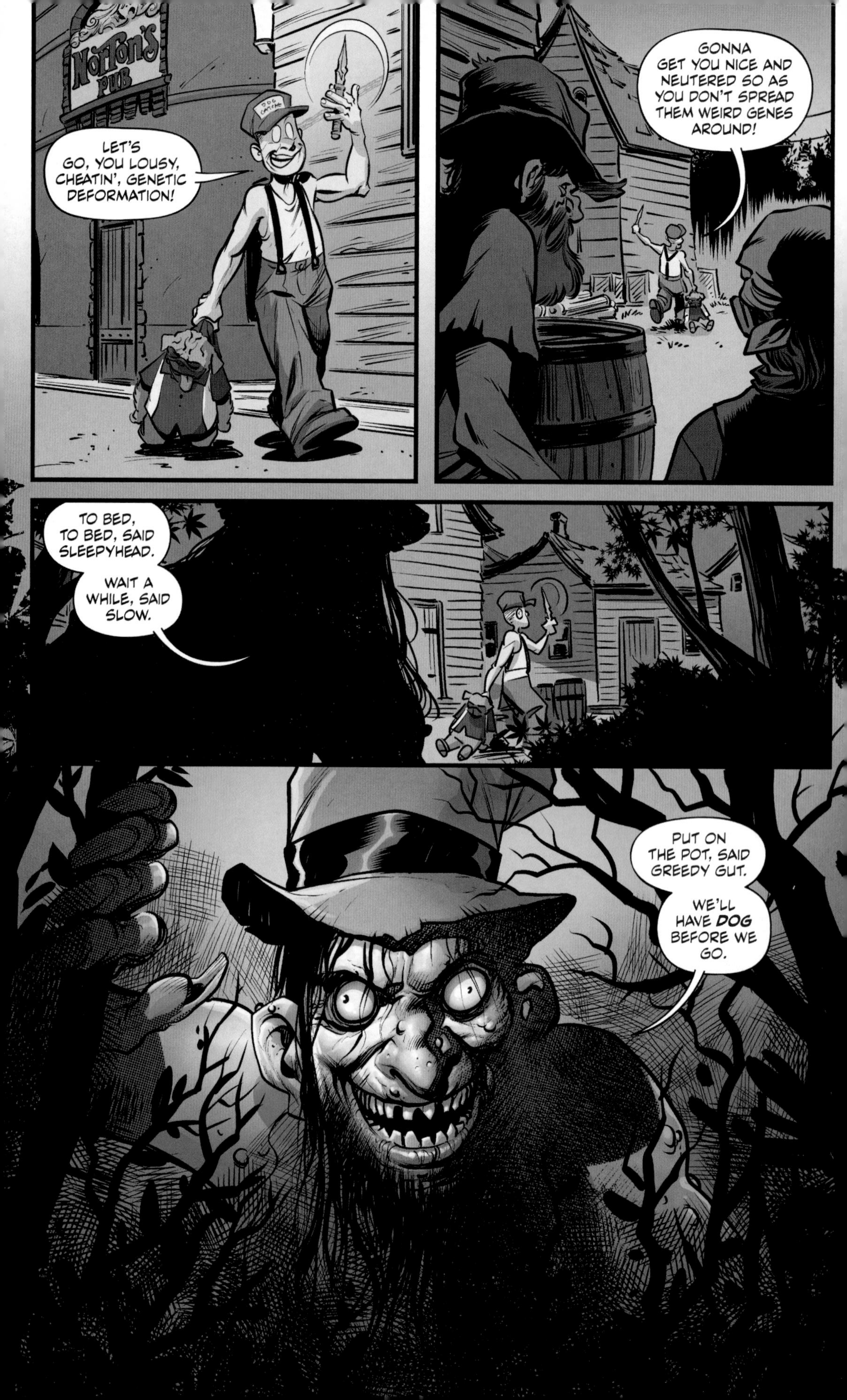
NORTON'S PUB
DOG CATCHER
LET'S GO, YOU LOUSY, CHEATIN', GENETIC DEFORMATION!
GONNA GET YOU NICE AND NEUTERED SO AS YOU DON'T SPREAD THEM WEIRD GENES AROUND!
TO BED, TO BED, SAID SLEEPYHEAD.
WAIT A WHILE, SAID SLOW.
PUT ON THE POT, SAID GREEDY GUT.
WE'LL HAVE **DOG** BEFORE WE GO.

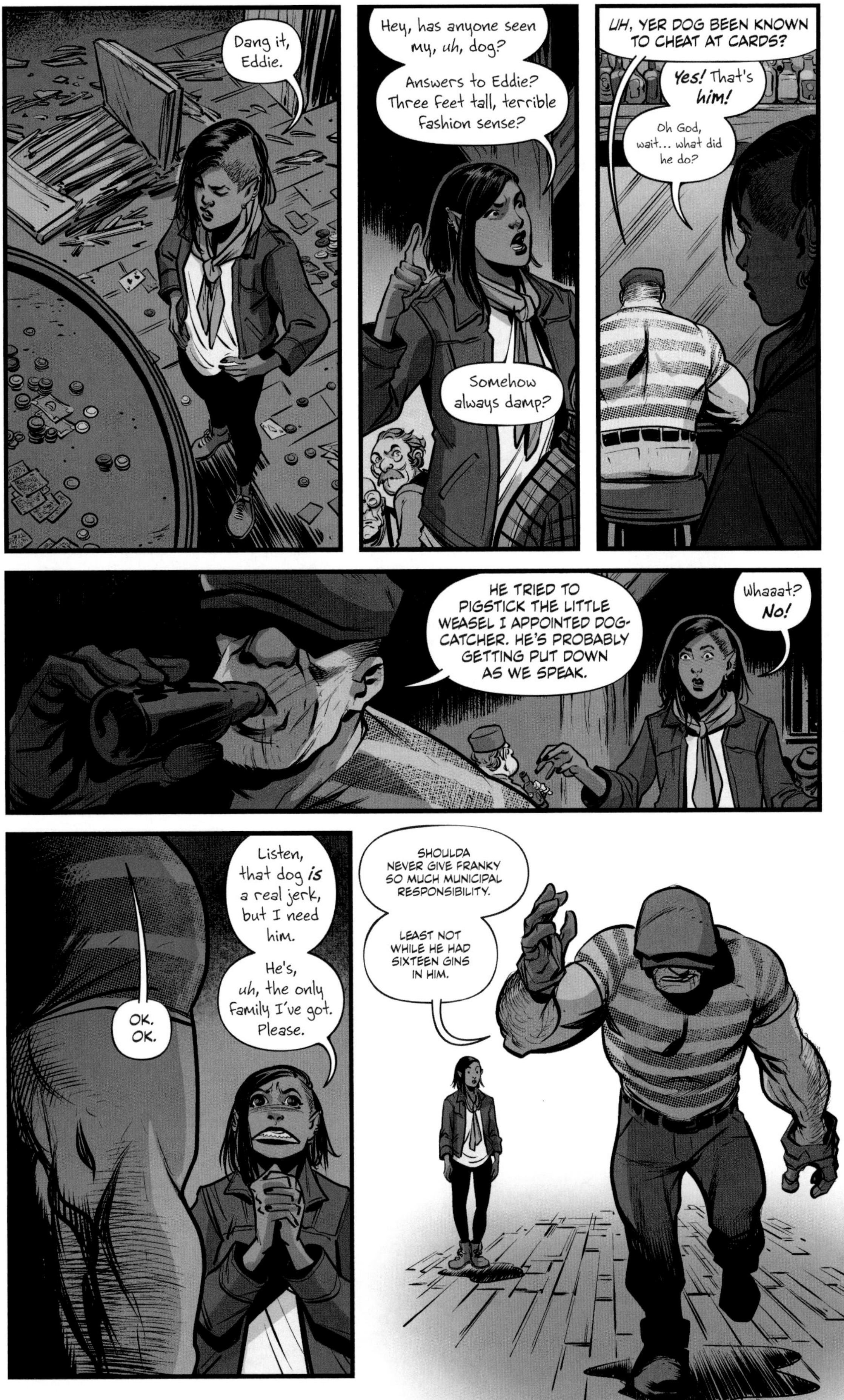
Dang it, Eddie.
Hey, has anyone seen my, uh, dog?
Answers to Eddie? Three feet tall, terrible fashion sense?
Somehow always damp?
UH, YER DOG BEEN KNOWN TO CHEAT AT CARDS?
Yes! That's him!
Oh God, wait... what did he do?
HE TRIED TO PIGSTICK THE LITTLE WEASEL I APPOINTED DOG-CATCHER. HE'S PROBABLY GETTING PUT DOWN AS WE SPEAK.
Whaaat? No!
Listen, that dog is a real jerk, but I need him.
He's, uh, the only family I've got. Please.
OK. OK.
SHOULDA NEVER GIVE FRANKY SO MUCH MUNICIPAL RESPONSIBILITY.
LEAST NOT WHILE HE HAD SIXTEEN GINS IN HIM.

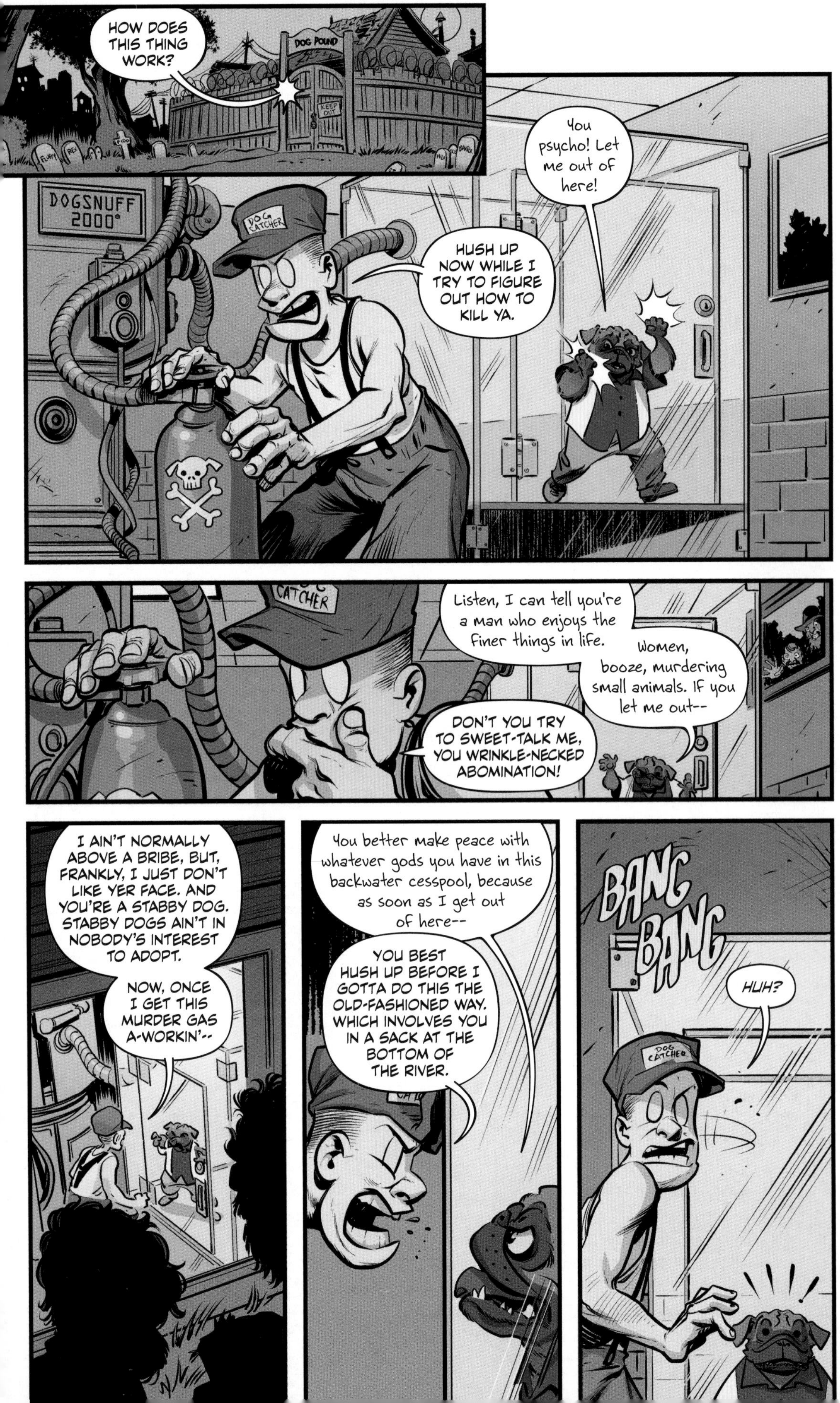
HOW DOES THIS THING WORK?
DOG POUND
KEEP OUT
FLUFFY
REX
FIDO
DOGSNUFF 2000®
DOG CATCHER
You psycho! Let me out of here!
HUSH UP NOW WHILE I TRY TO FIGURE OUT HOW TO KILL YA.
Listen, I can tell you're a man who enjoys the finer things in life.
Women, booze, murdering small animals. If you let me out--
DON'T YOU TRY TO SWEET-TALK ME, YOU WRINKLE-NECKED ABOMINATION!
I AIN'T NORMALLY ABOVE A BRIBE, BUT, FRANKLY, I JUST DON'T LIKE YER FACE. AND YOU'RE A STABBY DOG. STABBY DOGS AIN'T IN NOBODY'S INTEREST TO ADOPT.
NOW, ONCE I GET THIS MURDER GAS A-WORKIN'--
You better make peace with whatever gods you have in this backwater cesspool, because as soon as I get out of here--
YOU BEST HUSH UP BEFORE I GOTTA DO THIS THE OLD-FASHIONED WAY. WHICH INVOLVES YOU IN A SACK AT THE BOTTOM OF THE RIVER.
BANG BANG
HUH?
DOG CATCHER

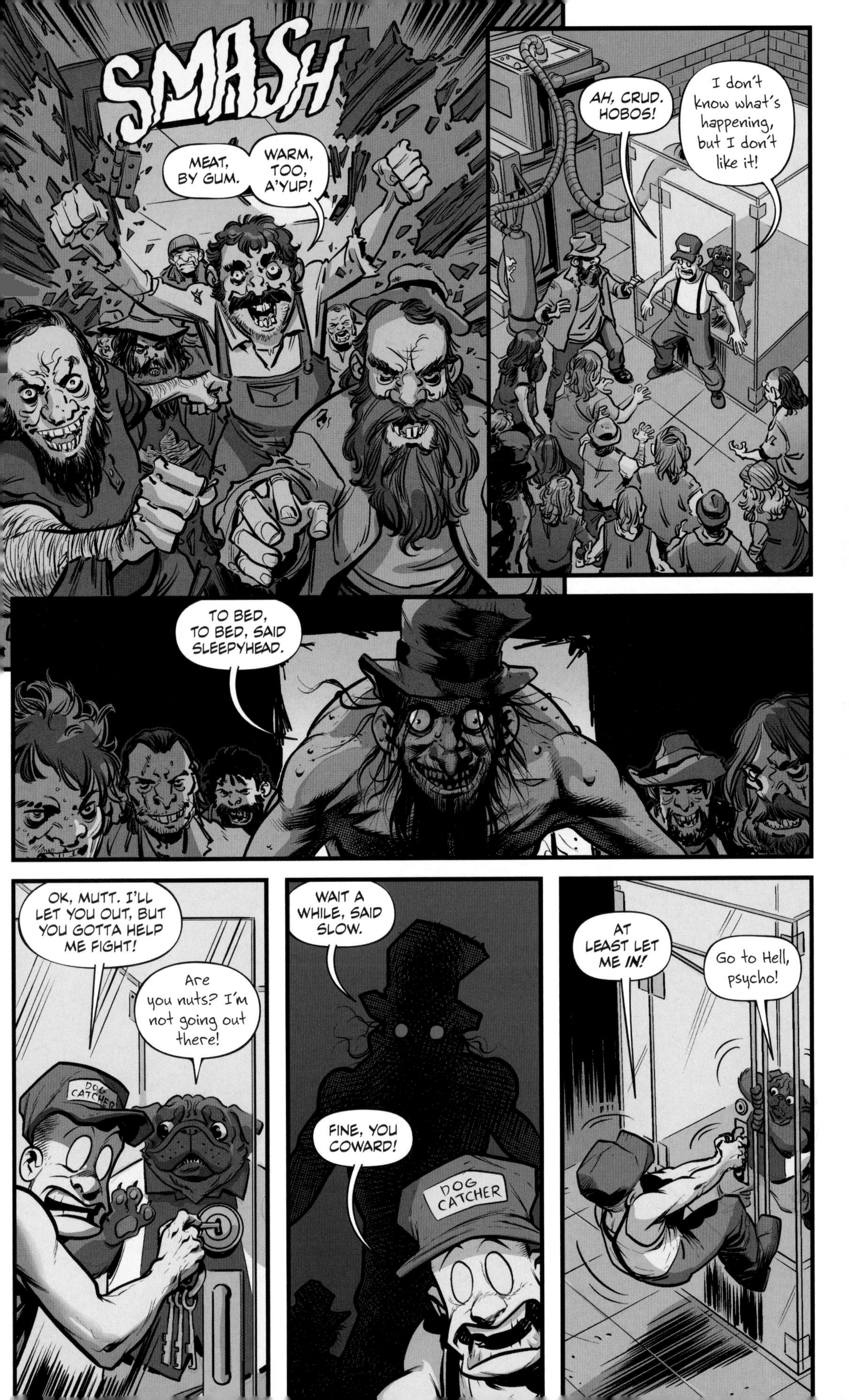
SMASH
MEAT, BY GUM.
WARM, TOO, A'YUP!
AH, CRUD. HOBOS!
I don't know what's happening, but I don't like it!
TO BED, TO BED, SAID SLEEPYHEAD.
OK, MUTT. I'LL LET YOU OUT, BUT YOU GOTTA HELP ME FIGHT!
DOG CATCHER
Are you nuts? I'm not going out there!
WAIT A WHILE, SAID SLOW.
FINE, YOU COWARD!
DOG CATCHER
AT LEAST LET ME IN!
Go to Hell, psycho!

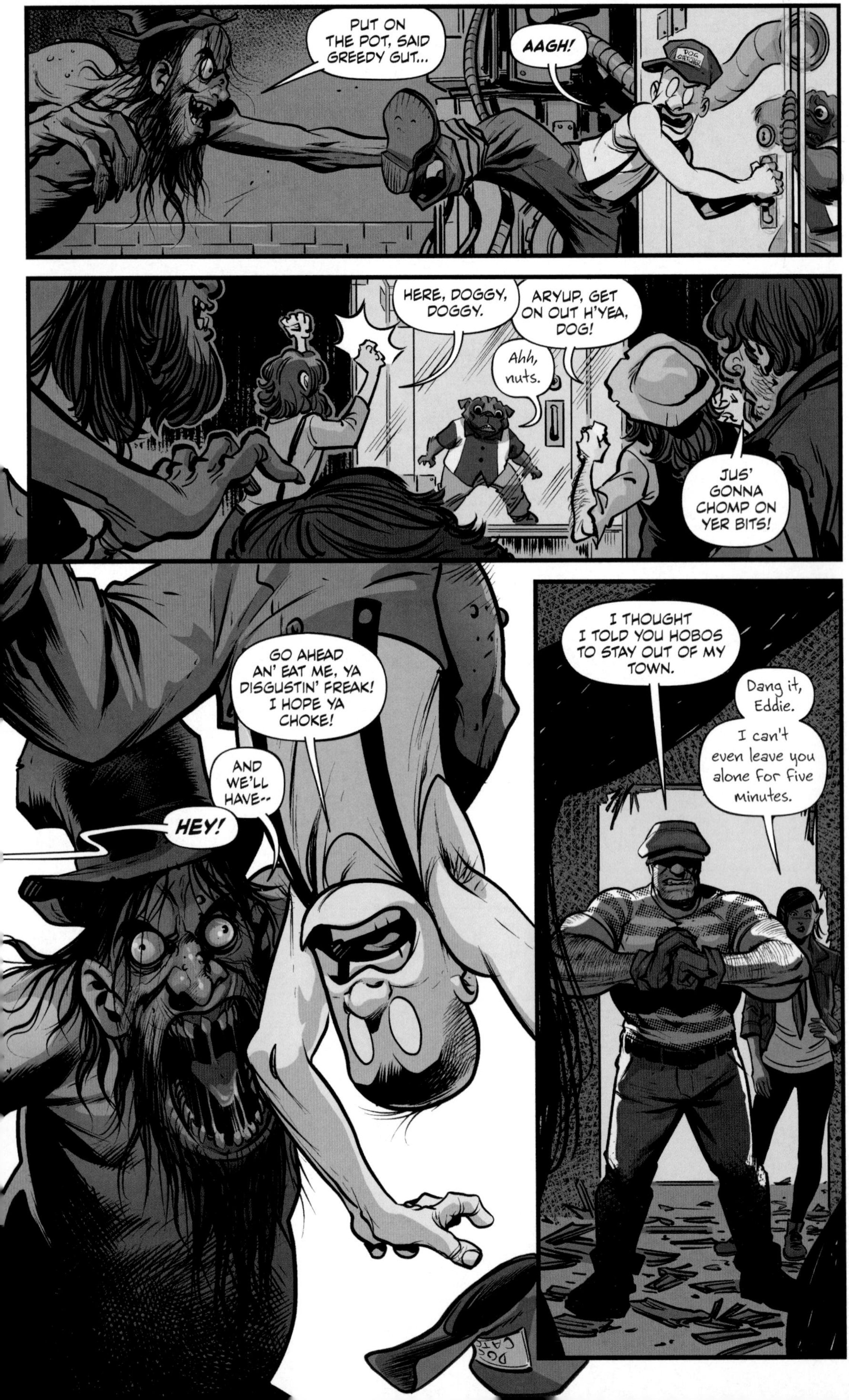
PUT ON THE POT, SAID GREEDY GUT...
AAGH!
HERE, DOGGY, DOGGY.
ARYUP, GET ON OUT H'YEA, DOG!
Ahh, nuts.
JUS' GONNA CHOMP ON YER BITS!
GO AHEAD AN' EAT ME, YA DISGUSTIN' FREAK! I HOPE YA CHOKE!
AND WE'LL HAVE--
HEY!
I THOUGHT I TOLD YOU HOBOS TO STAY OUT OF MY TOWN.
Dang it, Eddie.
I can't even leave you alone for five minutes.

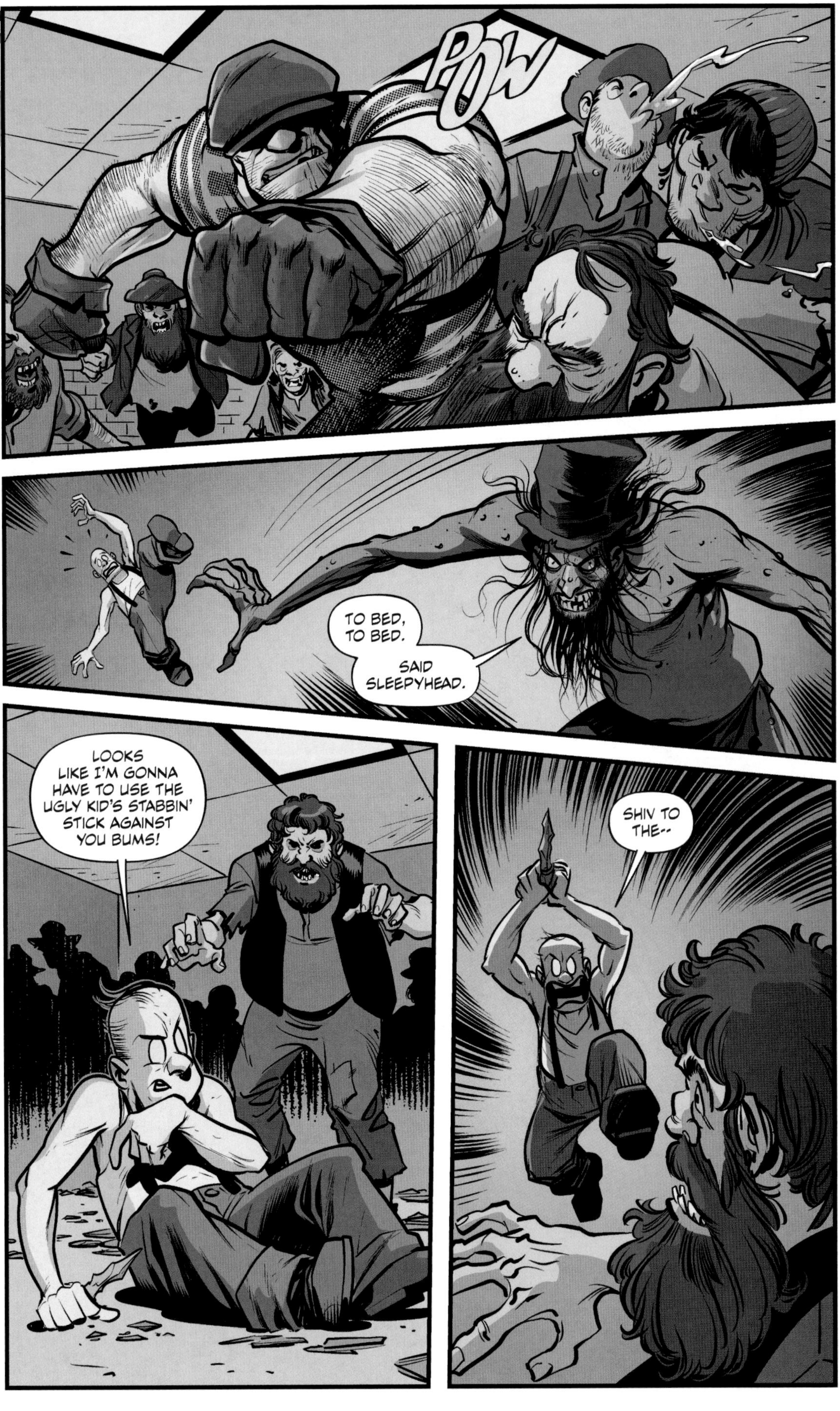
POW
TO BED, TO BED.
SAID SLEEPYHEAD.
LOOKS LIKE I'M GONNA HAVE TO USE THE UGLY KID'S STABBIN' STICK AGAINST YOU BUMS!
SHIV TO THE--

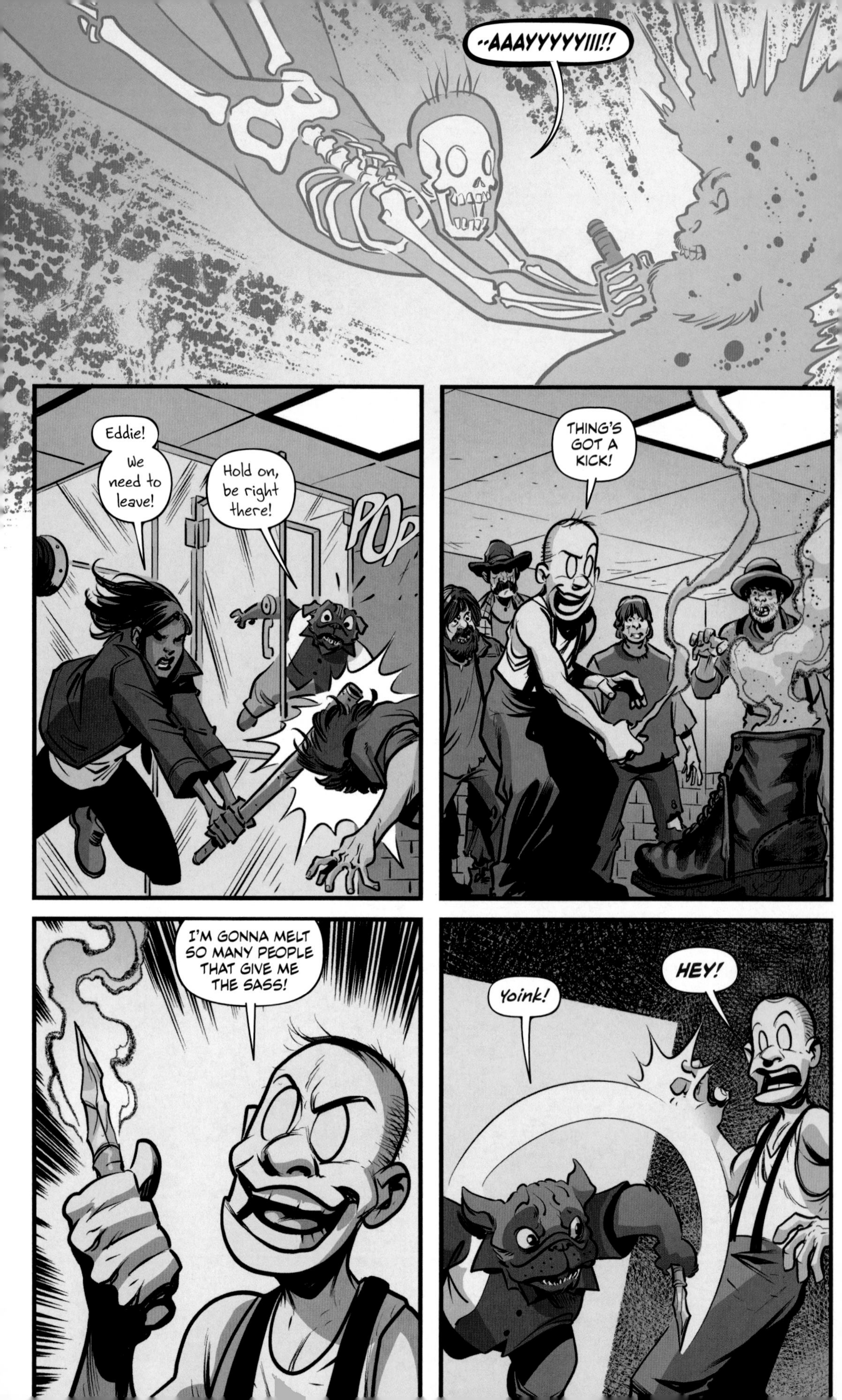
--AAAYYYYYIII!!
Eddie!
We need to leave!
Hold on, be right there!
POP
THING'S GOT A KICK!
I'M GONNA MELT SO MANY PEOPLE THAT GIVE ME THE SASS!
Yoink!
HEY!

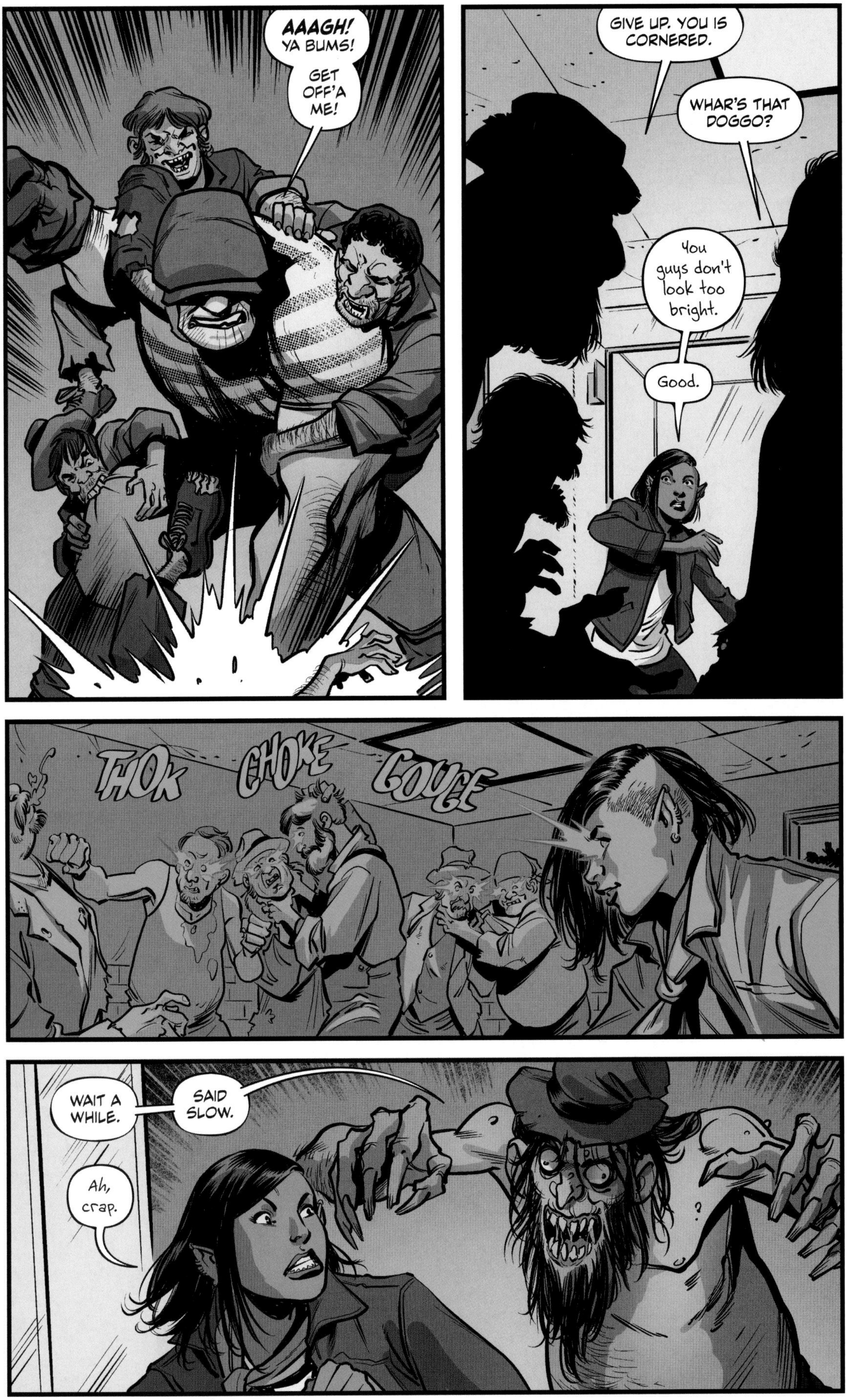
AAAGH! YA BUMS!
GET OFF'A ME!
GIVE UP. YOU IS CORNERED.
WHAR'S THAT DOGGO?
You guys don't look too bright.
Good.
THOK
CHOKE
GOUGE
WAIT A WHILE.
SAID SLOW.
Ah, crap.

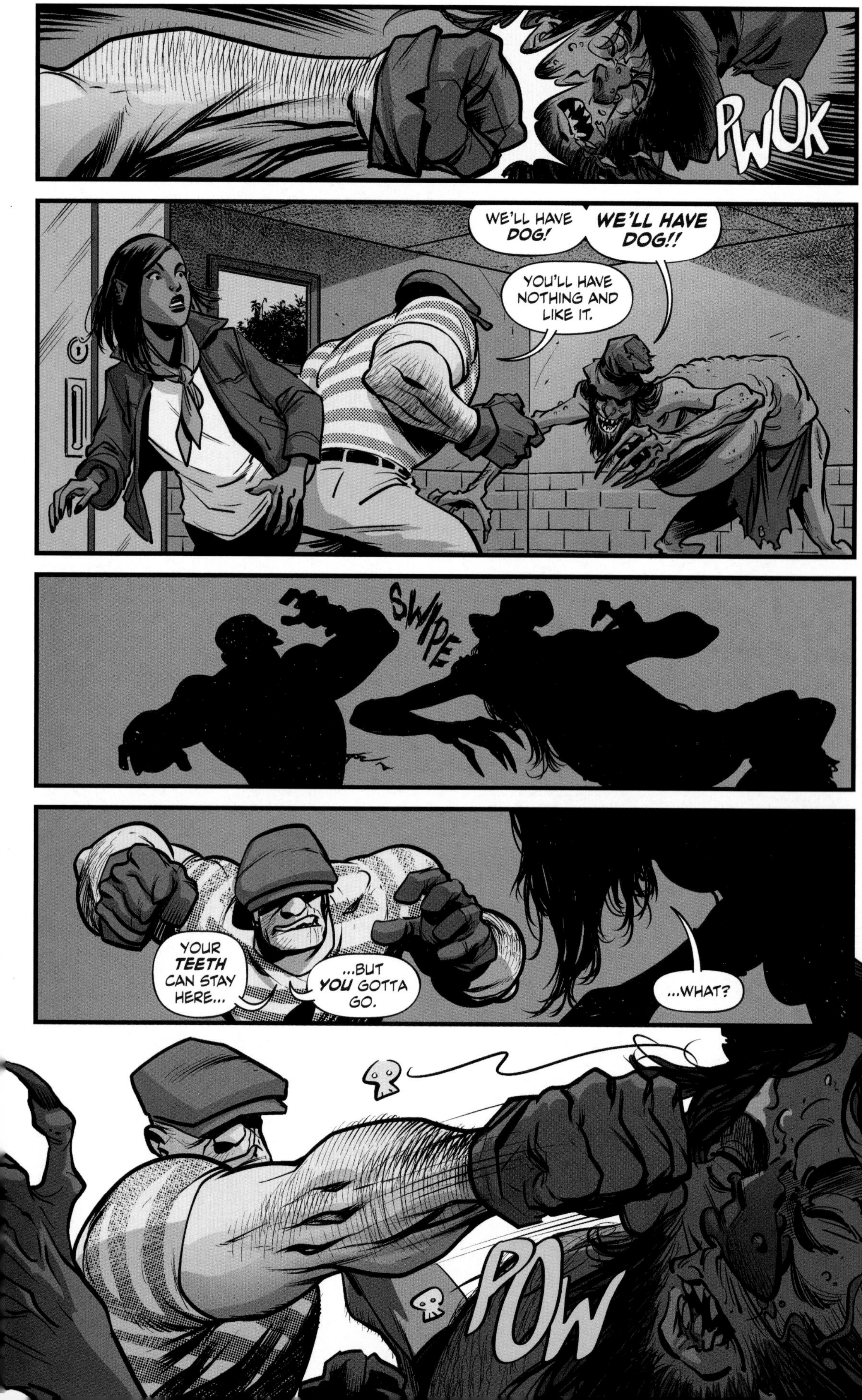
PWOK
WE'LL HAVE DOG!
WE'LL HAVE DOG!!
YOU'LL HAVE NOTHING AND LIKE IT.
SWIPE
YOUR TEETH CAN STAY HERE...
...BUT YOU GOTTA GO.
...WHAT?
POW

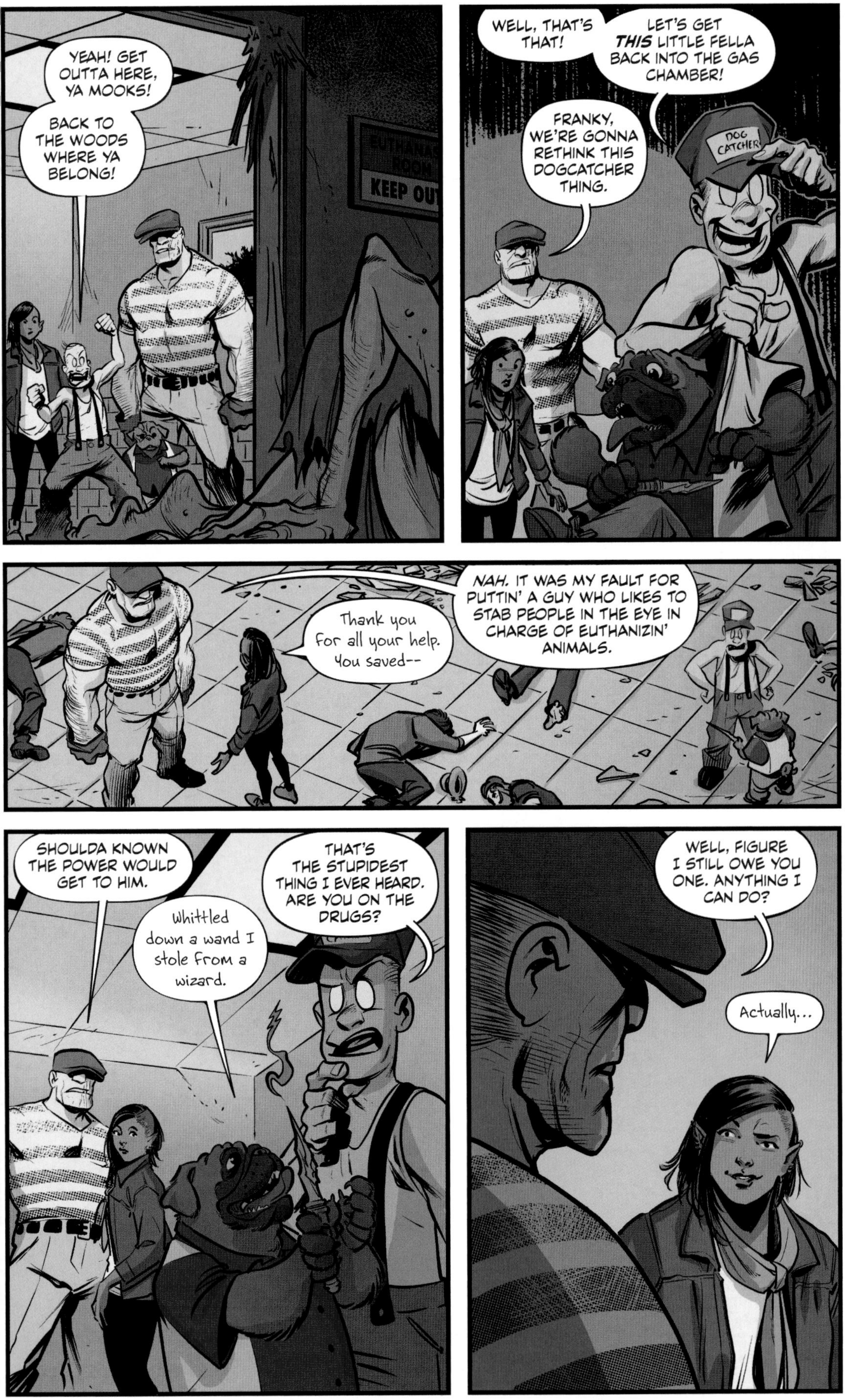
YEAH! GET OUTTA HERE, YA MOOKS!
BACK TO THE WOODS WHERE YA BELONG!
KEEP OUT
WELL, THAT'S THAT!
LET'S GET *THIS* LITTLE FELLA BACK INTO THE GAS CHAMBER!
DOG CATCHER
FRANKY, WE'RE GONNA RETHINK THIS DOGCATCHER THING.
Thank you for all your help. You saved--
NAH. IT WAS MY FAULT FOR PUTTIN' A GUY WHO LIKES TO STAB PEOPLE IN THE EYE IN CHARGE OF EUTHANIZIN' ANIMALS.
SHOULDA KNOWN THE POWER WOULD GET TO HIM.
Whittled down a wand I stole from a wizard.
THAT'S THE STUPIDEST THING I EVER HEARD. ARE YOU ON THE DRUGS?
WELL, FIGURE I STILL OWE YOU ONE. ANYTHING I CAN DO?
Actually...

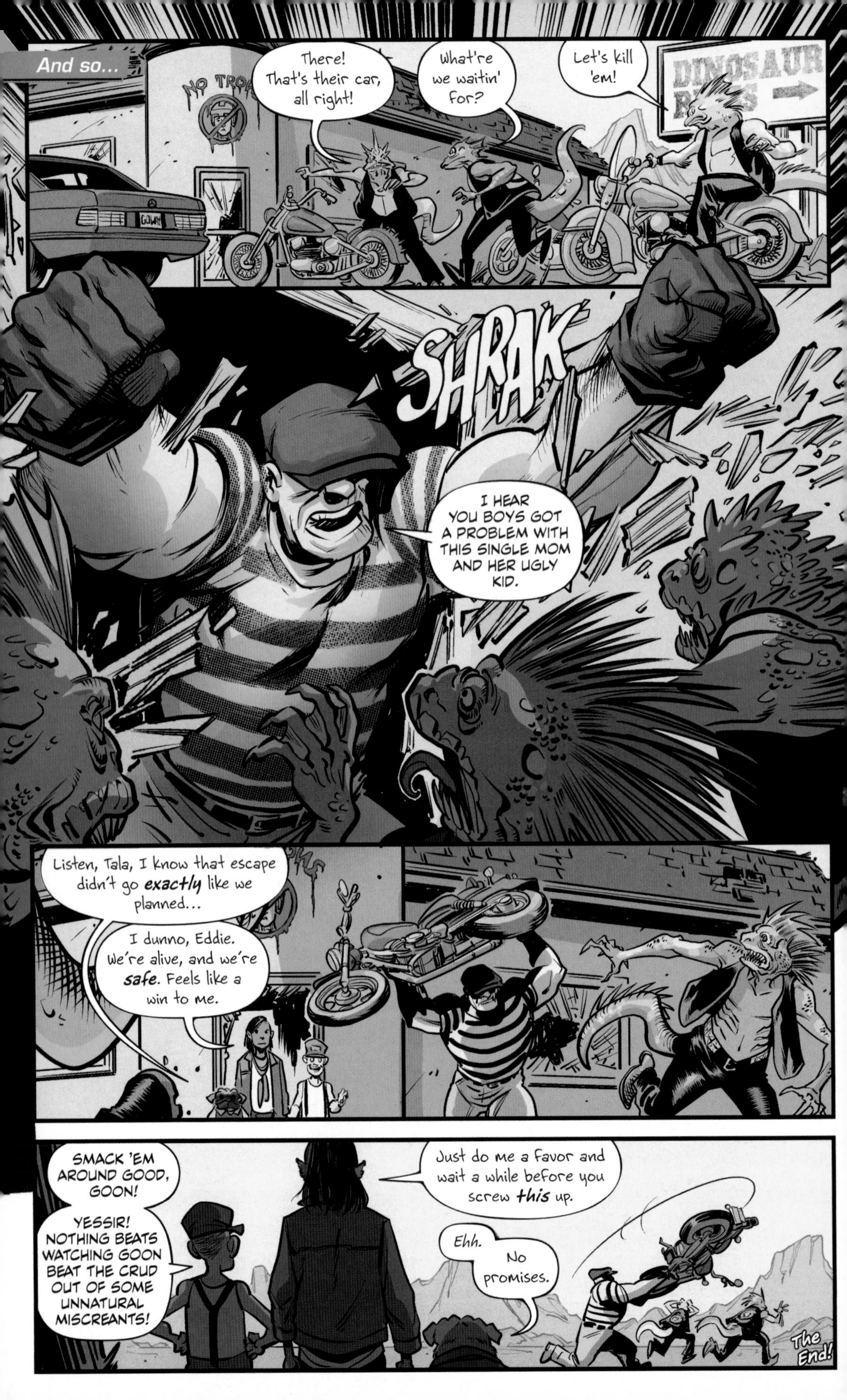
And so...
There! That's their car, all right!
What're we waitin' for?
Let's kill 'em!
DINOSAUR
SHRAK
I HEAR YOU BOYS GOT A PROBLEM WITH THIS SINGLE MOM AND HER UGLY KID.
Listen, Tala, I know that escape didn't go exactly like we planned...
I dunno, Eddie. We're alive, and we're safe. Feels like a win to me.
SMACK 'EM AROUND GOOD, GOON!
YESSIR! NOTHING BEATS WATCHING GOON BEAT THE CRUD OUT OF SOME UNNATURAL MISCREANTS!
Just do me a favor and wait a while before you screw this up.
Ehh.
No promises.
The End!

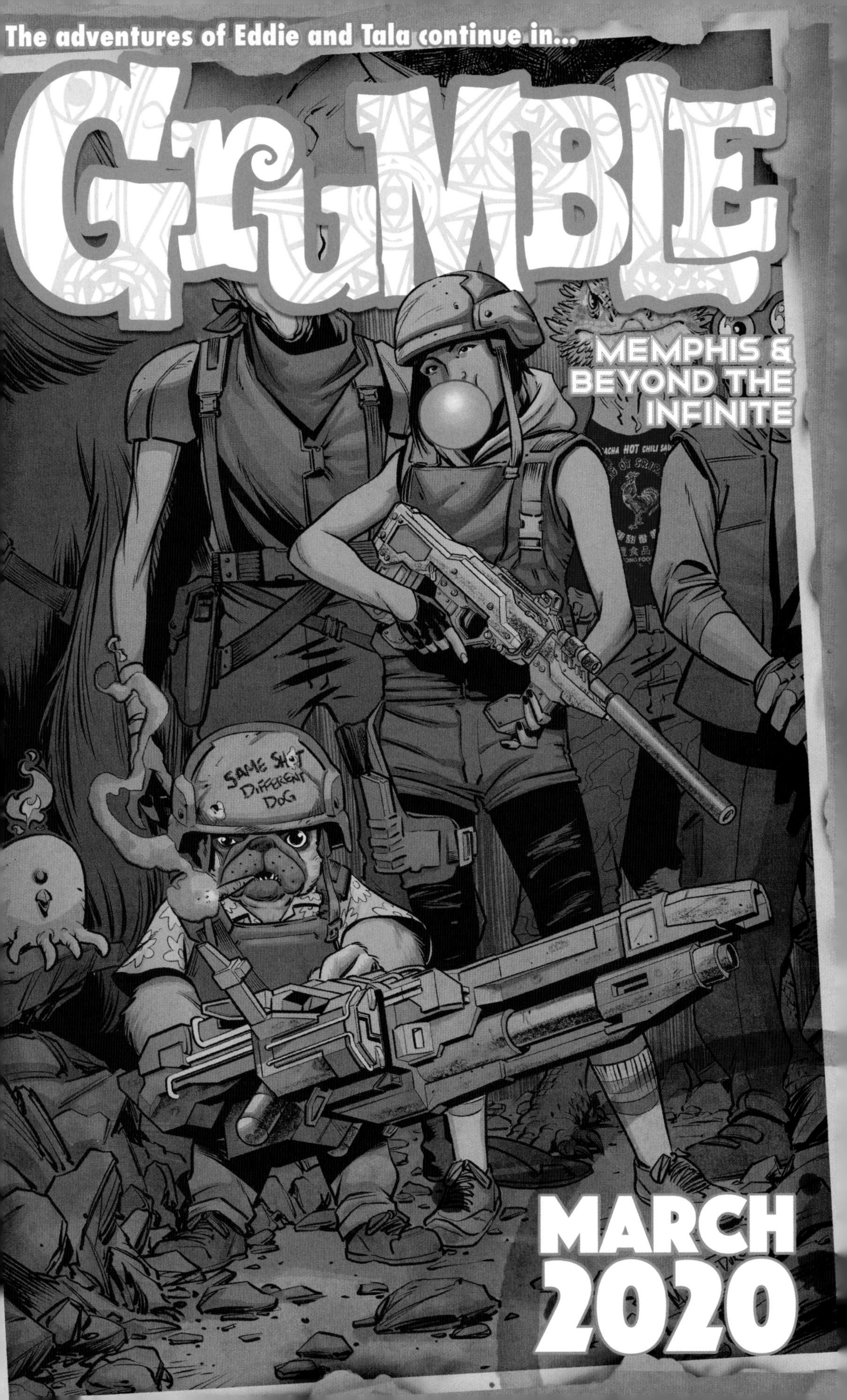

The adventures of Eddie and Tala continue in...
GUMBLE
MEMPHIS & BEYOND THE INFINITE
MARCH 2020

THE CREATORS

Rafer Roberts is the writer and co-creator of **Modern Fantasy**, published by Dark Horse Comics, and was the writer on **A&A: The Adventures of Archer & Armstrong** and **Harbinger: Renegades** for Valiant Comics. His self-published work includes the long running **Plastic Farm**, **Nightmare the Rat**, and the Tumblr famous **Thanos and Darkseid: Carpool Buddies of Doom.**

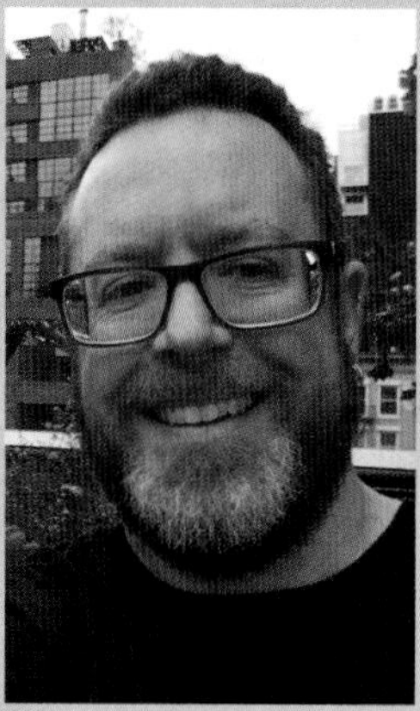

Mike Norton is the creator of the Eisner and Harvey award-winning webcomic **Battlepug** and the co-creator and artist of **Revival.** He has worked for Marvel, DC, Dark Horse and just about everybody else. He has a webcomic called **Lil' Donnie** about the worst president in US history. He lives in Chicago with his wife, two pugs, and a fridge full of beer.

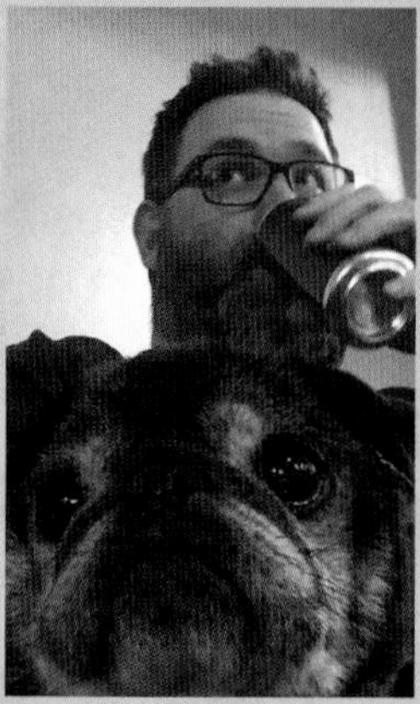

Marissa Louise is a colorist for DC, Dark Horse, Image, and others. She also does a twice monthly Curse of Strahd podcast called Bite Club, wherein she plays multiple loveable scamps.

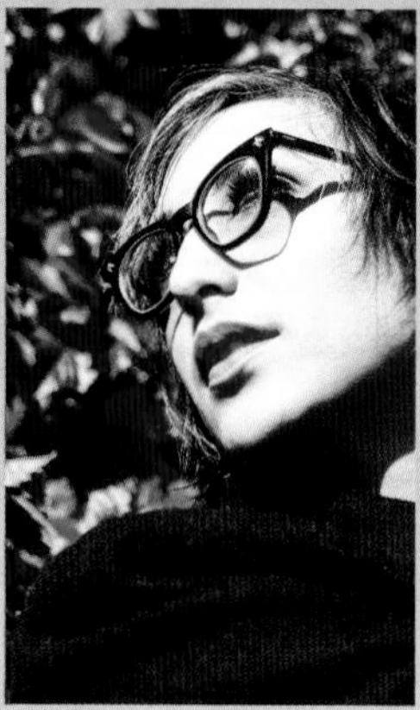

Christopher Crank (crank!) letters a bunch of books put out by Image, Dark Horse, Oni Press, Dynamite, and elsewhere. He also has a podcast with comic artist Mike Norton and members of Four Star Studios in Chicago (crankcast.com) and makes music. (sonomorti.bandcamp.com)

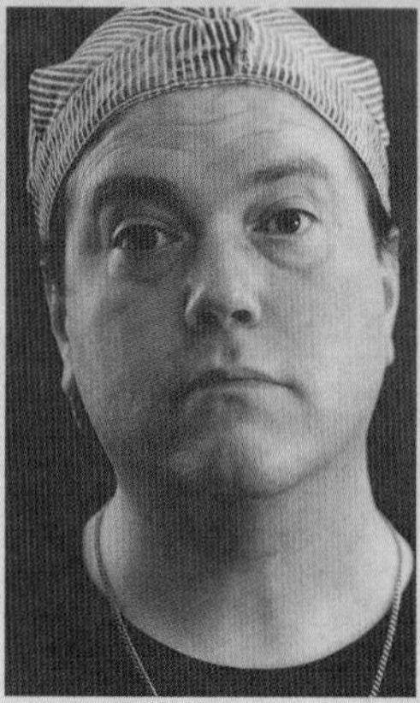

Addison Duke is an artist based in Chicago, IL. After graduating with a BFA in illustration from Academy of Art University, Addison began his professional career working as a Production Artist at Image Comics. Coloring work has included **Curse Words** (Image Comics), **Barbarella/Deja Thoris** (Dynamite Comics), **The Mall** (Vault Comics), as well as work for **Heavy Metal**

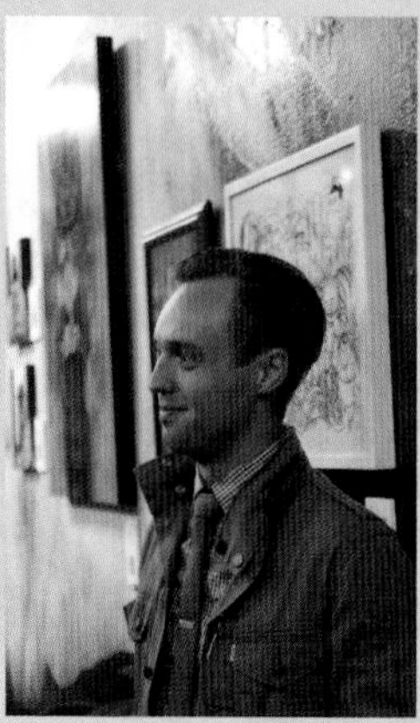

In addition to Grumble, Alejandro Arbona currently edits **Lazarus: Risen, Black Magick,** and **The Old Guard** for Image Comics, and recently edited **Ghost in the Shell: Global Neural Network** for Kodansha/Penguin Random House. He also wrote the non-fiction kids' books **Awesome Minds: Video Game Creators** and **Awesome Minds: Comic Book Creators.** Alejandro lives in New York City with a dog who only speaks Spanish.

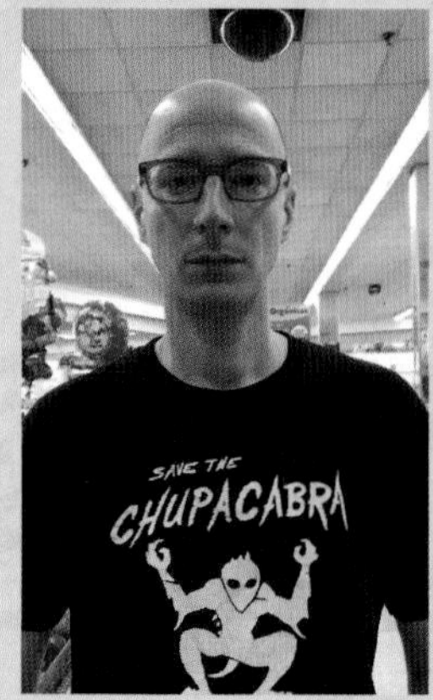
SAVE THE
CHUPACABRA

LOOK FOR THESE OTHER ALBATROSS TITLES!

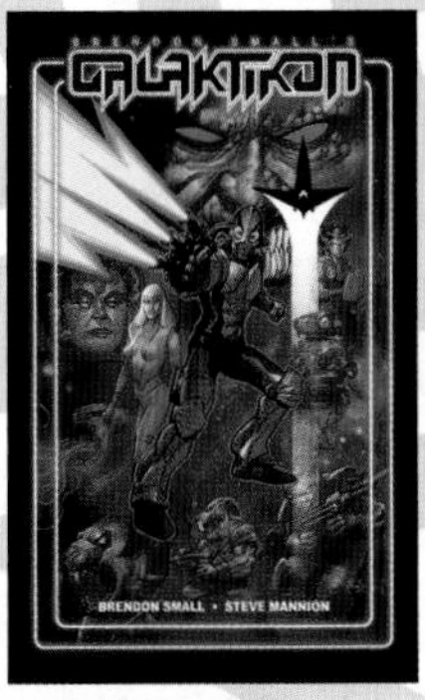
GALAKTIKON
BRENDON SMALL • STEVE MANNION

GALAKTIKON
ISBN: 978-0-9983792-5-8
$17.99

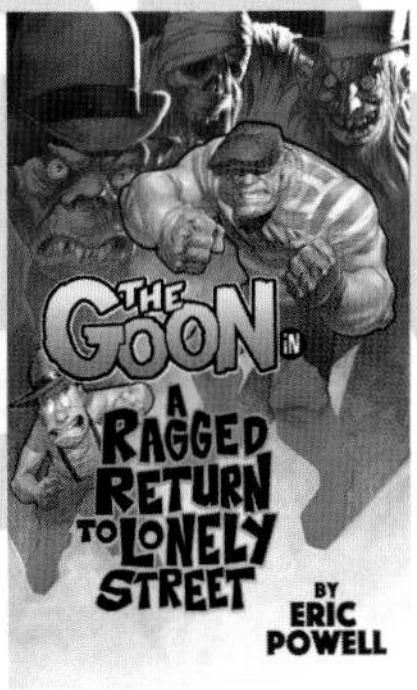
THE GOON IN
A RAGGED RETURN TO LONELY STREET
BY ERIC POWELL

THE GOON VOLUME 1
ISBN: 978-1-949889-92-5
$17.99

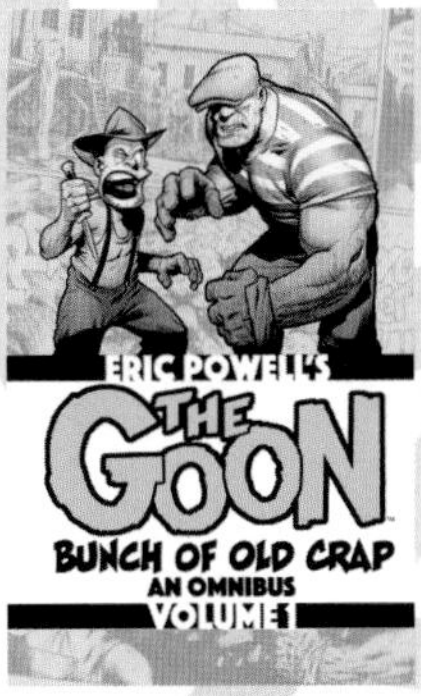
ERIC POWELL'S
THE GOON
BUNCH OF OLD CRAP
AN OMNIBUS
VOLUME 1

THE GOON
BUNCH OF OLD CRAP
AN OMNIBUS VOLUME 1
ISBN: 978-0-9983792-9-6
$29.99

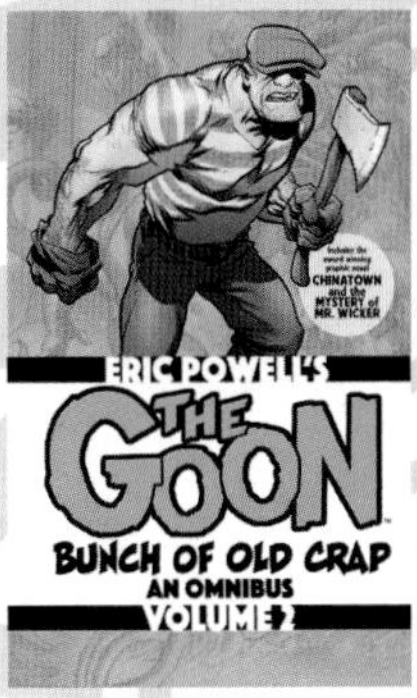
ERIC POWELL'S
THE GOON
BUNCH OF OLD CRAP
AN OMNIBUS
VOLUME 2

THE GOON
BUNCH OF OLD CRAP
AN OMNIBUS VOLUME 2
ISBN: 978-1-949889-93-2
$29.99

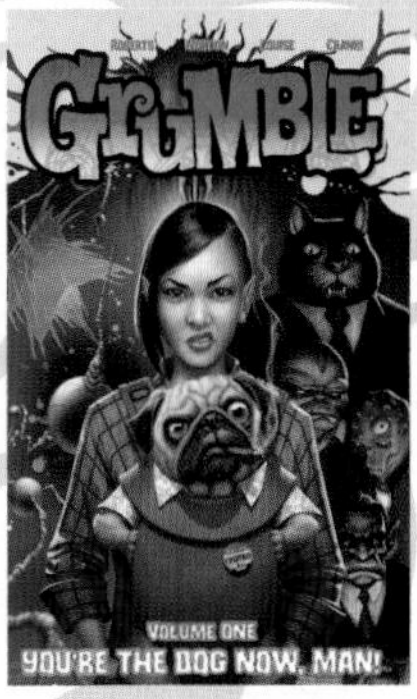
GRUMBLE
VOLUME ONE
YOU'RE THE DOG NOW, MAN!

GRUMBLE VOLUME 1
ISBN: 978-1-949889-90-1
$17.99

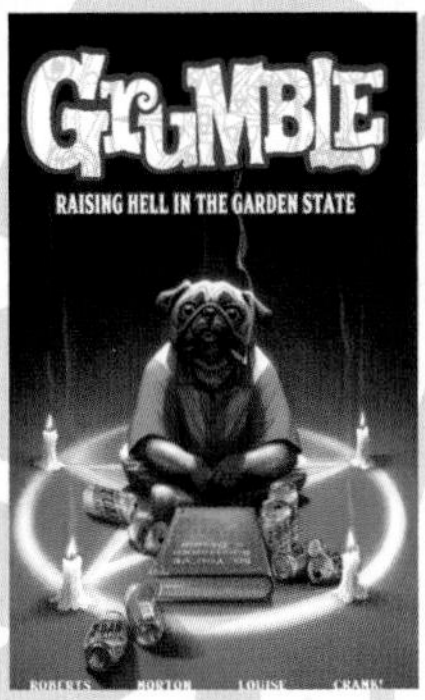
GRUMBLE
RAISING HELL IN THE GARDEN STATE

GRUMBLE VOLUME 2
ISBN: 978-1-949889-82-6
$17.99

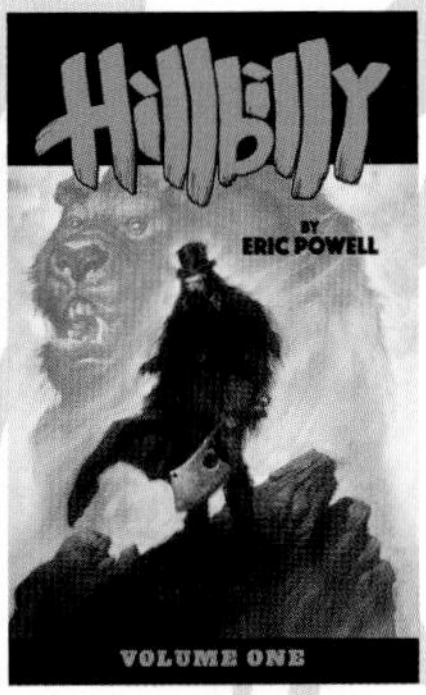
Hillbilly
BY ERIC POWELL
VOLUME ONE

HILLBILLY VOLUME 1
ISBN: 978-0-9983792-0-3
$17.99

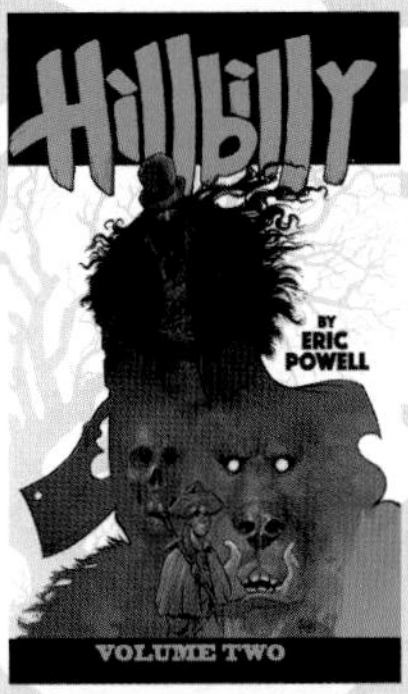
Hillbilly
BY ERIC POWELL
VOLUME TWO

HILLBILLY VOLUME 2
ISBN: 978-0-9983792-3-4
$17.99

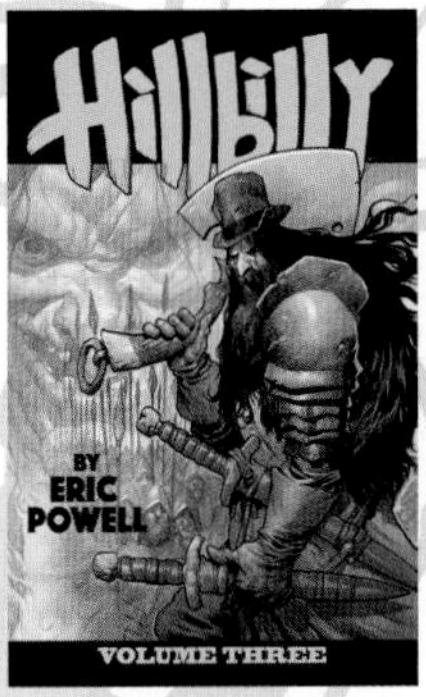
Hillbilly
BY ERIC POWELL
VOLUME THREE

HILLBILLY VOLUME 3
ISBN: 978-0-9983792-4-1
$17.99

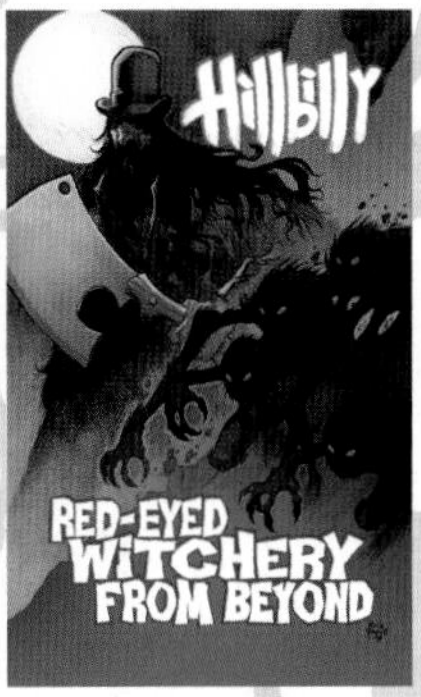
Hillbilly
RED-EYED WITCHERY FROM BEYOND

HILLBILLY VOLUME 4
ISBN: 978-0-9983792-8-9
$17.99

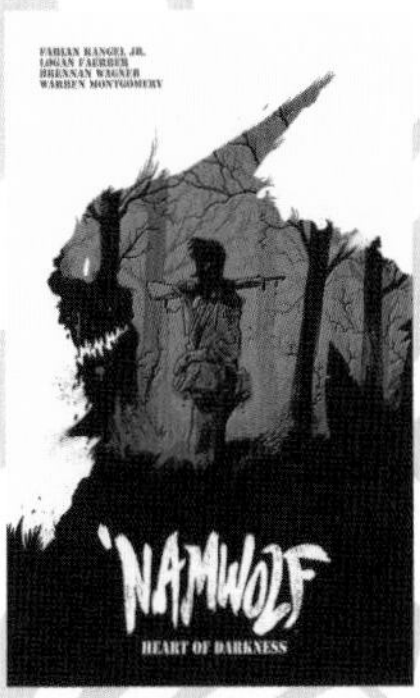
'NAMWOLF
HEART OF DARKNESS

'NAMWOLF
ISBN: 978-0-9983792-2-7
$17.99

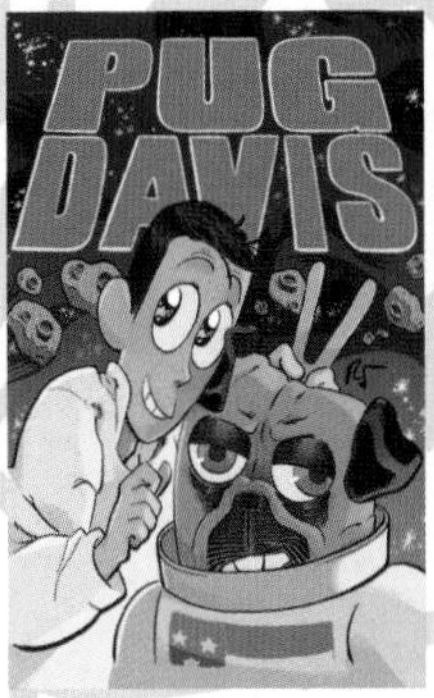
PUG DAVIS

REBECCA SUGAR'S PUG DAVIS
ISBN: 978-1-949889-91-8
$17.99

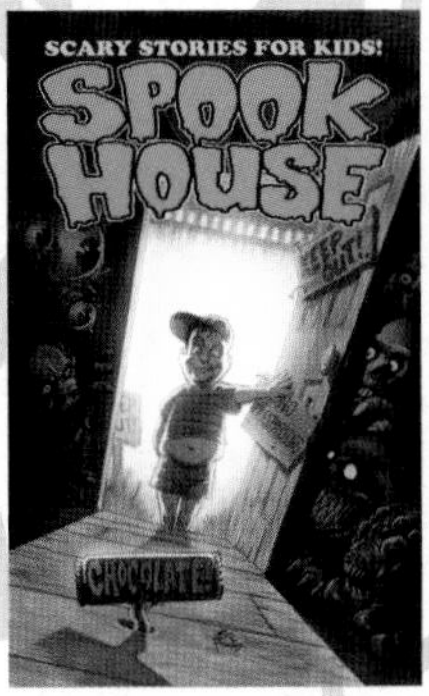
SCARY STORIES FOR KIDS!
SPOOK HOUSE

SPOOK HOUSE VOLUME 1
ISBN: 978-0-9983792-1-0
$17.99

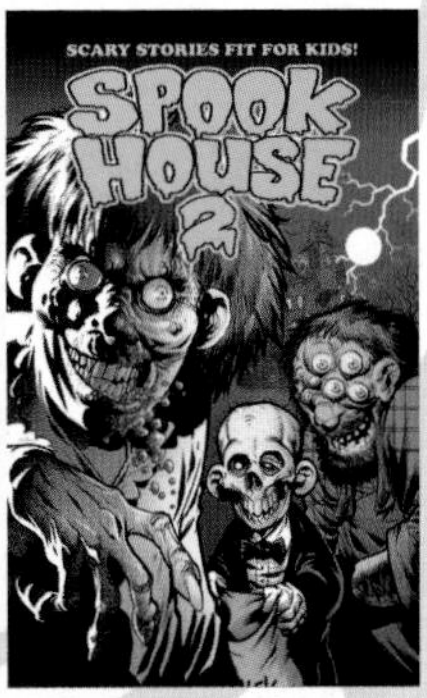
SCARY STORIES FIT FOR KIDS!
SPOOK HOUSE 2

SPOOK HOUSE VOLUME 2
ISBN: 978-0-9983792-7-2
$17.99

ALBATROSSFUNNYBOOKS.COM

ALBATROSS
FUNNY BOOKS™

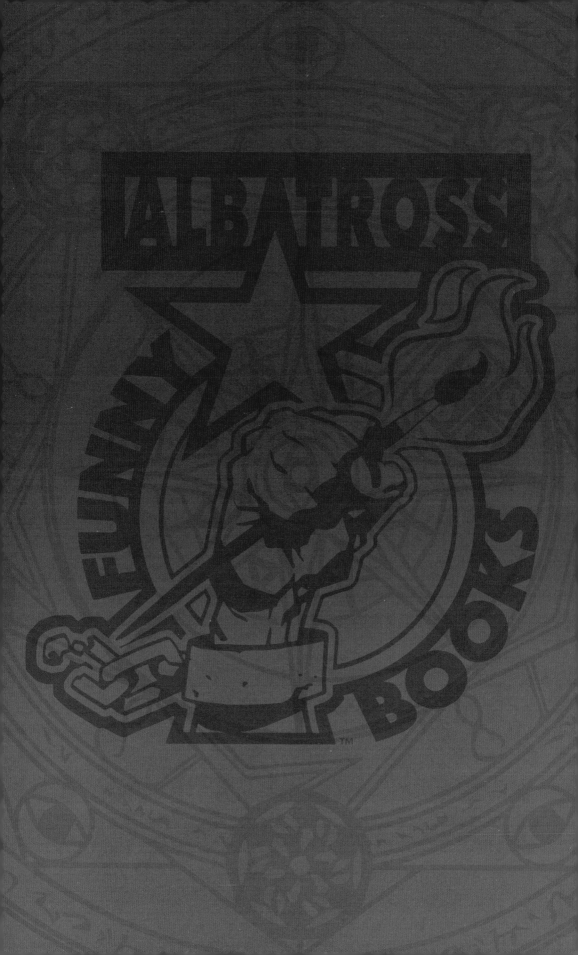